D1602493

UK arms control in the 1990s

UK arms control in the 1990s

edited by

Mark Hoffman

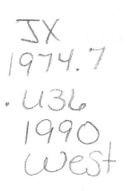

JX
1974.7
. U36
1990
West

Manchester University Press

Manchester and New York

Distributed exclusively in the USA and Canada by St. Martin's Press

Copyright © Mark Hoffman 1990

Published by Manchester University Press
    Oxford Road, Manchester M13 9PL, UK
and Room 400, 175 Fifth Avenue,
New York, NY 10010, USA

Distributed exclusively in the USA and Canada
by St. Martin's Press, Inc.,
175 Fifth Avenue, New York, NY 10010, USA

British Library cataloguing in publication data
UK arms control policy in the 1990s.
    1. Great Britain. Nuclear weapons. Arms control
    I. Hoffman, Mark
    327.1740941

Library of Congress cataloging in publication data
UK arms control policy in the 1990s. / edited by Mark Hoffman.
        p. cm.
    ISBN 0-7190-3186-9
    1. Nuclear arms control—Great Britain. 2. Arms control.
I. Hoffman, Mark, 1957–   .
JX1974.7.U36   1990
327.1'74'0941—dc20   —dc20   89-77463

ISBN 0 7190 3186 9 *hardback*

Typeset in Linotron Sabon
by Northern Phototypesetting Co Ltd, Bolton
Printed in Great Britain
by Biddles Ltd, Guildford and King's Lynn

Contents

Part II: Arms control issue areas

Part III: Conclusions

Acknowledgements

The essays in this volume developed out of a series of workshops and seminars held at the University of Southampton and the London School of Economics. The contributors would like to thank the Department of Politics at the University of Southampton and the Department of International Relations and the International Research Fund at the London School of Economics for providing resources and financial support. We would also like to thank the graduate students who attended the seminars and workshops whose comments contributed both to the liveliness of the discussions and the revisions of the individual chapters. In particular, we would like to thank Terry Terrif who read the whole of an earlier version of the manuscript and provided useful suggestions for highlighting the underlying themes. Thanks are also due to Manchester University Press for their patience and perseverance in dealing with the numerous revisions required to keep pace with a moving target.

Preface

Since the manuscript for this book was finished and went to press, a series of dramatic changes have taken place in Eastern Europe as one Communist regime after another was swept from power – sometimes peacefully and sometimes with considerable bloodshed. These changes have taken place at a tempo that few would have imagined, let alone predicted in the late summer and early fall of 1989. The implication of these changes for the future of Europe are profound and have yet to be fully worked through. One thing is clear: they call into question the very foundations of the Cold War security system established in Europe in the post-war period and have set in motion a significant restructuring of the political, strategic, economic and social architecture of European security.

It might be thought that such dramatic changes would undercut the arguments of much that was written in the field of security, defence and arms control prior to these events. This may well be the predicament for much of the literature. But in the case of this set of essays, the events of 1989 have reinforced the argument regarding the 'bonfire of the certainties' which runs as a theme through all the essays. While some of the detail may now seem dated (for example, the concern with the question of the modernisation of short-range nuclear forces stationed in Germany), the essential argument – that a series of profound changes in the political and strategic context can be identified which constitute the basis for a fundamental reassessment of the UK's security and arms control policy – is wholly sustained, if not made more vigorous.

In addition to the dramatic changes in Eastern and central Europe, the pace of domestic change within the Soviet Union has continued. A new constitution has been approved and an executive Presidency established which is intended to provide Gorbachev with the power necessary to accelerate the pace of reforms and to direct the restructuring of the Soviet state while separating his fortunes from the declining legitimacy of the Communist Party. Gorbachev's 'new thinking' has carried forward into the Soviet attitude towards eastern Europe, including the acceptance of democratically elected non-communist regimes and the withdrawal of Soviet troops from Czechoslovakia and Hungary. A further implication of these changes is that the military and strategic realities on the ground are likely to outpace the efforts of arms control negotiators to either control them or codify them.

The UK's limited response to these changes can be seen with regard to the question of the modernisation of short-range nuclear missiles. Since 1988, many observers have argued that the military and political justification for the modernisation of SNF in Europe were difficult to sustain. Nevertheless, the Thatcher government continued to push for modernisation, causing a serious split within the Alliance which was side stepped under the Bush compromise proposal at the May 1989 NATO summit. This was largely in response to Chancellor Kohl's desire to postpone the decision on a follow-on to the Lance missile until after the West German elections. However, with the changes in central and Eastern Europe at the end of 1989, the question of short-range nuclear forces stationed on German soil and a follow-on to the Lance became dead issues. Yet, until the March 1990 elections in East Germany, which gave the clear signal that German unification was an inevitability, the Thatcher government maintained, at least publicly, an unwillingness to countenance a 'third zero'.

In the aftermath of these elections the UK government seemed to accept that, given the outcome and the likely unification of Germany, the question of modernising SNF no longer arises. This, however, constituted only a partial and belated recognition of the magnitude of change in the European political and strategic environments which have been unfolding since the late 1980s. The limitations of the government's response to the changes in Europe are indicated by its stated policy that a unified Germany must be a member of NATO and that Allied troops and nuclear weapons must continue to be stationed on German soil. As the pace of change within Europe continues, it is an open question as to how long such policies are likely to remain credible.

The desire of the Thatcher government to leave in place as much of the old Cold War security framework as is deemed possible and desirable was reiterated during the March 1990 state visit of Czechoslovakia's President, Vaclav Havel. In her after-dinner speech the Prime Minister disagreed with Havel's call for a new European security order, reasserting the necessity for NATO, US troops in Europe and even the WTO. The CSCE framework, she argued, should be strengthened, but only as a framework complimentary to the continuing existence of Alliance structures. These views were repeated during the meetings with Chancellor Kohl at the end of March 1990.

These views are also to be found in the Defence White Paper (1990) published at the beginning of April. The limitations of the UK's response are also evident in the government's intended use for whatever 'peace dividend' occurs as a consequence of the changes in Europe. Unlike the US or the Germans, who plan substantial reductions in manpower and procurement, the Thatcher government intends to use it to relieve the financial pressures on the defence budget so as to allow the continued funding of expensive weapon platforms, rather than shifting financial resources to domestic spending.

The limitations of the UK's thinking are further indicated by its continued insistence on the necessity of nuclear deterrence as the basis of European security and as a means of dealing with 'uncertainties and change' in Europe. This continued emphasis on the necessity of nuclear deterrence in Europe has become embodied in a new focus on the role of the UK's 'sub-strategic capabilities'. This, in turn, has come to provide the justification for the decision to pursue the modernisation of a stand-off air launched theatre nuclear missile as a replacement for the aging WE-177 gravity bomb.

Thus, despite the changes in the Soviet Union during the last few years of the 1980s and in Eastern Europe in the closing months of 1989, the UK government has continued to maintain its view that nuclear deterrence is necessary to prevent conventional war in Europe. The difficulty the UK faces is in formulating and articulating the nature of European nuclear deterrence in the 1990s. It is no longer clear what the nature of the 'threat' is which will continue to justify the UK's status quo-oriented security and arms control policies. The Thatcher government has offered several possible justifications: the continued threat from the Soviet Union as a major

European military power; the instabilities in the Soviet Union which might lead either to the fall of Gorbachev and his replacement by a neo-Stalinist government or which might spill over into Europe; the instabilities and ethnic violence in Eastern Europe and the Balkans; and their value as 'insurance' against the 'uncertainties and instabilities' of an unknowable future, for which many read a concern over a united Germany at the centre of Europe. How convincing these will be militarily, in terms of the future structure of the UK's nuclear and conventional capabilities and force deployments, and politically, either to allied governments or a domestic population concerned with cuts in social services, remains to be seen.

Instead of clinging to old policies, the changes in Europe and the Soviet Union should be producing a reorientation of UK security and arms control policy. As the requirements of deterrence become less stringent, both at the national and European level, so too do the capabilities required to fulfil the deterrent function. The implication of these changes is that the question of the military balance between NATO and the WTO can no longer be the focal point of European security. Instead, the important issues for European security will be the structure of its political and economic architecture. This means that the UK's and the Alliance's strategic doctrines need to be rethought.

The difficulty for NATO is that the nuclear assumptions and necessities of extended deterrence, Flexible Response and Forward Defence, are no longer applicable to the likely contours of European security in the 1990s and require major rethinking. Indeed, in light of the changes in Europe, including the disintegration of the WTO as a credible threat, the continued existence of NATO itself – as a military and political alliance – is in jeopardy and will have to be rethought. Movement towards some kind of pan-European security framework which includes the Soviets as well as the US seems the most logical and practical course of events.

The difficulty for the UK is not only at the European level, but also at the strategic level. In 1989, the Thatcher government laid down three conditions for UK participation in future strategic arms control: a conventional arms control agreement, cuts removing the imbalances in conventional capabilities in Europe, and a chemical weapons treaty. As Stuart Croft notes in his chapter, the link between these three areas and the UK deterrent is tenuous at best. But even if the tenuous linkages are granted, the difficulty for the

Thatcher government is that all are likely to be achieved by the mid-1990s, if not in time for the US presidential election campaign in 1992. The UK government will have little left to hide behind in its continuing effort to ensure that the UK deterrent is kept out of strategic arms control negotiations. All the diplomatic, political and strategic barricades and justifications which the UK has erected around and underneath the UK deterrent will have fallen and the UK will face considerable pressure to participate in START negotiations.

What follows from the above is the need for the UK to rethink its strategic objectives. Its current objectives, as outlined in Stuart Croft's chapter, are now contradictory. The first objective – the desire to maintain Britain's nuclear status – and the third objective – the desire to maintain a degree of influence on questions of European security and the outcome of arms control processes – will not square in the 1990s with the second objective of keeping the UK's nuclear and conventional forces out of arms control processes. It will become increasingly difficult for the UK to keep a low-profile in arms control negotiations – at either the strategic or European level – if it wishes to affect the outcome of these and other European security processes. The self-exclusion from arms control processes in the 1970s and 1980s advantage, which arguably worked to the UK's, is no longer a credible policy option in the 1990s.

The events of the last few years of the 1980s, let alone the last few months of 1989, are unlikely, in the 1990s, to work to the advantage of the status quo orientation of the UK's security and arms control policies. The implications are clear: the need for a reorientation and redefinition of the UK's security needs and concomitant defence policy combined with a fully fledged defence review. Without such changes, the UK is in danger of being left with an overall force structure that lacks any coherent justification and which is too expansive in relation to the conceivable threats it will face. This shift in orientation needs to take place at two levels. At the strategic level it entails a movement away from the 'Moscow criterion', a reassessment of the UK's modernisation programme and the inclusion of the UK nuclear deterrent in strategic arms control negotiations. Additionally, its entails a reassessment of the 'special relationship'. This has already taken place, at least from the perspective of the US, as the Bush Administration has come to increasingly focus on the Germans as the central actor in European security at the strategic, political and economic levels. It may well be that the UK will also have to reassess the 'special relationship' coming to similar conclusions about the central role of Germany in determining the future of European security.

At the European level, it entails a movement away from the continental emphasis of the UK's security policy and military structure, resulting in the partial or complete withdrawal of BAOR. It also means cuts in expensive weapons platforms which were geared towards a set of military conditions which no longer obtain. The most likely candidates for reconsideration are: the number of EFA's ordered, if not the project as a whole; the replacement for the Challenger tank; the size of the surface fleet; and the modernisation and deployment of the UK's nuclear strategic and sub-strategic deterrent.

The danger of the Thatcher government's approach is that it relies on 'old thinking'; provides no positive support for the processes already in motion; and, most importantly, prevents the UK from playing a positive role in the restructuring of European security. It represents an attempt to assert the continuing validity of the Cold War security system or, more disappointingly and dangerously, an attempt to reassert the validity of nineteenth-century traditional balance-of-power thinking.

The adherence to artificial barriers to negotiations and to creative thinking about European security are aspects of UK security and arms control policy which may come back to haunt not only the UK, but the whole of Europe. What is needed, but so far lacking, is 'new thinking' on the part of the UK. This 'new thinking' would seek to influence the dramatic changes which are unfolding in Europe and reflect the intellectual, political and security challenges of a new era in European and Atlantic relations. The UK needs to develop security objectives and arms control policies which take advantage of the new challenges and opportunities in Europe. This means a serious reconsideration of the UK's strategic objectives as well as the best course of action and the nature of the capabilities needed to achieve them. In the 1990s, the risks are too great, the opportunity too momentous to justify the continuation of the UK's traditional status quo-oriented policy.

Mark Hoffman

Notes on the contributors

Stuart Croft is Lecturer in the Centre for Defence Studies at the Graduate School of International Studies, University of Birmingham.

David H. Dunn is Lecturer in Defence and International Affairs at the Royal Military Academy, Sandhurst.

Mark Hoffman is Lecturer in the Department of International Relations at the London School of Economics.

Darryl Howlett is the Information Officer on the Programme for the Promotion of Nuclear Non-Proliferation at the Department of Politics, University of Southampton.

Wyn Rees is Lecturer in Defence and International Affairs at the Royal Military Academy, Sandhurst.

John Simpson is Reader in International Relations and Co-Director of the Programme for the Promotion of Nuclear Non-Proliferation at the Department of Politics, University of Southampton.

Joanna Spear is Lecturer in the Department of Politics at the University of Sheffield.

Nicholas J. Wheeler is Lecturer in International Relations in the Department of Politics at the University of Hull.

Phil Williams is Senior Lecturer in the Department of Politics at the University of Southampton.

List of acronyms

ABM	Anti-ballistic Missile
ASMP	Air-Sol Moyenne Portée
ASW	Anti-Submarine Warfare
ATTU	Atlantic to the Urals
BAOR	British Army on the Rhine
BMD	Ballistic Missile Defence
BW	Biological Weapons
BWC	Biological Weapons Convention
CBW	Chemical and Biological Warfare
CDE	Conference on Disarmament in Europe
CDEE	Chemical Defence Experimental Establishment
CDNWT	Conference on the Discontinuance of Nuclear Weapons Tests
CFE	Convention Forces in Europe
CND	Campaign for Nuclear Disarmament
CoCom	Coordinating Committee on Export Controls
CSCE	Conference on Security and Cooperation in Europe
CTBT	Comprehensive Test Ban Treaty
CW	Chemical Weapons
CWT	Chemical Weapons Treaty
DESO	Defence Export Service Organisation
DSO	Defence Sales Organisation
DTI	Department of Trade and Industry (UK)
EEC	European Economic Community
ENDC	Eighteen Nation Conference on Disarmament
ENMOD	Environmental Modification Convention
EURATOM	European Atomic Energy Agency
FCO	Foreign and Commonwealth Office

FRG	Federal Republic of Germany
GCD	General and Complete Disarmament
IAEA	International Atomic Energy Agency
ICBM	Intercontinental Ballistic Missile
ICC	International Consultative Commitee
INF	Intermediate Nuclear Forces
INFCE	International Nuclear Fuel Cycle Evaluation
JVE	Joint Verification Experiment
MBFR	Mutual and Balanced Force Reductions
MoD	Ministry of Defence (UK)
MUF	Material Unaccounted for
NATA	North Atlantic Treaty Organisation
NNWS	Non-Nuclear Weapon States
NPT	Nuclear Non-Proliferation Treaty
NTM	National Technical Means
NWS	Nuclear Weapon States
OSI	On-Site Inspection
PNE	Peaceful Nuclear Explosion
PRC	People Republic of China
PRO	Public Records Office
PTBT	Partial Test Ban Treaty
R&D	Research and Development
SALT	Strategic Arms Limitation Talks
SDI	Strategic Defence Initiative
SIPRI	Stockholm International Peace Research Institute
SLBM	Submarine Launched Ballistic Missile
SNF	Short-range Nuclear Forces
START	Strategic Arms Reduction Talks
SVA	Separate Verification Agreement
THORP	Thermal Oxide Reprocessing Plant
TTBT	Threshold Test Ban Treaty

1 *Mark Hoffman*

UK arms control in the 1990s: introduction

During the course of the 1980s we have witnessed some of the most dramatic changes in the international and strategic environments in the whole of the post-war period. Indeed, the 1980s have been an almost exact chronological reversal of the pattern set in the 1970s. By the end of the 1980s we have witnessed:

1. the signing of the INF Agreement, an almost unprecedented arms control agreement eliminating a whole category of weapons;
2. several US-Soviet summits, including one at which the elimination of all ballistic missiles over a ten-year period was seriously contemplated;
3. dramatic changes in the Soviet Union including generational changes in its leadership engaging in domestic policies of *glasnost* and *perestroika* while proposing radical arms control initiatives;
4. the contemplation of the 'denuclearisation' of Europe via a 'third zero' which would remove short-range nuclear forces (SNF);
5. the likelihood of major arms control breakthroughs in conventional weapons, chemical weapons, strategic weapons and further restraints on nuclear testing;
6. democratically elected non-communist regimes in Eastern Europe.

So dramatic have these changes been that we almost forget that the first half of the decade was characterised by the virtual collapse of detente, heightened concerns about the implications of increases in Soviet military capabilities, the bellicosity of the first Reagan administration, the Strategic Defence Initiative, resurgent fears of the increased likelihood of nuclear war, and an underlying pessimism about the possibilities of and prospects for arms control. So far reaching have the changes been that most books, conference volumes and journal articles dealing with arms control and strategic issues over the past three or four years now read like period pieces.

The essays in this volume set out to examine UK arms control policy in the light of these changes. They argue that there are a set of strategic, political and economic constraints that any UK government, regardless of its political complexion, will have to face in the closing decade of the twentieth century. As becomes clear from a reading of the contributions, the underlying factor which conditions UK policy in all areas of arms control is Britain's status as a nuclear weapons state and its desire to preserve that status. This has promoted at best a status quo orientation in arms control negotiations and at worst a negative approach presented under the guise of 'assisting' superpower dialogue. The implications of the analysis in each of the chapters is that it will become increasingly difficult for Britain to maintain and defend such attitudes and policies. The conclusion which is drawn from the examination of UK arms control policy across a wide spectrum of issue areas is that, in the light of the changing international and strategic environments, any UK government will be compelled to take a more constructive approach to arms control in the 1990s. Any government that attempts to maintain the UK's traditional approach to these issues will squander the opportunity to play a central and constructive role in the restructuring of European security.

The first part of the book examines the contexts and constraints which condition UK arms control policy. In the first chapter, Phil Williams discusses the 'bonfires of the certainties'. He argues that all the certitudes on which British security and arms control policy are premised are now being severely undermined; the nature of the 'special relationship', the balance of forces within the NATO Alliance, the nature of the Soviet threat, and the stability of the cold war security framework in Europe. The implication is clear: in the light of the demise of these certainties the UK can no longer rely on its status quo orientation, its reactive policies. Instead, it must develop innovative, proactive arms control policies which take advantage of the new opportunities and challenges in Europe. Most importantly, UK security and arms control policy now needs to be geared towards crisis stability rather than deterrence.

Nicholas Wheeler picks up on several of these themes in the second chapter in which he discusses the 'dual imperative' of the UK's nuclear status: the Soviet threat and Anglo–American relations. Wheeler assesses the impact of changes in these two areas, particularly the implications of changes in the nature of the Soviet threat. He notes that the UK's status quo arms control orientation has been legitimised and justified by the Soviet threat. These attitudes developed in the immediate post-war period were reinforced during the Cold War, have became enshrined in the 'Moscow criteria' and provided part of the basis for the decision to purchase Trident. Arguing that these views might have been justified in the period from 1945 to 1985, Wheeler addresses the implications for UK policy of the changes taking place in Soviet domestic, foreign and defence policy and the degree to which these may validate alternative arms control policies. Importantly, he argues that changes in the Soviet threat may not lead to any substantial changes in UK policy. The reason for this is that the UK's policy has more to do with the Alliance and the 'special relationship' than the Soviet threat, but that these justifications are much more difficult to sell convincingly to the public. The outcome is a UK government pushing for nuclear force modernisations while the US and Soviet Union pursue substantial cuts in their nuclear forces. The result is that the UK could be seen to be a 'spoiler' in the developing momentum of arms control.

In the third chapter setting the context in which arms control decisions will take place in the 1990s, Stuart Croft and David H. Dunn examine the economic constraints facing British defence policy and how these might affect the UK's attitudes and approaches to arms control. They highlight two contrasting views on dealing with the tensions between commitments and resources: management or reform. The former argues that the tensions are manageable and require little change in policies. The latter argues that they are insuperable and require a redefinition and reorientation of Britain's traditional defence role. However, it is not clear that arms control provides a way out of the morass. Instead, what is required is a full-scale defence review co-ordinated with a reassessment of UK defence and arms control policies.

The second section of the book examines UK arms control policy in six specific areas: strategic and theatre nuclear; conventional and European security; non-proliferation; comprehensive test ban; chemical weapons; and conventional arms transfers. In the discussion of Britain's policy on nuclear arms control, Stuart Croft notes that Britain has traditionally professed its support for multilateral arms control. Yet the UK has never participated in strategic nuclear arms negotiations. Instead it has been the fortuitous beneficiary of its 'special relationship' with the US and has played upon the distinction between 'theatre' and 'strategic' weapons. These have ensured that the UK deterrent never came on to the negotiating table. However, the twin basis of UK policy are being called into question. The 'special relationship' has in some important senses broken down. The changed arms control environment means that it will be increasingly difficult to rely on the theatre/strategic distinction. The implication is that as we move towards a post-START world, there will be increasing pressure on Britain to participate in multilateral nuclear arms control processes.

David H. Dunn examines a similar set of problems in relation to conventional arms control, theatre weapons and European security in the post-INF world. He argues that Britain's policy has been profoundly cautious and conservative. Britain has continually reacted against any proposal that might undermine the NATO Alliance's traditional approach to European security based on nuclear weapons. This concern underpins Britain's attitudes to a 'third zero', its fear of denuclearisation and its emphasis on linking conventional arms control as a prerequisite for further nuclear arms control. But, as Dunn notes, if the hope was that this would forestall any major changes, these have been dashed by the speed with which the CFE negotiations have moved. The implication is the need to develop innovative policies that take account of and channel the changes taking place in the structure of European security.

The conservative position of Britain's arms control policies are once again highlighted in John Simpson's discussion of Britain's non-proliferation policy. Since 1945, the UK has adopted the position that it must possess nuclear weapons for its own security. The cornerstone of UK weapons policy is its agreement with the US on the transfer of nuclear technology. Once it gained possession of the bomb, UK policy pursued two interrelated tracks: one to ensure its continued possession of nuclear weapons and the other to prevent or dissuade other powers from developing them. In any clash between the two, the latter comes a poor second. This is evident in its changing attitudes and policies on a Comprehensive Test Ban, limitations on fissile material and the Non-Proliferation Treaty. But even this environment is changing and UK non-proliferation policy will come under pressure from a number of directions: the UK will be affected by and have to adjust to any constraints, such as a CTB, enhanced threshold treaty or redefined ABM Treaty, negotiated by the US and the Soviet Union; the pressures between commercial policy and its desire to forestall the development of other national nuclear capabilities; and pressure within the NPT review conferences to seriously pursue Article VI.

These pressures are further discussed by Wyn Rees, John Simpson and Darryl Howlett in their chapter on the Comprehensive Test Ban Treaty. This appears to be one of the few areas where Britain might lay claim to genuine efforts towards positive and constructive arms control policies. However, as the chapter makes clear, Britain's policy has historically been conditioned by its possession of nuclear weapons and its desire to safeguard that status. Its enthusiasm has been conditional on the state of modernisation of the UK's nuclear forces, of the superpower strategic balance and of its fear of being left behind. Its policy on a CTBT has also been conditioned by its technological reliance on the US. These objectives and constraints have lead to the UK's emphasis on the problems of verifying a CTBT and, later, the necessity to maintain some level of testing in order to ensure stockpile reliability. The result is a positive approach at the level of declared policy, but one which in reality severely undermines the likelihood of ever achieving a CTBT.

Britain's possession of nuclear weapons plays a prominent role in accounting for its policies on chemical and biological weapons. The UK is ostensibly committed to the objective of general and complete disarmament in the area of chemical and biological weapons. Once again, this would appear to be an arms control area where the UK could claim to have played a positive role. Indeed, the UK would appear to be a 'model' state, being one of the few countries to unilaterally disarm an offensive chemical weapon stockpile. But as Howlett argues, this policy had less to do with universal moral considerations than with factors specific to the UK: namely, the economic costs of developing nuclear weapons in the 1950s and its possession of nuclear weapons as an alternative security guarantee to the possession of chemical and biological weapons. This raises difficult questions regarding how suitable a role model Britain is for non-nuclear weapon states. Nevertheless, the UK has played a significant role in the negotiations on biological and chemical weapons, proposing complete bans, and novel approaches to overcoming apparently insurmountable differences between the US and the Soviet Union and international bodies for inspection. More problematic is the likelihood that once the US and the Soviet Union are convinced of the merits and possibilities of a treaty, they will develop their own 'watered-down' version of UK proposals, with the

UK compelled by virtue of the 'special relationship' to acquiesce to US policy.

The final issue area examined is the control of conventional arms transfers. Joanna Spear notes Britain's ambivalent attitude towards conventional arms transfers and conventional arms transfer controls. What is apparent is that the UK has no coherent policy in this area, judging transfers on a case-by-case basis. The constraints that the UK faces on conventional arms transfers derive from three areas. First is the changing nature and structure of the international arms market. There has been an increase in the number of arms suppliers with the rise of second and third generation arms manufacturers, such as Eastern European countries or Brazil and Argentina; increasing emphasis on co-production; and the transfer of technology along with weapon systems. Second, there has been mounting pressure from the US to limit and control the transfer of technology, particularly to the East. Third, there has been increasing concern over the transfer of ballistic missile technology. The dynamics of all three areas create competing pressures on UK policy: on the one hand, the need to effectively compete in the increasingly competitive arms markets and on the other, a concern over the rapid proliferation of advanced weapons technology which provides the possibility of advanced weapon delivery systems being transferred to third parties. On the basis of these pressures and previous efforts at multilateral control of arms transfers, Spear concludes that the prognosis for the future is not good.

The final chapter returns to some of the themes identified in Phil Williams's chapter and relates these to various problems identified in the other chapters. Starting with the characterisation of UK arms control policy as essentially reactive, it discusses possible alternatives for UK arms control policy in terms of conservative, managerial, reformist and radical traditions. Possible alternatives for UK arms control policy in the 1990s are: a conservative approach which seeks to limit the possibilities for any substantive restructuring of the strategic environment through an essentially ambivalent, if not hostile, attitude towards arms control; a managerial approach which seeks to encourage major reductions in US–Soviet strategic arsenals while making no changes in UK status; a reformist approach which would include UK nuclear weapons in multilateral negotiations while promoting substantial cuts in conventional weapons with the long-term goal of directing and contributing in a positive fashion to the restructuring of European security; and a radical approach which pursues unilateralist measures in an effort to disengage the UK from its strategic relationship with both the US and NATO and the elimination of the bloc structures as the basis of European security. It argues that the conservative approach is unnecessarily pessimistic in the light of changed political and strategic circumstances; that the managerial approach does not go far enough in recognising the nature of these changes and seeking to encourage them; and that the radical approach has become marginalised in the context of a post-INF and post-START world. It argues in favour of the reform approach, with an emphasis placed on policy approaches being developed and justified in the context of a contribution to the necessary rethinking of the nature of European security in the 1990s and into the twenty-first century.

The political and strategic environments of the 1990s are likely to create considerable pressures on the UK's status quo security policies. It may be that the traditionalists with the UK will be able to draw some comfort from the end of visionary arms control under the Bush administration. But this is true only at the level of strategic arms control and only for a relatively short-lived period of time. Once a START agreement is in hand, there will be immense pressure on Britain (and other middle-range nuclear powers) to participate in START II. The speed with which CFE negotiations are moving and the political changes in Eastern Europe means that Britain's position on a number of arms control issues will be out of step with the US and the rest of its NATO allies. Concerns about the proliferation of nuclear and advanced conventional weapons technology will place increasing pressures on the UK's ambivalent policies. The most effective way of dealing with these pressures is a reorientation away from the UK's traditional security policies which allows the UK to take advantage of and participate in the developing and ongoing processes of restructuring European and international security.

Part 1:

Changing contexts

British security and arms control policy: the changing context

The security debate

The British debate on security and arms control during much of the post-war period has been confined within narrow limits and characterised by a broad bipartisan consensus. During the 1950s and the 1980s, however, the debate widened. The Campaign for Nuclear Disarmament in the 1950s and the Peace Movement in the late 1970s and the early 1980s injected more radical ideas into the discussion of security issues. On both occasions the Labour Party became committed, if only for a short time, to unilateral disarmament. These periods of controversy highlighted fundamental differences between two schools of thought – conservative and radical – both of which have deep roots in British thinking about international politics. These two schools reflect divergent traditions in the approach to foreign policy and defence issues, offer very different assessments of the problems of national and international security, and equally divergent recommendations as to what should be done about these problems.

The conservative approach emphasises short-term considerations and is concerned primarily with upholding and managing the status quo. Its starting point is the assumption that the international system is Hobbesian and that in such a system, challenges to security are endemic. To contain these threats, a balance of power approach is essential. Power politics, scorn for visionary ideas of international reform, and a preoccupation with the narrow requirements of national security, dominate what is essentially a pragmatic approach. The problem is that concern with short-term management inhibits long-term assessment and stifles any sense of vision.

The radical tradition, in contrast, is the tradition of dissent and long-term vision. It rejects the pessimism of the Hobbesian school and offers proposals for reform and change in the international system. Existing mechanisms for maintaining order and security, such as deterrence, are regarded at best as inadequate and at worst as dangerous and provocative. While nuclear weapons have given an added urgency to radical thinking about international politics, the tradition can be traced back to the liberal idealism of the nineteenth century exemplified in the writings of Cobden and Bright. Subsequently, this idealism merged with socialist ideas and became particularly important during the inter-war period. During much of the period since the Second World War, it was muted, but was resuscitated in the 1980s by a Labour Party which argued once again that Britain could give a moral lead to the world.

The radical and conservative traditions lead to very different conceptions of the arms control process. The radical approach sees arms control as being of value primarily as something which might lead to disarmament. Agreements designed simply to uphold the status quo and stabilise nuclear deterrence have little utility and are dismissed as perpetuating a system that requires much more fundamental reform. The arms control process in the 1970s was seen in this way whereas unilateralism was an effort to move beyond status quo oriented arms control and bring about more far-reaching change. From this perspective, arms control has value only if it generates a dynamic towards disarmament.

The conservative approach is equally circumspect about arms control, but for different reasons. From a conservative perspective, arms control *per se* is not a good thing. Specific negotiations and agreements have to be assessed in terms of their contribution to British security, not according to whether they promote more far-reaching measures of disarmament. In other words, the conservative approach to arms control varies from issue to issue and from negotiation to negotiation: it is not necessarily hostile to arms control but, in certain circumstances, it may be.

During the 1980s, the British debate about security and arms control has been polarised by a Conservative government which used the idea of multilateralism to cloak its hostility to anything other than very modest forms of arms control which were effectively designed to uphold the status quo, and a Labour Party which enunciated a unilateralist stance that appeared so extreme that it became an electoral liability. As a result, the Labour Party has moved back towards the mainstream (but without adopting the conservative approach to security of arms control issues). Yet this has coincided with trends and developments in East–West relations which suggest that far-reaching changes in the security order in Europe might not be as remote as they have appeared in the past. Indeed, a Labour government with sympathy for radical ideas could well find the security environment of the 1990s rather congenial, whereas a Conservative government will find it discomfiting.

In the past, of course, the Labour Party, once in government, has eschewed radicalism in favour of more cautious policies based very much on short-term considerations. Indeed, British defence policy has traditionally been based on a set of stable assumptions about the nature of security and how it is best achieved. The Soviet threat, the US guarantee, the role of nuclear weapons, and the primacy of NATO have provided the basic parameters within which defence policy has been formulated by both parties. Many of the underlying judgements and assumptions have been evident since the late 1940s and though there has been a contraction in the geographical presence of UK forces and a recognition that Britain no longer plays a global role, defence policy has been marked, above all, by continuity. On several occasions Britain has had to engage in painful defence reviews in order to bring commitments and capabilities in line with each other and to adjust to reduced economic circumstances. Nevertheless, these reviews have not led to an abandonment of the basic assumptions underlying British policy.

As Britain enters the 1990s, it is confronted with what George Robertson, the Labour Party's deputy spokesman on foreign affairs has termed a 'bonfire of the certainties'. The evidence is that the post-war international order is disappearing. The implications of this for British defence and arms control policies remain uncertain and in some respects unpredictable. The purpose of this chapter is to identify the major changes that are taking place and to consider how this will impinge on British arms control policy in the 1990s. It is less concerned with providing definitive answers or solutions to the impending problems, than with highlighting some of the choices that the UK will have to make in an environment that is more unpredictable than at any time since the immediate post-war period. The international system of the 1990s is likely to have a degree of fluidity that contrasts very starkly with the static quality of the last forty years. The key question for policy-makers and planners in the UK, therefore, is whether they should adjust to these changes by adopting new policies and perhaps forging new institutions and management mechanisms, or should they resist the changes in an effort to uphold existing security structures and patterns of co-operation.

Part of the problem of adjustment is a conceptual one. Although Britain prides itself on a pragmatic approach to security policy, this often disguises an innate conservatism which leads to a reluctance to contemplate change and to adjust to new circumstances. In the 1990s, however, it will be necessary either to develop new concepts or, at the very least, to adjust and modify old concepts to new circumstances and conditions. Before examining possible reactions, however, it is necessary to discuss more fully some of the changes that are taking place in the context within which the United Kingdom has to formulate its security and arms control policies.

The changing context

After almost forty years of stability, the security environment has become more dynamic and exciting. Major changes have occurred in the nature of the threat to security and the US commitment to Western Europe, in the Anglo-American 'special relationship' and in the impact of arms control on defence policy.

Since the Second World War the principal preoccupation of British policy-makers and planners has been with those challenges posed by the Soviet Union. The values which infused the Soviet economic, social and political system, and which, it was generally believed, the Soviet Union was ideologically committed to propagate, were regarded as antithetical to those of Western democracies. Moreover, the Soviet Union and its allies possessed formidable military capabilities which are regarded as a direct military threat to Western Europe. This is not to suggest that British policy-makers believed that the Soviet Union was intent on conquering Western Europe through military invasion. It is simply that given the antipathies between Soviet and Western systems, it was important not to provide opportunities either for direct military action or for coercion based upon military superiority. As the Statement on the Defence Estimates in 1986 expressed it:

The Soviet Union presents us with the paradox of a country obsessed with its own security but unwilling to acknowledge the implications of its massive

military forces for the security of others. There is, moreover, sufficient
evidence of Soviet ruthlessness, both against internal dissent and against
what are seen as external threats, to justify a permanent degree of Western
caution ... whether Soviet actions are interpreted as ... a communist crusade
or as a search for security, it is essential that we and our allies continue to
provide an adequate political and military counter-weight to Soviet nuclear
and conventional strength. Only in this way can we be certain of protecting
the freedom and lifestyle that we have chosen.[1]

This has been the prevailing judgement since the late 1940s when
much of the framework for British defence planning and policy-
making was established.

In the second half of the 1980s, however, this judgement was
increasingly challenged. The changes in Eastern Europe and flexibility of the Soviet Union under Mikhail Gorbachev called into
question traditional assessments of the Soviet threat. Moreover,
although the British government established a series of litmus tests
for Gorbachev, it has been faced with difficulties when he has met
them. Soviet withdrawal from Afghanistan, for example, made it
much more difficult for Britain, and indeed, its allies, to use the war
as an excuse for continuing with hard-line policies towards
Moscow. Perhaps even more importantly, Gorbachev has taken
steps to ease Western anxieties over Soviet military capabilities. The
flexibility he displayed in agreeing to asymmetrical cuts on Intermediate Nuclear Forces has been followed by substantial unilateral
cuts in Soviet conventional forces, including those in Eastern
Europe. Such measures greatly alleviate fears over the Soviet
capacity for surprise attack, something that has long been a major
concern for NATO. They seem to accord with Gorbachev's idea of
reorienting Soviet defence capabilities to a level of reasonable
sufficiency.

There have been several responses to Gorbachev in Britain. His
policies have sometimes been dismissed as simply a more subtle
variant of traditional Soviet desires to split the Western Alliance
and to achieve a position of dominance over Western Europe.
Simply because the Soviet bear has learned how to smile, it is
argued, it does not mean that it has ceased to be a bear. Yet the
extent of the changes within the Soviet Union itself and the moves
towards democratization in Eastern Europe have cast doubt on the
wisdom of maintaining an approach to security that was essentially
a response to the Soviet Union of Joseph Stalin. Very few officials

are yet willing to accept that the threat has disappeared, or that Britain should abandon its traditional approach to security. At the same time, Gorbachev has had a significant impact at the level of public opinion and in the last few years of the Reagan administration consistently obtained higher ratings in opinion polls throughout Western Europe than did the US President. The British government has also had to contend with the fact as a consequence of the changes in Eastern Europe that some of its major allies appear to be engaging in far-reaching reappraisals of the requirements of security in the 1990s.

In view of all this, it is not surprising that there are elements of confusion and uncertainty in the British debate over security. The situation is reminiscent in many respects of the lines written by the nineteenth-century Greek poet, Gavafy, to describe the confusion that reigned in ancient Rome when the threat from the Barbarians did not materialise:

Why this sudden bewilderment, this confusion? Why are the streets and squares emptying so rapidly, everyone going home lost in thought? Because night has fallen and the barbarians have not come. So what is going to happen to us without the Barbarians? They were, those people, a kind of solution!

Even though there is still a need to provide countervailing power against the Soviet Union which, for all its internal problems, is likely to remain the largest single power on the European continent, planning assumptions based upon the Soviet threat are no longer either as stable or as compelling as they once were. Since the late 1940s the Soviet Union has been a kind of solution for British defence policy-makers and planners; it may be far less of one in the 1990s.

The downgrading of the Soviet threat will intensify familiar pressures on money and manpower for defence. The Federal Republic faces the economic costs of unification, while defence policy-makers and planners in other NATO countries, including Britain, have to contend with serious economic and political constraints. In the past, governments have attempted to overcome these constraints. One result of the Gorbachev phenomenon, however, is that it will be increasingly difficult for governments to justify higher spending on defence in a period when the threat has diminished, especially when the demands for greater resources from health, education and welfare are becoming increasingly insistent. There is also a feeling that, with the increases in defence spending resulting from the NATO commitment to the three per cent target in 1978, defence had it too good for too long.

A second area of change is in the US commitment to Western Europe. Although there is unlikely to be any dramatic shift in the tectonic plates of US foreign policy – especially with a Bush administration which is very Atlanticist in its orientation – there are trends which suggest that the US is likely to be less willing to underwrite the security of Western Europe to the same extent in the 1990s as it has in the past. Indeed, there are several developments which imply that the period in which Western Europe has been predominantly a security consumer is coming to an end and that increasingly Western Europe will have to accept greater responsibility for its own security. One reason for this is the relative decline of the US in the international system. West European dependence on the US was understandable in the 1950s when American hegemony was unchallenged. During the 1960s and 1970s, however, the economic recovery of Western Europe and Japan and the Soviet attainment of strategic parity challenged that hegemony. Yet in many respects, the Atlantic security arrangements are still based on the assumptions of the 1950s. During the early 1990s the anachronistic nature of these assumptions will become more apparent as a consequence of the changes in Europe.

These changes will reinforce domestic pressure for defence cuts in order to deal with the US budget deficit. With less money available for defence, the choices within the US defence budget will become more acute. Although there are very obvious areas, such as the SDI programme, where cuts are already being made, and there are other obvious candidates for savings either through cancellation or stretching out the acquisition process (eg the B-2 stealth bomber), the US troop level in Europe is unlikely to be sacrosanct. The Bush initiative to reduce US forces in central Europe to 195,000 as part of a negotiated deal on conventional arms control depends on the Soviet union being prepared to make a much larger cut. Nevertheless, the very existence of the initiative suggests that the time when the US was willing to provide its European allies with security on the cheap has passed – and is unlikely to return.

British policy has always been designed to prevent a serious – let alone an agonising – reappraisal of the US commitment to Western

Europe. In order to ensure this, Britain has placed great weight on
the Anglo–American 'special relationship'. This relationship is
based on patterns of co-operation which reflect 'ties of history and
kinship' but which were cemented during the Second World War
and have remained in some form ever since. Although the relationship is often described as an asymmetrical one and being of far
less importance to Washington than to London, co-operation has
been both close and extensive. According to former US Secretary of
State, Henry Kissinger, successive British governments were able to
establish

a pattern of consultation so matter-of-factly intimate that it became
psychologically impossible to ignore British views. They evolved a habit of
meetings so regular that autonomous American actions came to seem to
violate club rules. Above all, they used effectively an abundance of wisdom
and trustworthiness of conduct so exceptional that American leaders saw it
in their self-interest to obtain British advice before making major decisions.
It was an extraordinary relationship because it rested on no legal claims; it
was formalised by no document; it was carried forward by succeeding
British governments as if no alternative were conceivable.[2]

The 'special relationship' encompasses the nuclear connection,
and co-operation on a wide range of military and intelligence
activities, including, most significantly, anti-submarine warfare
(ASW) operations. The patterns of co-operation have provided
Britain with a Polaris SLBM force and with its replacement, the
Trident D5 missile, at a relatively modest cost. Moreover, the
practice and procedures of co-operation have been developed at a
variety of levels. 'Beyond the diplomatic and political links, an
intricate network has, over the years, been established' in which
British and American policy-makers and officials work closely
together.[3] This is evident in a variety of fora including NATO
where, according to one former American diplomat, British and
American officials attempt to co-ordinate their approaches on a
variety of issues.[4]

Although successive British governments have embraced the idea
of a 'special relationship', it not a relationship devoid of problems
and is not always popular in Britain itself. Some critics have
asserted that the relationship has had a largely negative effect on
British policy, encouraging continued pretensions about Britain's
role and status in the world, an undesirable ambivalence towards

ventures in European defence co-operation, and an uncritical attitude towards the US. The contention that Britain has slavishly supported ill-chosen US policies was especially marked during the 1980s, and the Thatcher government's backing for President Reagan on a variety of controversial issues was characterised as 'poodleism'. British public opinion polls revealed a decline of faith in the US as an ally. Part of this reflected an antipathy towards President Reagan and on very few occasions in Gallup polls taken in Britain between 1981 and 1986 did Reagan have a positive rating as a 'good president'. The negative ratings peaked in 1982 and 1983 and became pronounced again after the US attack on Libya in 1986. There is also a continuing concern with the quality of American leadership, and since 1978 there has been a fairly consistent pattern of poll results indicating a lack of faith in the American ability to 'deal wisely with present world problems'.

A second problem is that, Kissinger's comments notwithstanding, the wielding of influence by Britain is often made problematic by the turbulence of the American political system. The executive branch guards its power jealously against the Congress, and the President and his key advisers are often unwilling to engage in advance consultation with Capitol Hill, let alone the allies. Much of the process of wielding influence, therefore, has to be done on a personal level. Meetings between the Prime Minister and the President are often crucial, as are the contacts between the Foreign Secretary and the US Secretary of State, and between the UK Minister of Defence and the US Secretary of Defence. This places a premium on the relationship between the leaders, especially Prime Minister and President. When their personal rapport is good, the relationship appears to be strong; when they get on less well together, the relationship can appear rather more fragile. If this accounts for short-term fluctuations, however, there also seems to be a long-term trend away from the 'special relationship'. In the final analysis, Washington's most important ally in Western Europe is not Britain but the Federal Republic of Germany and the US connection with Bonn has become more important as the pace of change in Eastern Europe has accelerated, culminating in the redrawing of the political and security map of Europe. In the 1990s, therefore, there must be question marks about both the supposed uniqueness of Anglo–American relations and the British ability to act as intermediary between the US and Western Europe.

The other area where the 'bonfire of certainties' has had major impact is on the role of nuclear weapons in underpinning NATO strategy and Western European security. The challenge here has come from several separate directions. One was the upsurge of anti-nuclear sentiment that greeted NATO's 1979 decision to deploy Cruise and Pershing 2 missiles. Anti-nuclear sentiment was evident in most states of Western Europe, and in Britain it destroyed the consensus on defence, as the Labour Party (as in the 1950s) embraced unilateral disarmament. Although this challenge to the existing policy receded as unilateralism proved to be a vote loser for Labour in 1983 and 1987, two other challenges became more insistent.

The first of these was from the US, which during much of the 1980s appeared to relegate the role of nuclear weapons in European security. The antipathy of the Reagan administration towards nuclear weapons was evident initially in SDI and subsequently in the negotiations at the Reykjavik Summit and in the INF Treaty which eliminated all nuclear missiles in Europe with a range between 500 and 5000 kilometres. At the formal level, the INF Agreement between the superpowers was endorsed by the West European allies including Britain. Yet, it also generated much concern in certain quarters about a possible weakening of the US guarantee to Western Europe and about American reliability as an alliance leader. Part of the problem was that the long-range theatre nuclear forces, which were deployed as a result of the 1979 decision, were regarded by European governments, especially the British government, as an important means of strengthening or reaffirming the coupling between the US and Western Europe. In an era of strategic parity they helped to ensure that extended deterrence retained its validity. Consequently, their removal appeared as a weakening of extended deterrence – although certainly not an abandonment of it.

The other challenge to the nuclear component of NATO strategy and to the British government's faith in nuclear deterrence came from the Federal Republic of Germany – and resulted from Bonn's response to the new opportunities offered by Gorbachev and the new dangers resulting from the INF Agreement and subsequent plans for the modernisation of short range nuclear forces. In the aftermath of the INF Treaty there was a strong feeling in Bonn that West Germany had been singularised and was now bearing an inordinate share of the risk. In the past, NATO strategy had always been ambiguous about the likelihood of escalation and the uncertainty had meant that the burden of risk appeared to be distributed amongst the allies in a fairly equitable manner. The removal of Cruise and Pershing meant that, apart from aircraft, the bulk of NATO's nuclear forces in Europe were short-range and would be used either on West Germany itself or on East Germany. Demands for Bonn to agree to deploy a follow on to the Lance (FOTL) missile system, which would need replacement by 1995, accentuated German neuralgia. Consequently, Mrs Thatcher's emphasis on the need for modernisation and the importance of avoiding a 'third zero' or indeed even negotiations on short-range systems placed her on a direct collision course with Bonn. The NATO Summit was able to forge a compromise on this issue, but it was a compromise which moved away from the commitment to modernise and emphasised the commitment to negotiate. Mrs Thatcher claimed that a third zero had been formally ruled out, but the possibility of a further downgrading of nuclear weapons in NATO's force posture now seems very likely.

These challenges to the British belief that nuclear weapons are critical to the European security order have gone hand in hand with the challenge to the British assumption that while arms control can be a modest but important supplement to unilateral efforts to attain security it cannot be a substitute for these efforts. Conservative governments in Britain have traditionally emphasised the primacy of force planning considerations over arms control and attempted to ensure that arms control was not allowed to erode the Alliance's apparatus for deterrence and defence vis-a-vis the Soviet Union. They accepted that arms control might enhance stability, but regarded it as tangential to the real basis of security. Not surprisingly, therefore, the Thatcher government became apprehensive about the more reformist approach to arms control adopted by the Reagan administration – and was anxious that the role of nuclear weapons not be downgraded too far. Although it is somewhat happier with a Bush administration which has adopted a less visionary and more pragmatic approach to arms control, the Federal Republic of Germany has now adopted a more ambitious and visionary approach to arms control – albeit one rooted in the peculiarities of German security concerns and vulnerabilities as a consequence of the changes in Eastern Europe.

The difficulties faced at the nuclear level have been compounded by the problems posed at the conventional level. The talks on Conventional Forces in Europe (CFE) have raised crucial questions about the extent of conventional force reductions in light of the changing structure of European security. There is some argument that these units have to be structured to meet certain force to space requirements almost irrespective of the shape of the Soviet military threat. The implication is that even large scale reductions in Soviet military capabilities will not permit concomitant cuts in NATO forces. Yet, as the negotiations develop a momentum, this may be difficult to avoid.

The other development which provides part of the emerging context for British defence policy in the 1990s is serious negotiation between Moscow and Washington on the reduction of strategic forces. A START Agreement which reduces Soviet and American strategic arsenals by around 35 per cent (i.e., the nominal 50 per cent cut) would still leave large superpower arsenals, but would enhance the significance of French and British forces. There would almost certainly be increased pressure, therefore, for including these forces in a second START forum. Britain could be particularly susceptible to pressure, given that it depends on the US for the supply of the Trident D5 missile.

While each of these trends seems manageable when looked at in isolation, the danger is that the divergences between the US and the European allies as well as among the Europeans themselves could take on their own dynamic and generate splits in Atlantic relations that will prove difficult to contain. There are several developments – the European reluctance to do more for security, as well as the German process of unification – which could feed into the American debate about NATO in a way that is particularly harmful and divisive. The American Congress, disillusioned about the lack of European burden-sharing and quick to fashion slogans such as 'no nukes, no troops' could become far more insistent in its demands for reductions in the American military presence in Western Europe.

The implication of all this is that the familiar and relatively static security order in Europe that Britain helped to create is eroding. How far this erosion will go is uncertain. What is clear is that Britain will not be able to uphold the existing order rather than accommodate and promote change within it. Much will depend on the composition of British governments during the 1990s. Whatever government is in power, however, it will need to grapple with the changes that are taking place and to devise a coherent response. The problem, however, is far easier to state than to solve.

The conceptual crisis

The main difficulty for the UK is less the practical problems that have arisen than what might be termed a conceptual crisis in British security policy. The trends outlined above have challenged the orthodoxies of post-war British policy and have raised doubts about the appropriateness of the traditional British approach, dominated as it has been by the conservative tradition. They have also raised in a far more pointed way than ever before fundamental questions about the nature of security and the role of both nuclear weapons and arms control in a changing Europe and a changing world. There are several key questions, therefore, that successive British governments in the 1990s will have to confront if they are to manage this crisis and shape a new security policy that is relevant and appropriate to new circumstances.

Perhaps the first and most basic question that has to be answered concerns the nature and meaning of security. Britain has clung to a traditional security paradigm which has been based on clear identification of friend and foe, unilateral and collective defence efforts to maintain a balance of power, the need to deter premeditated attacks, the central role of nuclear weapons in providing that deterrent, and the subordination of arms control to strategy and force planning. In the late 1980s key components of this paradigm were called into question and an alternative paradigm of common or reciprocal security has been enunciated.

The notion of reciprocal security is based on the assumption that even enemies can have common interests and that, in particular, they have a mutual interest in achieving stability. Moreover, the problem of security is not defined simply in terms of thwarting the ambitions and potential aggressiveness of an enemy state, but is seen instead as the need to control dangerous and insidious interaction processes which result from the security dilemma in which each side's attempts to enhance its security have the perverse effect of increasing the insecurity of the other side. It is also believed that stability depends less on deterrence – and some proponents of this alternative paradigm see nuclear weapons as part of the problem rather than the solution – than on reassurance, on a capacity to prevent crises and, in the event that they occur nonetheless, on an ability to manage them successfully and avoid inadvertent escalation.

The traditional notion of security and the idea of reciprocal security are not mutually exclusive. Establishing force postures, mechanisms and procedures in which they are blended together, however, is not easy. Similarly, it is difficult to decide on the appropriate criteria for strategy and force posture, in view of the changing nature of the Soviet threat. In the past, the most obvious danger has been premeditated aggression; in the future this seems far less likely than political instability resulting from developments in Eastern Europe. The US is sometimes described as Europe's American pacifier; by the same token, the Soviet Union has acted as pacifier in Eastern Europe. Although it has done this in a repressive way, the easing of this repression has allowed old tensions, rivalries and conflicts to resurface. In these circumstances, an exclusive focus on deterrence seems misplaced while the need to improve the capacity for crisis prevention and crisis management in Europe appears more important than ever.

The changing international context also highlights the need to distinguish more carefully between ends and means in the European security equation. Flexible response, deterrence and the need to maintain NATO cohesion are often discussed as if they were the ends rather than simply the means to security. This is understandable in view of their enduring role in maintaining stability on the European Continent. Yet the security arrangements we have now are very much a product of the Cold War and the period of unquestioned American dominance in the international system. As these conditions alter so there should be adjustments in the security arrangements to reflect new realities. Furthermore, no military strategy should be regarded as sacrosanct, while even security arrangements embodied in collective political and military organizations like NATO are not immutable. The reluctance to reappraise something that has been eminently successful is understandable. Yet by clinging to security mechanisms that, in the light of changing circumstances, may be less appropriate than they were, there is a danger that opportunities to enhance both security and stability will be lost. On the other hand, there are dangers in moving from one set of security arrangements to another and it is important that some kind of safety net be maintained – and that this be given a credible public rationale.

It is not sufficient to argue that nothing has changed in terms of European security and any government which attempts to do this is unlikely to maintain popular support.

Closely related to all this is the most fundamental question of all for British policy-makers and planners – should they regard change as inevitable and simply accommodate themselves to it while simultaneously attempting to channel it in desired directions, or should they resist change and attempt to maintain the status quo against those trends and developments that are now discernible. This question arises at both the political and military levels and requires that greater attention is given to future models of European security. What kinds of security order will exist by the year 2000? How will this differ from the existing order? What elements of the existing arrangement should be retained and what can be dispensed with? Is negotiated arms control something that will facilitate change or will it inhibit flexibility? Would unilateral measures be a more effective way to proceed? To what extent are the changes likely to be controllable, or will they involve processes which, once set in motion, take on a dynamic or momentum of their own and become virtually unstoppable?

Questions such as these cannot be answered in any final or definitive way. It should be possible, however, to identify several principles which seem relevant for the 1990s and could appropriately be reflected in British policy.

Security in the 1990s

It is important to recognise that deterrence is likely to be much easier in the environment of the 1990s than it has been for most of the post-war period. Although the likelihood of Soviet aggression against Western Europe may have been more remote than official British and NATO assessments suggested, in the past the ideological character of the regime combined with massive Soviet military capabilities in ways which were not conducive to trust in Soviet restraint. The Soviet Union of Gorbachev, however, is certainly not the Soviet Union of Stalin, or even of Brezhnev. The internal changes taking place in the Soviet Union have demonstrated that the repressive ideological monolith has become less repressive, less ideological and less monolithic, while Gorbachev's willingness to reduce forces unilaterally and to display unprecedented flexibility in negotiations has started to diminish concerns over the Soviet capacity for a surprise attack.

Even so the West cannot become sanguine or complacent and it would be premature to abandon deterrence or to suggest that nuclear weapons have no role to play in maintaining European security. Yet, there has to be some recognition that the Soviet Union of the 1990s may be relatively easy to deter. The West German opposition to modernisation of Lance was based partly on the proposition that the requirements of deterrence are less stringent than in the past and that NATO does not need to deploy the full panoply of nuclear systems to inhibit Soviet actions inimical to West European security.

To argue against a Lance follow on, however, is not to campaign against deterrence. Indeed, it is possible to oppose the FOTL while recognising that nuclear weapons must continue to play a crucial role in the European security order of the 1990s. Nuclear deterrence has an immediacy and an impact that conventional deterrence lacks. If the balance is purely conventional, there is always the possibility that military victory might be achieved at an acceptable cost. The problem with conventional deterrence is the absence of the element of terror. When nuclear weapons are brought into the equation, winning no longer has much attraction. It is crucial therefore to ensure that the UK's force posture retains a nuclear component. After all, nuclear weapons instil prudence, and relations between adversaries who possess nuclear powers are generally based on mutually understood conventions or codes of conduct.

Nuclear weapons would help to ensure that the inhibitions on high risk behaviour are maintained against a background of shifting relationships that could result in widespread unrest and political turmoil. They would not only ensure that prudence continues to look attractive to Moscow, but would also provide a residual guarantee against changes in Soviet policy and the possible reversion to a more hostile approach. How this general principle translates into specific operational requirements is, of course, more problematical. If it is assumed that deterrence is easy then the requirements are not very stringent. If, on the other hand, it is assumed that deterrence is hard and that the Soviet Union is held in check only by NATO's ability to deter and defend at every level then this has to be reflected in its force posture.

If the importance of nuclear deterrence is accepted for the 1990s, the question still remains as to how many nuclear weapons need to be deployed in Europe and for what purposes. If it is believed that the effectiveness of deterrence depends on having nuclear weapons which can be used for battlefield purposes such as destroying Soviet force concentrations, then short-range systems are crucial. If, though, it is believed that what counts is the capacity to use nuclear weapons for political effect in changing Soviet calculations about the advantages of persisting with aggression, then the most important systems are of longer-range – such as those on aircraft.

Another possibility is that what counts is not the details of NATO's nuclear posture, but the fact that Western Europe is part of the overall superpower relationship. The presence of US troops in Europe guarantees US involvement in any conflict in Europe. Inherent in such a clash is the possibility of uncontrolled escalation between two powers with vast nuclear forces. While there is no guarantee that escalation would occur – and the superpowers would obviously want to avoid it – the possibility that it might is a powerful deterrent and, in the 1990s, might well be all that is required.

The difficulty with this is that it seems to hark back to the trip-wire strategy and to place all the risk on the US. Some nuclear weapons deployed in Europe may be important, therefore, not so much to deter the Soviet Union but to reassure the US that its allies are prepared to share the risks as well as the benefits of nuclear deterrence. At the same time, the existing spectrum of forces seems increasingly unacceptable to the Federal Republic. A compromise might be possible, however, in which NATO adopts a posture that has a less comprehensive range of nuclear forces but is politically robust. An agreement to dispense with nuclear artillery and abandon the follow on to Lance, in return for a German commitment to permit the continued basing on German territory of nuclear aircraft for use against Soviet targets, could provide the basis for a sustainable long-term posture. This would be an approach which allows for the continued role of nuclear weapons deployed in Europe but which also reflects the broader political changes that are taking place in East–West relations.

While nuclear deterrence remains relevant, it deals only with the threat of premeditated aggression. Yet there are other types of threat that seem more relevant in the 1990s – especially those stemming from instability in the Soviet Union and Eastern Europe. The implication is that NATO has to change its planning assumptions. Whereas in the past NATO planned to deal with a major and premeditated aggression that was very unlikely, in the future it will face a somewhat greater probability of much lower level conflict that results not from calculation but from misperception and misunderstanding in a crisis in central or Eastern Europe.

The implication is that NATO force posture should be predicated somewhat less on deterrence and rather more on the need for crisis prevention and crisis management. One important requirement of the security order of the 1990s, therefore, is a risk reduction centre, established in Geneva and staffed by civilian and military officials from both NATO and the Warsaw Pact. This would have the task of monitoring troop movements and ensuring compliance with both arms reduction agreements and confidence-building measures. In periods of rising tension it would also facilitate discussion between NATO and the Warsaw Pact. The existence of staffs on both sides with experience of practical co-operation, well-established procedures for monitoring and verification, and the availability of additional and familiar communication channels could all help to minimise prospects for miscalculation, misperceptions and misunderstandings.

Closely related to this is the need to develop force postures which are responsive to the requirements of crisis stability. The kinds of force reductions initiated by Gorbachev, as well as those being considered in the current CFE talks on conventional force reductions, will do much to enhance the prospects for crisis stability through reducing the Soviet capacity for surprise attack, and minimising the need for speed in a crisis. At the same time, there is a danger that new instabilities will arise. If the two alliances draw down front line forces and depend more on reserves and mobilisation capabilities, an increase in tension might generate a mobilisation race as both alliances attempt to re-establish their military effectiveness. Such a drawdown of front-line forces would also leave NATO vulnerable to Soviet capacity to disrupt resupply and reinforcement from the UK and the continental US, while pre-positioned equipment and stocks of war material would be an extremely attractive target to Soviet military planners.

In other words, unless great care is taken, one set of security instabilities can all too easily be replaced by different and perhaps more insidious forms of instability. At the very least it will be necessary for NATO to ensure that US POMCUS stocks, which will become particularly important in the event of a reduction in the US military presence in Europe, are well protected against pre-emption. The implication of this is that force reductions *per se* will not necessarily enhance stability and may even detract from it, unless accompanied by appropriate compensatory measures. Although NATO is already heavily engaged in thinking and planning for a post-CFE world, the requirements of stability in such a world remain to be delineated and this task should be treated as a matter of some urgency.

The other adjustment that will have to be made in the 1990s is internal and involves what is sometimes described as the orderly devolution of power and responsibility within NATO from the US to Western Europe. It is clear that although the US has no intention of abandoning Western Europe – and the Bush administration is particularly Atlanticist in its orientation – Washington in the 1990s will be unwilling to underwrite West European security to the same extent as it has in the past. This is evident in both the congressional pressures which are as much about the shedding as the sharing of burdens and in the Bush proposal to limit US troops in Europe to 195,000 as part of a CFE agreement. It is important that the governments of Western Europe recognise that a reduction in the size of the American contingent on the European continent does not mean a diminution in the US commitment to Western European security.

At the same time, the allies must demonstrate that they continue to take their security seriously and that they are prepared to shoulder more of the responsibilities of the Alliance. This can be done partly through greater West European defence co-operation and collaboration. The creation of a West European defence identity will require a thickening of bilateral links, co-ordination of policies in the Western European Union, and greater collaboration in the production and acquisition of weapons. This process will be a natural accompaniment to the creation of a single European market by the end of 1992 and will help to ensure that European economic strength is reflected in the defence field. At the same time, this process will require careful management so that the US is not alienated by what appears to be a Fortress Europe.

Assessment

It is indisputable that the parameters of European security are changing. Far less certain are the consequences of these changes or the implications for British policy. If it is believed that the changes are desirable then it is arguable that British policy should be more flexible and accommodating than it has appeared in recent years. Mrs Thatcher's hard-line position on nuclear weapons, for example, has not been conducive to harmony in an Alliance which, in the final analysis, depends for its effectiveness as much on political cohesion as on military strength. Similarly, the ambivalence that has been evident in the government's approach to European co-operation, whether in economics or security, does not augur well for the orderly devolution of responsibility from the US to Western Europe. Indeed, if it is believed that the government should not only welcome these changes, but encourage and shape them in ways that enhance mutual security in Europe, then a Labour government would be far better attuned to the developments of the 1990s. Radical thinking encourages both a receptivity to change and an ability to harness it in positive directions. The danger is that a more radical government would not attempt to maintain those elements of the existing security order that deserve to be preserved – although the fact that the Labour Party in the late 1980s has moved back towards the centre on security and arms control issues suggests that a Labour government might be more cautious in its policies than might have been expected a few years ago.

If, on the other hand, it is believed that the 'bonfire of the certainties' poses more dangers than opportunities and that the key to security in Europe in the 1990s is the maintenance of the existing arrangements as intact as possible, then a Conservative government might be more appropriate. Certainly, Mrs Thatcher has been the last bastion of security orthodoxy in a Europe in which traditional ideas about security have been challenged from many quarters. Yet the very nature of the conceptual crisis that is currently besetting British security and arms control policy suggests that the old solutions are no longer adequate. The challenge for the 1990s, therefore, is to retain those aspects of the security order that remain of value, while grasping new opportunities to restructure security relations in more positive directions between East and West and between the US and Western Europe. The requirement is for a British government which can combine the prudence of the conservative tradition with the imagination and sense of vision that has characterised much radical thinking about international politics.

Notes

1 *Statement on the Defence Estimates 1986*, Vol. 1, Cmnd.9763–I, HMSO, London, 1986, p.2.

2 H. Kissinger, *White House Years*, Weidenfeld and Nicolson, London, 1979, p.90.

3 D. Newsom, 'Consultation in Anglo–American relations', *International Affairs*, LXIII, 1986–87, p.229.

4 *ibid.*

The dual imperative of Britain's nuclear deterrent: the Soviet threat, alliance politics and arms control

Introduction

The bedrock assumption which has underpinned Britain's nuclear strategy is that the UK could not afford to be nuclear free in a nuclear armed world. This assumption is rooted in its wartime experiences and perceptions.[1] The result of these experiences and perceptions has been a 'dual imperative'[2] in the development of Britain's nuclear strategy: British perceptions of the Soviet threat and of Anglo–American/Alliance relations. The effect of this dual imperative is that successive British governments have justified Britain's nuclear capabilities as an 'independent', national deterrent to the Soviet Union, as a contribution to an Alliance deterrent posture, as a means of influencing US strategic and defence policies, and as insurance against the withdrawal of the US commitment towards Western Europe.

The context in which Britain's nuclear deterrent has developed over the last forty years has shifted from interdependence with the US, to technological dependence on the US due to economic costs, to an effort to reassert independence, despite this technological dependence, as a second centre of decision-making within the Alliance.[3] Behind these shifting rationales has been the pursuit of an independent nuclear deterrent as a hedge against the collapse of the Atlantic Alliance. The anxiety of an isolated Britain exposed to Soviet nuclear, chemical or conventional threats has been a constant theme in the legitimisation of Britain's possession of nuclear weapons. This theme was used with great success in the 1987 General Election, when Margaret Thatcher claimed that Neil Kinnock underestimated the threat of Soviet nuclear blackmail. The implementation of Labour's proposed non-nuclear defence policy, the Prime Minister claimed, would leave Britain helpless in the face of a determined Soviet aggressor.

However, as Soviet momentum in the diplomatic and arms control areas continues in the Gorbachev era, the Thatcher government is coming to be seen as a 'spoiler' in the pro-arms control spirit engendered after the INF agreement. More importantly, the recent changes in Soviet foreign policy are likely to prompt renewed debate about the nature of the Soviet threat to British and Western security and its implications for defence and arms control policies. It is the perception of the Soviet threat and the implications of its modification for UK policy which form the primary focus of this chapter.

Foreign policy vs military threats

A threat is 'an intention, perceived or otherwise, on the part of one state to inflict injury, in some circumstances, on the interests and values of another.'[4] Booth and McGwire have argued that threats are best conceived of as a level-of-analysis problem, drawing a distinction between threats at the foreign policy and the military contingency levels.[5] Threats at the foreign policy level are concerned with intentions and probabilities: what action might another country take in pursuit of its interests in a particular situation? Threats at the military contingency level are concerned with capabilities and possibilities: what is another country capable of doing in military terms?

There are several points which follow from these distinctions. On the one hand, what is seen as a 'threat' at the foreign policy level might not be significant at the military level. On the other hand, what a contingency planner might define as a possible threat in the event of conflict might have little or no significance from the perspective of the foreign policy analyst. This means that analysts should hesitate before interpreting changes in force structure as an indication of escalation at the foreign policy level of threat. It also means that if the threat assessment is made at the level of foreign policy characterised in terms of ideology, then any reductions in capabilities are unlikely to undermine or alter the threat perception.

The implications of these distinctions are clear in addressing the question: why is the Soviet Union perceived by British policy-makers and military planners as a threat? The Soviet Union is perceived as a threat at either the ideological level of intention (ie that it is a revolutionary, expansionist power) or at the level of military capabilities (i.e., it has offensive capabilities). However, it is not simply a case of 'either/or'. Rather it is the case that the British assessment of the Soviet threat is based on an integration of both intentions and capabilities: the Soviet Union is seen as a hostile power at both the foreign policy and military contingency levels of threat. The early assessment of the character and aspirations of the Soviet regime as an ideological threat provided the context in which the 'capabilities' of the Soviet Union – both real and potential – were evaluated and seemingly exaggerated. This, in turn, reinforced the threat assessment at the 'ideological' or foreign policy level. This intertwining of threat assessments has important implications for Britain's attitude towards arms control processes in the post-war period.

Threat assessment in the Cold War period

As noted above, the assumptions underpinning Britain's nuclear strategy can be traced back to wartime perceptions. The Maud Report of 1941 had placed the development of an atomic energy programme in the context of the post-war strategic environment, stating that 'No nation ... would care to risk being caught without a weapon of such decisive possibilities.'[6] By the later stages of the Second World War, British concern had shifted from anxiety about the risk of Nazi Germany acquiring the bomb to the prospect that the Soviets might develop atomic weapons. In mid-1943, Churchill argued that Britain's interest in nuclear expertise and capabilities resulted from its concern to maintain its 'future independence in the face of international blackmail that the Russians might eventually be able to employ.'[7] This early concern about exposure to a future Soviet nuclear threat is one of the essential premises of Britain's post-war nuclear strategy.

In the immediate post-war period, the Chiefs of Staff argued that:

... the Soviet conception of an inherent conflict between social democracy and totalitarian Communism, the official and unofficial pronouncements of the Soviet leaders, and the attitude of the Soviet press make it abundantly clear that the Soviet Union must be regarded as a potentially hostile power.[8]

Accepting the notion that expansion was endemic in the nature of the Soviet regime, one planning paper argued that lasting security was impossible between ideological foes. The only prescription was the complete removal of the Soviet regime and the best possible means of accomplishing this goal would be the targeting of Soviet state power.[9] Thus, the Chiefs of Staff quickly articulated both a justification for Britain possessing its own deterrent capability and a rudimentary doctrine of deterrence.

These views were not shared by the new Prime Minister, Clement Attlee. He offered a radically different prescription for dealing with Britain's strategic predicament in the nuclear age. He reasoned that the advent of the atomic bomb had transformed the nature of international politics and that '... if mankind continues to make the atomic bomb without changing the political relationships of states sooner or later these bombs will be used for mutual annihilation.' Attlee believed in 1945 that the only hope for the future lay in realising international relationships in which war was ruled out as an instrument of state policy. Thus, at the very beginning of the atomic age, a British Prime Minister articulated the view that nuclear weapons had rendered war obsolete as an instrument of state policy.

Although prepared to accept that some type of international control of nuclear weapons might be desirable, the Chiefs of Staff were much exercised by the practicalities of such negotiations. They were concerned with the risks of Soviet cheating and especially with the dangers of the West giving up atomic weapon production while secret development might be continued in the Soviet Union. The Chiefs of Staff insisted on the need for full rights of inspection but argued that '... how this is to be achieved under the present Soviet system is the crux of the problem.'[10] The implication of this view was that unless there was a change in the nature of the Soviet regime it would be dangerous to facilitate the establishment of a system of international control.

This view was supported by the Foreign Office. In early 1946 it had supported Attlee's hope that the UK and the Soviet Union might reach a diplomatic accommodation. But by the end of 1946, Foreign Office officials agreed with the Chiefs of Staff that the Soviet Union was the only 'foreseeable' enemy. The threat assessment of the Chiefs of Staff and Foreign Office was based on a view of Soviet ideology, which was seen as committing the Soviets to a revolutionary foreign policy, and the military possibilities open to such a regime possessing nuclear weapons. Thus, the initial British assessment of the Soviet threat was based primarily on the belief that the very nature of the Soviet regime meant that its intentions could not be benign, which reinforced a concern about it potential capabilities.

The dual imperative

While the origins of British nuclear strategy lie in its perceptions of a Soviet threat, the development of Britain's nuclear strategy is unintelligible without reference to the Anglo–American relationship. Although concern about Soviet nuclear capabilities was explicit in the strategic formulations of the Chiefs of Staff, it was relations with the Americans which loomed largest in the actual decision to develop the British bomb in January 1947.[11] Attlee agreed with Bevin that British atomic weapons were essential if the UK was to have a measure of influence over the US, at a time when American policy towards Europe was both uncertain and hesitant. Britain perceived that Western Europe's conventional weakness relative to that of the Soviet Union demanded a nuclear countervailing capability – a capability that was in the late 1940s entirely in American hands. Alliance concern was not only evident in Attlee's decision to build the bomb, but in the British decision to proceed with a hydrogen bomb programme. Although a number of studies of this period have suggested that the development of a doctrine of British independent deterrence was linked to the emergence of hydrogen weapons,[12] the greatest emphasis was given by civilian and military leaders to the political necessity for such a weapon as a means of influencing US security policy in the nuclear age.[13] Thus, from its earliest days, British nuclear strategy was conditioned by a 'dual imperative' to influence both ally and adversary.

Britain's nuclear strategy thus developed in the context of what might be termed 'deterrence in concert',[14] in which Britain sought to make a contribution to US deterrent capabilities. At the same time, Britain's desire for a stockpile of H-bombs also reflected a series of overlapping, and at times contradictory concerns: a fear that the American nuclear guarantee might be found wanting in an era when the Soviet Union could retaliate with H-bombs against the US; a concern about the dangers of becoming overly dependent upon the US; and an underlying fear that the US and the Soviets might do a deal on nuclear tests which would leave Britain out of the thermonuclear club. Finally, although the emphasis was on the *political* need for thermonuclear weapons in the context of Anglo–American relations, there was also a belief in the defence establishment that a

British H-Bomb capability was the only '... conceivable method of deterring a thermonuclear armed Soviet Union from aggressive action'[15] against the UK.

By the late 1950s, the pace of Anglo–American co-operation enabled the Macmillan government to achieve its nuclear objectives at a cheaper cost and within a much shorter time scale than would otherwise have been possible. Britain crossed the thermonuclear threshold, leaving France and China on the other side. If British officials had been sceptical of pursuing accommodation with the Soviet Union in the late 1940s and early 1950s, the development of an indigenous nuclear capability and the stability of the emerging US–Soviet strategic balance served to provide an essential measure of confidence and laid the basis for government efforts to reach a diplomatic accommodation with the Soviet Union. Despite NSC-68 and the American preoccupation with technological projections of Soviet strategic power, the Berlin and Cuban missile crises indicated to the Macmillan government that the dangers of war lay less in deliberate Soviet aggression or coercion against Western Europe, than in the risks of miscalculation and inadvertent escalation.

The Macmillan government sought to advance the normalisation of East–West relations through promoting arms control processes and achieved some success with the signing of the Partial Test Ban Treaty in 1963.[16] The Wilson government continued Britain's participation in these processes with its involvement in negotiating the Non-Proliferation Treaty in 1968.[17] However, while both treaties made a contribution to East–West nuclear stability, they also served Britain's more narrow national interests. In pursuing these agreements, both Conservative and Labour governments had the basic objective of ensuring that Britain's nuclear deterrent was not undermined by nuclear arms control negotiations. Indeed, Simpson has argued that Britain's international security policy in this period was governed by a three pronged strategy:

the achievement of the national atomic and thermonuclear weapon stockpile goals as rapidly as possible; the signing of a comprehensive test ban agreement and possibly a fissile material cut off, to achieve the inter-nationalist aims of both a halt in the arms race and the exclusion of further states from the nuclear club; and the pursuit of all measures which would limit the ability of the two superpowers to develop methods of neutralising atomic and thermonuclear weapons and thus once more relegate Britain to an inferior military position.[18]

The bipartisanship which underpinned this three-pronged approach and which dominated post-war British defence and arms control policy was premised on the belief that, in the nuclear age, a nuclear capability was the ultimate guarantee of British security. The maintenance of an independent nuclear deterrentwas also seen as an essential precursor to the pursuit of co-operation with the Soviet Union, as well as providing the basis for influencing US policy. Thus, it was not seen as inconsistent that British security policy should seek to foster superpower detente in the late 1960s and early 1970s, while embarking on a modernisation of its strategic forces which would enable Britain to target the Soviet Union into the 1990s.

Chevaline, Trident and the Moscow criterion

Britain's acquisition of Polaris missiles from the US in 1962 was a direct consequence of the crisis over the cancellation of the American Skybolt system. The earlier decision to rely on an American stand-off system rather than develop an indigenous ballistic missile capability was seen by many as the nadir of Britain's nuclear independence. The increasing dependence on American nuclear technology, and now delivery systems, resulted from primarily economic considerations. Nevertheless, there were compelling strategic rationales related to survivability and targeting for making a shift from the V-bomber force to a sea-based ballistic nuclear force. With regard to targeting policy, it was believed by the late 1950s that if Britain was to pose a unilateral deterrent threat against the Soviet leadership, the targeting of the British force would have to be designed so as to raise the costs to Moscow of any aggression against Western Europe.

A clue to thinking on British nuclear targeting can be found in recently released records from the 1940s which discuss plans for counter-regime attacks designed to destroy Soviet state power and dismember the Soviet state itself. The status of such plans in the late 1940s and early 1950s is unclear, since operational planning at this time focused on the requirement to destroy key counter-force targets in a damage limiting first strike in conjunction with US nuclear capabilities.[19] Nevertheless, it seems that targeting Soviet state power came into prominence in the 1960s as British sought to square the circle of the national and alliance justifications for its deterrent contained in the 1962 Nassau Agreement. The concept which was put forward to achieve this was the argument that Britain's nuclear deterrent constituted a 'second centre of decision-making'. This in turn required that it be able to pose an 'independent' threat to Soviet state power which was defined in terms of the 'Moscow criterion'.

Almost as soon as Britain's Polaris system become operable, its ability to meet the 'Moscow criterion' was threatened as the Soviets began to deploy an exo-atmospheric ABM system around Moscow. The anxiety which the Moscow ABM generated in the MoD and Cabinet created pressure to modernise the British nuclear deterrent in the form of the Chevaline programme. The Chevaline programme was designed to operate in the strategic environment of the late 1980s and 1990s, but it is worth noting that this capability was complementary with the ABM treaty signed between the United States and the Soviet Union in 1972. As Michael Charlton has put it, '... Chevaline and the ABM treaty were both judged necessary to make the British deterrent credible'[20], that is to say, capable of targeting Moscow.

The necessity of being able to target Moscow was summed up by Sir Herman Bondi, Chief Scientific Adviser to the British government in the early 1970s:

For [Britain] to resign ourselves to have a capability that is not only quantitatively small but *qualitatively second-rate* would severely diminish the political effect, within the Alliance, of having a deterrent at all. So the 'Moscow criterion' goes rather far. It's rather important in the context of alliance politics ... As far as 'the other side' is concerned, one is of course talking of a highly centralised system ... (and) the enormous importance of Moscow in the Soviet Union is quite clear. So abandoning 'the Moscow criterion' would be a very severe reduction in what one might call 'the quality of the deterrent' and its prime task of helping to keep the peace.[21]

Bondi's comments vividly illustrate the 'dual imperative' in British nuclear strategy. For Bondi, Britain's targeting of Moscow is significant not only in terms of influencing the behaviour of the adversary, but also that of the ally. The clear inference being that a British deterrent capability which was unable to target the lynch-pin of Soviet state power, would be a deterrent which was almost worthless in terms of influencing US security policy.[22]

This approach was reiterated and slightly modified by the Thatcher government. In its 1980 memorandum on the Polaris successor the government publicly announced the basis of the UK's deterrent posture:

The Government ... thinks it right now to make clear that their concept of deterrence is concerned essentially with posing a potential threat to key aspects of Soviet state power. There might, with changing conditions, be more than one way of doing this, and some flexibility in contingency planning is appropriate.[23]

The meaning attached by the Thatcher government to the phrase 'key aspects of Soviet state power' is unclear. In evidence to Parliament, Michael Quinlan suggested that Soviet state power might '. . . embrace a range of targets lying between hitting a large city and hitting a silo.'[24] The 1980 memorandum suggested that one approach to targeting was to consider '... what type and scale of damage Soviet leaders might think likely to leave them critically handicapped afterwards in continuing confrontation with a relatively unscathed US.'[25] Such a scheme pointed to Britain's targeting of ABM and air defence radars in a manner designed to convince the Soviets that in the event of a British attack, they would be more exposed to American nuclear strikes.[26]

Clearly, the idea of targeting Soviet state power was not new, but offering it as an explicit public rationale for Britain's strategic nuclear force was. More importantly, the decision to modernise Britain's deterrent with the Trident system offered enhanced targeting options for strikes against Soviet state power.[27] But this enhanced capability in Britain's targeting of Soviet state power is not seen as forming the basis for an offensive political strategy against the Soviet Union. Rather, it is seen by Whitehall as offering the ultimate means of deterring a Soviet leadership intent on European hegemony. Thus, the 1980 memorandum's public rationale for the UK's nuclear force has its roots in perceptions of the Soviet ideological threat in the late 1940s. More importantly, the implication of the 1980 document is that British threat assessment has not been revised since the late 1940s.

However, if there has not been an official revision of threat assessment, there has been a reassessment offered by those expert groups and academics operating within the broad umbrella of Alternative Defence. In the early 1980s, the Peace Movement, activists in the Labour Party, the SDP/Liberal Alliance and academic strategists articulated great concern about the breakdown in East–West relations and the apparent irresponsibility of the first Reagan administration in its approach to nuclear strategy and arms control. As in the early 1960s, the emphasis was not on the danger of deliberate Soviet aggression, but miscalculation and inadvertent escalation leading to nuclear war.[28]

Although the government's opponents did present a broad spectrum of opposition, the divisions between these groups and the inconsistencies and confusions within the Labour Party and SDP-Liberal Alliance defence policies hampered both in presenting their alternative security policies. Thus, despite being exposed to considerable criticism, the Thatcher government's victory in the 1983 General Election – the first election since 1964 in which the defence issue was hotly contested between the parties – ensured that the Prime Minister was in no mood to trim Britain's nuclear sails, or play down the ideological confrontation between East and West.[29]

The Gorbachev factor

With the accession of Mikhail Gorbachev to the Soviet leadership in 1984, the British government has found itself dealing with a leader whose diplomatic statements and proposals in the foreign policy and arms control arena do not conform to a traditional 'Stalinist' image of the Soviet Union. As Christopher Coker notes: 'Gorbachev's rise to power changed everything overnight'.[30] These changes have increased the pressure for a revised assessment of the Soviet threat.

Despite this, the Thatcher government has been averse to reassessing the modalities of British security policy in the Gorbachev era. The government's view is that 'new thinking' was forced on Moscow as a result of Western political, economic and military strength. With regard to the latter, maintaining the Alliance nuclear deterrent is seen as essential to continued stability in Europe. As a result, Mrs Thatcher has been a staunch supporter of modernisation of short-range nuclear forces (SNF), a stance which has won her few friends in West Germany, and even placed strains on the Anglo–American relationship since President Bush sought at the 1989 NATO June summit to conciliate West German sensitivities on the SNF issue.[31]

Nevertheless, the emphasis of the Bush administration is on progress in conventional and chemical weapons before further reductions in nuclear weapons. This is in conformity with the Prime Minister's views. At the June summit, Mrs Thatcher was adamant that reductions in short-range nuclear forces should not be undertaken until conventional force reductions (CFE) had been agreed and fully implemented. However, if Mrs Thatcher considered that CFE talks would be painstakingly slow, or even go the way of MBFR, the pace of progress in Vienna has been little short of breathtaking. Normally, the negotiators of treaties are the least optimistic, but the noises coming out of Vienna suggest that there could be a phase 1 agreement by the end of 1990. President Bush has stamped his own authority on the CFE process, with his initiative for the inclusion of combat aircraft and helicopters in the common ceilings, thereby meeting a long-standing Soviet demand. But it is the willingness of the Soviet Union to accept massive asymmetrical cuts in its forces which has led to the breakthrough in conventional arms control negotiations.

In the past, the Soviet Union sought to make a distinction between a defensive political strategy and an offensive operational military posture, arguing that the latter provided an essential insurance against the risk of war, and should not be seen as indicating offensive intent. However, as part of the Soviet 'new thinking', Gorbachev and his supporters have come to question the wisdom of an offensive conventional posture, which in frightening neighbours and stimulating counter-responses carries with it such a high political, military and economic price tag.[32] Michael McGwire traces the origins of such ideas to the early 1980s, but they have received their fullest articulation and initial application under Gorbachev. The professed goal of 'reasonable sufficiency' is already leading to changes in Soviet strategic culture and even force structure. The most notable example of this is the unilateral reductions in Soviet forces announced by Gorbachev in December 1988 and the withdrawal of Soviet troops from Czechoslovakia and Hungary. These will lead to a significant reduction in the Soviet capability for a short-warning surprise attack against Western Europe.

Whatever the doctrinal upheavals taking place in the Soviet Union as Gorbachev and his supporters seek to over-turn the traditional assumption that national security depends upon strength and over-insurance, those 'Whitehall Watchers' entrusted with British threat assessment consider that while a CFE agreement which leads to parity in conventional forces in Central Europe will enhance European security, conventional parity does not obviate the requirement for some modernised short-range nuclear weapons. If short-range nuclear missiles and artillery shells were completely removed, the Thatcher government's fears focus on consequences for the US troop commitment in the FRG, as well as the danger that a future FRG government (perhaps a Green-SPD coalition) might seek to remove British and American airborne nuclear weapons from West German soil leaving NATO with no land-based nuclear deterrent.

It is in the light of fears about 'denuclearisation' that the Thatcher government's decision to modernise the RAF's free-fall gravity nuclear weapons must be understood. The government has decided to procure a successor to the ageing WE177 gravity bombs, and will probably buy a modified version of the SRAM II missile from the US. Although modernisation of Britain's airborne nuclear weapons is not particularly astonishing given the Thatcher government's nuclear proclivities, what is surprising is the doctrinal articulations which have been offered by the Ministry of Defence in support of such a decision. The 1989 Defence White Paper stated:

The UK ... will maintain the independent non-strategic contribution without which the value of our strategic force, which provides a separate second centre of nuclear decision making in support of Alliance strategy, would be seriously incomplete.[33]

Francois Heisbourg argues that the above is an official statement of the position that British non-strategic nuclear forces could be used independently of NATO commands, as has always been the case for Britain's strategic nuclear forces.[34] Thus, if the process of nuclear arms control in Europe should lead to an erosion of the US nuclear security guarantee, the government is determined to maintain a sub-strategic nuclear capability which will enable it to hold at risk Soviet targets. From the perspective of the Thatcher government, it is at a time when the Alliance nuclear edifice is crumbling that such a capability is most urgently needed. The need to communicate British sub-strategic nuclear thinking to both adversaries and allies alike probably explains the doctrinal statement in the 1989 Defence White Paper.

This theme of maintaining British nuclear capabilities despite pressures for arms reductions can also be seen in the Thatcher government's attitude to strategic nuclear arms control. Mrs Thatcher has stated that global nuclear disarmament is not a long-term goal of British security policy. In this, the British Prime Minister found herself out of step with both Reagan, who in his second term espoused the goal of visionary arms control, and Gorbachev who has made the search for nuclear disarmament a constant theme of his public speeches. At the Iceland summit in November 1986, Reagan and Gorbachev came close to agreeing to the elimination of *all* ballistic missiles over a ten year period, a move which would have left Britain high and dry without a Polaris successor, and which underlined the vulnerabilities of Britain's nuclear dependence on the US.

With President's Bush reassessment of US arms control policy, the abolition of ballistic missiles is a not a near-term proposition. However, the basis has been laid in the current strategic arms reductions talks (START) for deep cuts in strategic arsenals, although not the talked about 50 per cent reductions.[35] However, START is currently stalled and the emphasis placed by the Bush administration on conventional, chemical and nuclear testing negotiations means that a START treaty is receiving lowest priority. If there is a START agreement in the first Bush administration, the question of Britain's participation in a START II process could become salient. The Soviet Union has indicated that further reductions beyond START I will require the participation of the medium-sized nuclear powers. The declared position of the Thatcher government is that '... if Soviet and US strategic arsenals were to be very significantly reduced, and if no significant changes occurred in Soviet defensive capabilities ... Britain would want to consider how best she could contribute to arms control in the light of the reduced threat'.[36] More recently, the government has stated that there would have to be cuts greater than 50 per cent in strategic arsenals before the UK would consider participating.

Despite this, it is hard to envisage what Britain might actually do to further the strategic arms control process. Reducing the future Trident submarine force from four to three boats, as proposed by the Labour Party, would mean that Britain would reduce its warhead numbers from a proposed 512 warheads[37] to 384 warheads. Although this would be a significant reduction, it would require a change in the way Britain has operated its strategic nuclear force. In the past, the underlying premise of the deterrent force has been that Britain will have one boat on station at all times which requires a four boat force. However, if the UK was to operate a three boat force, it would not be possible to have one on station at all times. Consequently, Britain would have to depend at times upon a period of strategic warning to ensure that it had a boat on station if the need should arise. However, such a force requirement could be paralysing in times of crisis, as the government might confront a dilemma between scrambling a boat to sea in times of crisis and trying to avoid being overly provocative.

A more appealing option might be cuts in the number of submarine tubes or warheads on the Trident D-5 missile. The government has said that it will not operate the Trident force with more warheads than the eight it planned to operate on the Trident C-4 (the initial choice for Britain's Polaris successor), but it could go further and reduce the number of Trident warheads down to the level of 3 warheads on each missile as with the existing Polaris force. The Labour Party proposes to operate a three boat Trident force in this manner.[38] The alternative option of sealing missile tubes up in the submarines might be easier to verify than actual warhead reductions, although the latter may be verifiable by radiation detection. Such options might give the UK a role in a future START II deep cuts regime without affecting the survivability of the British nuclear force.

However, the prospect of START II deep cuts might start the alarm bells ringing in London about the erosion of American extended deterrence. In fact, a British government wedded to the strategic orthodoxy would probably consider that the threat to British security actually increased with deep cuts rather than being reduced. This was suggested by the Thatcher government in its 1988 Defence White Paper. As a result, the British requirement to hold at risk Soviet targets – especially the 'key aspects of Soviet state power' – might be seen as more urgent than ever. Furthermore, with regard to deep cuts, Britain would be even more anxious if reductions were not accompanied by continued constraints on ballistic missile defence (BDM) deployments.

Moscow is currently opposed to modifying the ABM Treaty to permit ballistic missile defence (BMD) deployments, but if a START II regime was to allow some BMD deployments, Britain would probably seek to take active steps to maintain an ability to hold at risk key Soviet targets. This might well include increasing the numbers of warheads on the Trident missiles. Deep cuts and relaxation of ABM Treaty constraints would be a nightmarish environment for British nuclear strategy to operate in, and the UK would be more determined than ever to avoid the inclusion of its deterrent in such a strategic arms reduction regime.

Conclusion

It is clear from the above discussion that continuity rather than discontinuity characterises British threat assessment. Successive British governments have perceived in the Soviet Union the only 'foreseeable threat' to Britain's security in the nuclear age. Even in the absence of ideological enmity, as the naturally dominant European nuclear power, the Soviet Union would pose a potential threat to Western security. However, Britain has perceived in the character and behaviour of the Soviet regime evidence of active *hostile intent*. Thus, Soviet intentions have not been deduced so much from an assessment of capabilities, as from a reading of the nature of the Soviet regime and the military possibilities open to it. Put differently, while greater sensitivity to threats as a level-of-analysis problem, as outlined at the beginning of this chapter, might provide for greater stability and predictability in the East–West relationship, it is unlikely that such sophistication on the part of those entrusted with British threat assessment would have led to a revision of views about the nature of the Soviet regime, or the military threat arising from it.[39]

However, if Britain has seen itself facing both an *intentions* and a *capabilities* threat, this has not precluded the search for accommodation with the Soviet Union. In the nuclear age, Britain has placed value on the arms control process as a means of engendering stability and predictability into the superpower relationship. Nevertheless, at no point in the arms control process has Britain been prepared to give up its own nuclear weapons. The theme of British security policy has been that possession of national nuclear weapons is not incompatible with superpower strategic arms control or the strengthening of barriers to further nuclear proliferation. Critics of Britain's nuclear strategy, especially in the 1980s, have castigated this policy as 'do as I say not as I do'. For those seeking a new European security order, Britain's nuclear capability remains a basic and lasting impediment to the construction of a new security regime.

While British perceptions of the Soviet ideological threat have been influential in shaping targeting strategy, it is also the case that Britain's nuclear strategy has been affected by its relations with the US. Although the publicly stated rationale for Britain's bomb has tended to focus on the existence of Soviet conventional and nuclear forces, it has been seen in private as providing London with influence over American nuclear policy-making. At one level, the 'Moscow criterion' can be seen as arising from Britain's perceptions of the nature and character of the Soviet state, but at the same time Britain's desire to hold the Soviet state hostage can be understood in the context of the Anglo–American nuclear relationship, and the belief in Whitehall that Britain's influence in Washington is strengthened by British possession of strategic nuclear weapons.

For these reasons, if in the 1990s, Gorbachev succeeds in radically altering public perceptions of the Soviet threat, it is not clear that Britain's nuclear strategy will be as responsive to change in the perceived nature of the Soviet threat as some might hope. If public support for the British deterrent erodes in the face of change in the Soviet Union and the momentum of nuclear arms control negotiations continues, a Labour or centre-left government would probably consider including Britain's deterrent in post-START negotiations. However, a conservative government is likely to maintain the traditional approach to British security policy, arguing that Britain could not afford to opt out of the nuclear business in the face of an uncertain strategic environment. While privately, anxieties might well focus on the long-term future of American extended deterrence in a post-CFE world, which in itself raises questions about how much influence Britain obtains in Washington through its possession of strategic nuclear weapons, policy-makers might well publicly emphasise the increasing spread of weapons of mass destruction to states in the Third World, and the consequent need for Britain to possess nuclear weapons as a deterrent to future nuclear blackmail. Publicly declared rationales which emphasise Britain's nuclear status would probably strike a chord with public opinion which continues to support Britain's deterrent even as public perceptions of the Soviet threat decline.

In fact, if Gorbachev continues to persuade Western public opinion of his good intentions, the British government could find itself in an analogous position to that which faced NATO over the INF decision in the early 1980s. The deployment of INF systems was legitimised in relation to the SS20 threat, but when the Soviets offered to remove the SS20s, NATO governments were forced to acknowledge that there were factors related to Alliance politics which necessitated modernisation of NATO's theatre nuclear forces independently of Soviet behaviour. Similarly, if the legitimising device of the Soviet threat weakens, the British government might find itself in the uncomfortable position of having to publicly defend the deterrent in terms which relate more to the uncertainties of the future strategic environment, especially with regard to the future behaviour of its American ally, than to anxieties about the Soviet threat. Thus, to expect the British nuclear deterrent to wither on the vine of a declining Soviet threat is to probably overstate the dependence of Britain's deterrent strategy on a particular image of the Soviet Union.

Supporters of the national deterrent but critics of the Thatcher government argue that the creation of a new security regime in Europe does not depend upon Britain giving up nuclear weapons. Rather, it is argued that Britain's continued possession of nuclear weapons is necessary to the process of managed change in a fluid and uncertain European security environment. In thinking about the relationship between threat assessment and Western responses, it may well be that the strongest rationale for British and French possession of a nuclear capability in the 1990s is the measure of reassurance such capabilities provide in the movement towards a mutual security regime, at a time when there are growing doubts in Bonn, Paris and London, not only about the long-term future of the American security guarantee[40] but also about the future evolution of the European security system itself.

Yet, if the argument for Britain's nuclear deterrent into the 1990s is a hedge against an unpredictable and uncertain future, this conviction sits uneasily with the improvement in East–West relations and the fundamental changes in European security relations which seems to make nuclear weapons of decreasing political value. While accepting the thesis of diminished political utility, Francois Heisbourg suggests that the trend towards a proliferation of nuclear weapons may increase the requirement for Britain and France to retain their strategic nuclear arsenals.[41] There seems to be a paradox between an emerging European security system in which Britain's nuclear capability might be of increasingly marginal value, and the clinging of the government to Britain's nuclear weapons as a guarantee of security and status in the global arena. The risk for British policy-makers is that they become so obsessed with maintaining Britain's nuclear status that it becomes an end in itself, to the detriment of the UK's long-term security.

Notes

1 See Ian Clark and Nicholas J. Wheeler, *The British Origins of Nuclear Strategy, 1945–55*, Oxford University Press, Oxford, 1989.

2 I have borrowed the concept from Edward A. Kolodziej, 'French and British nuclear forces: implications for arms control', Paper presented at 'New Weapons, Strategies and Mind-sets', SIPRI, June 1986.

3 This is discussed more fully in Lawrence Freedman, Martin Navias and Nicholas J. Wheeler, 'Independence in concert: the British rational for possession of strategic nuclear weapons', *Nuclear History Program, Occasional Paper 5*, Centre for International Security Studies, Maryland, 1989.

4 K. Booth, 'New challenges and old mind-sets: ten rules for empirical realists' in C. Jacobsen (ed.), *The Uncertain Course: New Weapons Strategies And Mind Sets*, Oxford University Press, Oxford, 1987, p. 46.

5 *ibid.*, p. 46 and M. McGwire, 'Prologue: the level of analysis and its effect on assessment', in M. McGwire (ed.), *Soviet Naval Developments: Capability, and Contest*, Praeger Publishers, New York, 1975, pp. 1–5.

6 M. Gowing, *Britain and Atomic Energy, 1939–45*, Macmillan, London, 1964, p. 396.

7 L.R. Groves, *Now It Can Be Told: The Story of the Manhattan Project*, Harper, New York, 1962, p. 132.

8 DEFE 5/6, COS. (47) 227, November 1947.

9 The paper stated that '...the complete removal of the Soviet regime will be an essential requirement for achieving allied war aims...We consider that effective air attacks upon the towns, in which are centres of control – political, administrative, and police – is the best method of creating conditions in which the Communist Party and the administrators could not control and the secret police could not suppress. When control is disrupted the armed forces will not be able to fight effectively.' See DEFE 4/22, J.P. (49) 59, 20 July 1949.

10 PREM 8/116, Chief Staff Officer to Minister of Defence, 10 October 1945.

11 The British decision to go ahead with an atomic bomb was taken by a small Cabinet sub-committee on 8 January 1947. The only dissenting voice against Britain's development of an atomic bomb was that of P.M.S. Blackett, wartime scientist and member of the Anderson advisory Committee on International control of atomic energy. Blackett was on the fringes of the British nuclear debate, but did have one or two discussions with Attlee during 1945–6.
The dominance of Alliance over national military considerations was exemplified by Foreign Secretary Ernest Bevin's statement that ' "Britain" could not afford to acquiesce in an American monopoly of this new development'. A few months earlier Attlee's atomic bomb committee had discussed the merits of developing a gaseous diffusion plant (to increase the supply of fissile material) and Bevin is reputed to have silenced dissenting voices in the Gen 163 committee with the comment that '... We've *got* to have this. ... We've got to have a bloody Union Jack flying on top of it.' Quoted in Peter Hennessy, 'We've got to have a bloody Union Jack flying on top of it', BBC

Radio Transcript, 1988.

12   Peter Malone, *The British Nuclear Deterrent*, Croom Helm, London, 1984. In addition, Andrew Pierre claims that '... strategic doctrine as it had been evolving in Britain supported the H-bomb as the apex of an independent nuclear deterrent'. Andrew J. Pierre, *The British Experience with an Independent Strategic Force*, Oxford University Press, London, 1972, p. 91.

13   The actual decision to build a British thermonuclear capability was taken by the Defence Committee on 16 June 1954. Prime Minister Churchill stated that '... we could not expect to maintain our influence as a world power unless we possessed the most-up-to-date nuclear weapons.' Pierre maintains that Churchill entertained the notion that whatever the US and the Soviet Union possessed, Britain must have also. However, although world power status was important, as with the original atomic bomb decision, relations with the US loomed largest in the deliberations. The Chiefs of Staff had emphasised throughout their review of defence policy in 1954 that '... it would be dangerous if the US were to retain their present monopoly since we would be denied any right to influence her policy in the use of this weapon'. The Lord President of the Council, Lord Salisbury, provided the clearest endorsement of such sentiments in his concern that Washington might '. . . plunge the world into war, either through a misguided intervention in Asia or in order to forestall an attack by Russia'. He argued that the Americans would '... feel more respect for our views if we continued to play an effective part in building up the strength necessary to deter aggression than if we left it entirely to them to match and counter Russia's thermonuclear strength'. See CAB 128/27, C.C. 48 (54), 8 July 1954.

14   See Clark and Wheeler, *op. cit.*

15   J. Simpson, *The Independent Nuclear State: Britain, the US and the Military Atom*, 2nd ed., Macmillan, London, 1986, p. 95.

16   See B.P. White, 'Britain and the Rise of Detente' in S. Smith and R. Crockatt (eds.) *The Cold War: Past And Present*, Allen and Unwin, London, 1987, pp. 102–4 and the chapter by Wyn Rees, John Simpson and Darryl Howlett in this volume.

17   See J.P.G. Freeman, *Britain's Nuclear Arms Control Policy In the Context Of Anglo–American Relations, 1957–68*, Macmillan, London, 1986, and the chapter by John Simpson in this volume.

18   J. Simpson, *The Independent Nuclear State.*

19   For a discussion of early British nuclear targeting see Clark and Wheeler, *op.cit.* and Martin Navias, 'Strengthening the Deterrent? The British Medium Bomber Force Debate, 1955–56', *Journal of Strategic Studies* II, 1988.

20   *ibid.*, p. 120.

21   M. Charlton, *The Star Wars History*, BBC Publications, London, 1986, p. 121. Emphasis in the original.

22   It is worth noting that there were critics of the 'Moscow criterion' inside the defence establishment. Dr David Owen, Foreign Secretary in the Labour Government, 1974–79, recalls that he and Lord Zuckerman, who was Chief Scientific Adviser to the Ministry of Defence, and several officials

at the Foreign Office produced a paper challenging the validity of the 'Moscow criterion'. They argued that the targeting of a few key Soviet cities would suffice for British deterrent purposes. 'A Bloody Union Jack on Top of It', Transcript of BBC Radio documentary presented by Peter Hennessy (programme 2), p. 12.

23   *The Future UK Strategic Nuclear Deterrent Force*, Open Government Document 80/23, Ministry of Defence, London, July 1980, pp. 5–6.

24   Lawrence Freedman, 'British Nuclear Targeting', in D. Ball and J. Richelson (eds.), *Strategic Nuclear Targeting*, Cornell University Press, Ithaca NY, 1986, p. 124.

25   *The Future UK Strategic Nuclear Deterrent Force*, p. 5.

26   Critics of the Government's nuclear policies were quick to assert that a British 'decapitation' strategy was in conformity with the Reagan Administration's bias towards nuclear war-fighting strategies of deterrence. However, while American strategy is premised on the possibility of manipulating the risks of nuclear war for political purposes, British strategy is essentially grounded in perceptions of weakness and not strength. In addition, Freedman argues that a 'decapitation' strategy was unattractive because of the lack of damage it inflicted on the Soviet state itself. See Freedman, *op. cit.*

27   The possibility with Trident of holding the Soviet regime, as distinct from the Soviet people, hostage seems to have been attractive to Quinlan and others seeking to apply principles of just war theory to the tenets of nuclear deterrence. See Freedman, *ibid.* for an insight into Quinlan's thinking on just war theory and nuclear deterrence.

28   Such criticism were more appropriate to the Reagan Administration than to the British Government, since Britain's threat assessment seems to have been more sensitive to fears of a nuclear 'Sarajevo' than to a nuclear 'Munich'. Nevertheless it is interesting to note the degree to which the rhetoric of the first Thatcher Government complimented that of the first Reagan Administration. See C. Coker, *Less Important than Opulence*, Institute for European Defence and Strategic Studies, London, 1988, p. 33.

29   *ibid.* Although this 'mind-set' has been implicit in the thinking of successive British Governments, Christopher Coker has pointed out that one of the most interesting features of the first Thatcher Administration was its willingness to portray the Soviet Union as the 'Empire of Evil'.

30   *ibid.*, p. 33.

31   See David H. Dunn's chapter in this volume.

32   M. McGwire, 'A Mutual Security Regime for Europe', *International Affairs*, LXIV, 1988.

33   See *Statement on the Defence Estimates*, vol. 1, HMSO, London, May 1989, p.12, para. 9.

34   François Heisbourg, 'The British and French nuclear forces', *Survival*, XXXI, 1989, p. 306.

35   START counting rules mean that the actual number of weapons reduced under START will be less than 50 per cent. Under START, penetrating bombers will only count as one despite the fact that bombers can carry a number of short-range attack missiles (SRAMs) and gravity bombs.

36 *Statement on the Defence Estimates* (Cmd 344–I), p. 10.

37 Calculated on the basis of four submarines, sixteen missile tubes and eight warheads on each Trident D-5 missile.

38 Under Labour proposals this would leave a UK submarine based deterrent force of 144 warheads compared to a potential of 640 warheads, using Trident's full capacity, or 512 warheads as is indicated by the statements of the Thatcher government.

39 This is not to devalue Booth and McGwire's framework, since attention to the problem of threats as a level-of-analysis problem provides a useful counter to concerns expressed by some strategic analysts that increases in Soviet military power will lead to shifts in Soviet risk-taking propensities.

40 Peter Jenkins considers that '... the reinsurance [British nuclear weapons] provide allows greater elbow room to move in the very directions in which Mr Kinnock wishes to go – towards the denuclearisation of NATO and the consummation of a new East–West detente.' Peter Jenkins, 'Raising Gaitskell's ghost', *Independent*, 9 June 1988.

41 Heisbourg, *op. cit.*, p. 319.

The impact of the defence budget on arms control policy

Introduction

It has become part of the conventional wisdom of the British defence debate that the conclusion of successful arms control agreements that lead to specific measures of disarmament will allow British policy-makers to offset the UK's perennial tension between commitments and resources. Implicit in this conventional wisdom is the expectation, or at least the hope, that such agreements may halt the decline in the status of the UK in the international system, a decline visible since at least the late 1940s. Yet the assumptions underlying this conventional wisdom are rarely analysed and represent only one side of the political debate.

The trade-off between military preparedness and its associated costs is not a new problem. Indeed, it is one which naturally follows from the perceptions of a threat, and judgement of the seriousness of that threat. There will always be incentives felt by some within a polity for enhancing defence preparedness; yet resources are always finite. For the UK, this problem has been compounded and deepened by what Professor Northedge called the 'Descent from Power'.[1] Britain, formerly a major world power, is now a medium-sized regional power. The transition has been painful, and it may be as yet incomplete. This is evident in a defence posture which owes more to historical circumstance than to strategic design. The UK has four divisions permanently stationed in Germany due to Treaty requirements and maintains one of the most extensive naval forces in the world. Furthermore, the UK, like the superpowers, has a full range of nuclear capabilities.

Since 1945 the dominant perception has been that British defence commitments have declined with the end of the empire and the fall in the country's financial ability to project its forces abroad. By 1988, as the *Statement on the Defence Estimates* noted, 'Over 95 per cent of the defence budget goes, directly or indirectly, towards carrying out our main defence roles in NATO. The great majority of our forces are committed to one or other of the three main NATO commands, Europe, Atlantic and Channel ...'.[2] Within this framework, Britain fulfils four main roles. First, the provision of nuclear forces, of which strategic forces are only one element. Second, defence of the UK base. Third, provision of land and air forces based in Europe and primarily in West Germany, together with the capability for reinforcement from the UK. Fourth, the provision of maritime forces in the Eastern Atlantic and Channel, with the capability to conduct operations in the Norwegian Sea.[3]

From the late 1970s, the UK attempted to maintain the forces adequate to fulfil these major roles through a commitment to increase defence expenditure by 3 per cent per annum. This commitment ended in 1985/86. But during this period, the defence budget grew at an average of only 2.2 per cent in real terms, excluding the Falklands commitment. From 1985/86, there was a planned reduction of some 5 per cent in real terms over the following three years.[4] Although there was hoped to be some offset in the form of a decline in funds needed for the defence of the Falklands, the House of Commons Defence Committee felt that 'other factors may increase this to some 7 per cent.'[5] In fact, 'by 1989–90 the percentage of GDP allocated to the MoD will have fallen to four percent compared with five percent in 1985–6'.[6] The onset of leaner times for the Ministry of Defence has increased the political salience of choices faced in the defence field. Yet despite ominous predictions the government in November 1988 was able to commit an extra £1660 million to defence over three years.[7] For 1989–90, this will mean an expenditure of some £20 billion.

At a time of limited resources there will be two particular pressures on the defence budget. One is a traditional concern, the other quite specific to the period at the turn of the decade. The traditional concern has been with the effects of increases in equipment costs. Colin McInnes estimated the average rate of inflation in defence equipment at some 50 per cent above the rate of inflation experienced in the rest of the economy.[8] The effect of this has been that the equipment allocation of the defence budget has risen from 33.5 per cent in 1975/76 to the present rate of 46 per cent.[9]

The specific concern has been the effects of the purchase of

Trident. During the key years at the turn of the decade Trident will account for far more than the government's figure of 3 per cent of the defence budget over Trident's eighteen year construction period. At that time, Trident will account for a significant proportion of the equipment budget, although possibly less than the procurement of Tornado at its peak.[10] This will occur at a time which is particularly demanding on the defence procurement budget generally. The RAF is in the midst of acquiring the two variants of the Tornado, the Harrier GR5, as well as the unexpected costs of the AWACS. The Royal Navy is building a new class of frigate, the Type 23, with a new helicopter, the EH 101. On top of this, the Army will spend some £1 billion on purchasing main battle tanks. In the long term costings, the Secretary of Defence will have to include the purchase of the European Fighter Aircraft (EFA) and an air launched sub-strategic missile to replace the WE 177 free fall nuclear bomb. The pressure on resources has been felt at all levels. There has been slippage (the failure to order ships in time to replace obsolete vessels in service) in the ship-building timetable resulting in reduced operational strength, a problem highlighted by Admiral Sir Julian Oswald, Commander-in-Chief Fleet, in the winter of 1988.[11] In March 1987 an Army officer complained in *The Times* that cost constraints were 'making it increasingly difficult for commanders at all levels to train their formations and units to the highest standard.'[12] And Air Vice-Marshal John Walker estimated that to stockpile enough weapons for each EFA to fly thirty missions would require an expenditure of two and a half times the cost of each aircraft.[13]

Yet the tension between commitments and resources can be exaggerated. The purchase of Trident will not prove to be the burden forecast by some critics, due to significant changes in the rate of exchange between sterling and the dollar, which has resulted in a fall of 'nearly £2 billion since the programme was first announced'.[14] Another unexpected factor which has also mitigated the worst predictions of the tension between commitments and resources has been the government's ability to increase defence expenditure, as it did in 1988. This unforeseen development was, however, a highly unusual, if not extraordinary, occurrence in the trend which is dominated by the upward spiral of cost inflation. It may also be possible to increase resources allocated to defence, as occurred in November 1988. Nevertheless the effect of all this may not be to offset the underlying tension between commitments and resources, but rather to delay the emergence of any crisis. The underlying pressures will remain: high inflation costs in defence equipment, pressures to modernise and buy expensive items, and the high relative cost of volunteer forces. Despite the unexpected improvements to the health of the defence budget, the tension between commitments and resources will remain, and will continue to require attention.

The last time a tension between commitments and resources became apparent in the UK, there was a major defence review. *The Way Forward*, presented to Parliament in 1981 by the then Secretary of Defence, John Nott, cut several billion pounds from the defence budget projection. This was planned despite the government's commitment at that time to increase spending by 3 per cent per annum. Nott identified two problems. First, he argued that there was an overall force structure that was too expensive, with planned force levels too high in relation to the resources available. Second, he criticised the capital stock for having too many large and costly weapons platforms at the expense of actual weaponry. Nott's proposed cuts focused on the Navy, but with the Falklands War, the defence review embodied in *The Way Forward* was effectively scrapped. Indeed, the Navy's proportion of the defence budget has risen from 13.5 per cent in 1980/81 to 14.2 per cent in 1986/87.[15] It is therefore clear that the problems Nott identified in 1981 have not been substantially dealt with in the intervening years.

There are two main views taken of the severity in this tension between commitments and resources. The first view argues that the tension is manageable. The *Statement on the Defence Estimates* for 1988 demonstrates the contours of this view by arguing that:

Past Statements have warned that the ending of the commitment to maintain real growth inevitably means that difficult choices have to be made between priorities in our forward plans; but we shall maintain our main defence roles. The extra resources now available provide greater room for manoeuvre at the margins of the programme, but will not avoid the need for some difficult decisions, of the kind we face every year in the course of our usual planning cycle.[16]

The second view argues that the tensions are insuperable. David Greenwood estimated that by 1990/91, with planned expenditure at £20 billion, current commitments will cost £25 billion.[17] There would therefore be a 'funding gap' of some £5 billion a year. This thesis (without the figures) was supported by the House of Commons Defence Committee in 1985. In 1987, Mark Urban of *The*

Independent estimated the gap to be £4 billion.[18] The implication of this view is that a major defence review is required. There is clearly no means for resolving these contrasting views. Differences on the severity of the problem lead to differences on the solution. Each approach implies an alternative way to accommodate the tension between commitments and resources.

The first alternative: management

Those who believe that the tension between commitments and resources is manageable seem to exist mainly in the Conservative Party and the Ministry of Defence. For the government, the tension can be resolved by better management of defence procurement. This will be achieved through a mixture of efficiency, competition and collaboration. The government believes that there is considerable waste in the procurement process. For all projects which had begun full development between 1979 and 1985, the House of Commons Public Accounts Committee found that the cost overrun was 28 per cent.[19] The head of procurement in the Ministry of Defence, Peter Levine, has claimed that a 10 per cent saving of the procurement budget may be possible within five years.[20] For the government, the way to achieve this improved efficiency is through an increase in competition. There has been an attempt to minimise cost plus payments contracts. The proportion of contracts let on this basis declined from 15 per cent in 1983/84 to 10 per cent in 1985/6.[21] Contracts have been advertised in the hope of increasing the number of companies bidding for Ministry of Defence work. Since Michael Heseltine introduced the 'Value for Money' scheme, the proportion of contracts let on a competitive basis has increased from 38 per cent to 64 per cent.[22] New management structures have been planned following the recommendations of Sir Robin Ibb's report on 'Improving Management in Government – The Next Steps'.[23] And there has been privatisation of state owned defence enterprises, such as the Royal Ordnance factories and Rolls-Royce.

The value of these measures to the government budget is questionable, however, since these companies are now profit-making concerns. There are also limits to the policy of competitiveness. There are only a certain number of companies equipped to compete in the highly specialised defence field. And the costs of rejecting a company's bid on economic grounds may be its bankruptcy. The consequences of the absence of government planning and patronage were all too well illustrated in the plight of Westland Helicopters.[24]

Such limits have also led the government to stress the third part of its policy – collaboration. Collaborative arrangements for military equipment currently in production or in service, exist in eighteen different forms of equipment. There are a further twenty items of equipment in development or earlier study phases.[25] These are largely Anglo-European ventures, although Britain also collaborates with the US. Such collaborative arrangements allow economies of scale and therefore help save costs. This effect, however, is often considered in practice to be less important than the political commitment that joint projects receive and the resulting inter-operability that is achieved as a consequence.

A further way of saving costs would be direct purchases of equipment from other nations. At present over 75 per cent of the British equipment budget is spent on national projects, 15 per cent on collaborative and 5 per cent on foreign purchases.[26] It is only by increasing the proportions of the latter two forms of investment, that the government might be able to control the increasing cost of defence procurement. For example, by purchasing the American F-18 rather than pursuing the development of the European Fighter Aircraft, the UK could save perhaps £7 million per copy. The purchase by Britain of the AWACS aircraft in preference to the home produced, yet over-budget and technically deficient AEW Nimrod provides an example of the benefits of buying a proven technology. Such deals need not necessarily be detrimental to British interests.[27] The final contract for the purchase of the AWACS involved a commitment on the part of Boeing to spend the equivalent of 130 per cent of the costs of the programme in the UK. However, obtaining the implementation of such high offsets in practice is another matter.

Critics of those who support the management approach oppose these procedures not in their own right, but because they are presented as solutions to the fundamental tension between commitments and resources. The result of adopting a management strategy, it is argued, would be the imposition of 'salami slicing' and slippage of contracts on the principle of 'equal misery for all'. Such tactics would mean that defence questions would be decided not on the basis of strategy, but on the basis of accountancy. For Greenwood, 'this is too important a matter to be left to the book-keepers'. Greenwood's approach has been supported by John Baylis:

(Greenwood's) critique the 'salami slicing', 'cheese paring' process and his advocacy of a more rational approach to establishing defence priorities in a strategic context have clarified in no small way the difficult task which British defence planners have faced: how to adjust to changing international and domestic circumstances.[29]

The conclusion of such critics is that a full defence review is necessary, and that tactics to delay it should be avoided. Jonathan Alford argued that almost any solution that prevented salami slicing, equal misery for all and the consequent fall in morale would be desirable.[30] Ron Smith has drawn a parallel between current policy and previous attempts to head off a full defence review. 'Previous defence reviews have been preceded by such periods of myopic book balancing, whose unfortunate consequences are still with us'.[31]

Yet given the declining cost of Trident, and the availability of more resources for defence, the criticisms of the management approach may have been overly severe. In addition, Gavin Kennedy has argued that with the growth of the British economy in the late 1980s, the government would be able to increase defence spending in real terms in order to keep it at the same percentage of Gross Domestic Product.[32] Kennedy calculated that growth in the economy could be of the order of 2–3 per cent per annum. This level of increase in defence spending would effectively close the funding gap. Indeed, this has partially proved to be the case. Given the improved performance of the British economy over the last few years, the government was able to announce in November 1988 an increase of 1.7 per cent for the defence budget in 1990/91, and 1.3 per cent in 1991/2.[33]

Whether any government would be able to mobilise sufficient public support for an increase in defence spending over the longer-term is not clear. The maintenance of a high priority accorded to defence spending in the face of Gorbachev's reforms and public concern over domestic spending (notably the National Health Service) is highly problematic. In any case, the spending increases of November 1988 only came about after long, hard and at times acrimonious argument within government. It is also not clear whether the British economy has the ability to sustain a growth rate of 2–3 per cent a year. Nor is it readily apparent that even if it did grow at this rate, defence inflation would be covered. But it is clear that were the economy to grow steadily and substantially, then those proposing a managerial approach to reconcile the tension between commitments and resources would have further options.

A final approach is simply to increase the defence budget to meet commitments at the expense of other high-spending government departments. Such an approach is implicit in Chichester and Wilkinson's *British Defence: A Blueprint for Reform*.[34] Chichester and Wilkinson argue for conscription, the modernisation of equipment and the restructuring of the BAOR into a strategic reserve. Certainly in the short term, such proposals would require the investment of greater resources in defence. Yet the costs of these proposals probably means that, short of a return to the depths of the Cold War, such suggestions will be likely to remain on the fringes of the political debate.

The second alternative: reform

An alternative approach to resolve the tension between commitments and resources is to reform British defence. This is proposed by nearly all the critics of the managerial response. Such reform can take one of two forms: either the UK could give up one of its commitments; or one of Britain's defence roles could be redefined.

Which of the four commitments Britain should sacrifice is often related to the political preferences of the analyst. Prior to the 1981 Defence Review, there was serious debate about the utility of the continental role versus the maritime role of Britain's defence posture. Supporters of the maritime strategy argued that although the European balance was stable, there was an increasing Soviet threat at the global level. The Europeans therefore needed to be less parochial in their approach to security. The maritime strategists' arguments also depended on the possibility that the conventional phase of hostilities in Europe would be protracted. If the short war thesis is wrong, or at least dubious, resupply and reinforcement by sea become very important factors to the conduct of war.

In contrast, those who wanted to maintain BAOR at existing levels pointed to the likely political effects on the US of a reduction in the strength of British forces in Germany. Weakening British forces in Germany would also seem to make it more likely that a conventional war in Europe would be short – either because the Soviet Union would win a quick victory, or because NATO would make use of nuclear weapons early in the war. With these calculations, sea borne resupply and reinforcement would be rendered irrelevant. As David Greenwood observed, 'A hedge against protracted hostilities is always handy. But to have nurtured the means to win tomorrow's battles is little comfort if you lost the war this morning.'[35] Air Vice-Marshal Norman Hoad put it more pithily, 'It is no good being able to keep open the Atlantic bridge if, by the time help arrives in Europe, the Russians are toasting their toes in the Channel ports'.[36] These calculations implied that in a choice between the two, it would be the Navy's role in the Eastern Atlantic that would be sacrificed in a major review. That option became more attractive with the potential replacement in the shape of an American Navy that made much progress towards, although failed to obtain, a 600-ship fleet.

The decision to remove the Royal Navy's role in the Eastern Atlantic, however, would be an extremely difficult one to take for several reasons. The Soviet Northern fleet has increased in range and power, raising serious questions about the viability of transatlantic reinforcement. In combatting such a threat, a major navy would seem to be required. This is especially true given the technical re-evaluation which has emphasised the promise of anti-submarine techniques using towed array and variable depth sonar and helicopters. All of these require surface platforms. To an extent, these developments render inappropriate the measures suggested by John Nott in 1981. Moreover, the fleet seemed at least partially defensible using light carriers with Sea Harriers, as evidenced in the Falklands conflict. There has also been the requirement for a truly amphibious capability for the Northern flank.[37] A reduction in the size and capability of the British naval fleet would throw the defence of Norway into question. Finally, a British role in the Eastern Atlantic may allow the UK to have some influence on the American Maritime Strategy which some feel could be strategically destabilising. On top of all this, the Navy has many supporters, and – as John Nott found to his cost – a decision to cut the Navy could have major political costs.

The argument has been made, however, that despite espousing the management strategy, the government has in reality been pursuing a reformist strategy in terms of reducing the size of the Navy by stealth. The House of Commons Defence Committee argued that 2.6 ships need to be ordered every year from 1988 for six years in order to maintain the size of the fleet.[38] Three were ordered in 1988 and it remains to be seen whether the full rate will be maintained through the 1990s. Captain Richard Sharpe, the editor of *Jane's Fighting Ships*, has argued that far from having a fifty-ship Navy, there are only twenty-eight fully operational frigates and destroyers at any one time.[39] In a report for *The Independent*, Mark Urban found only thirty-one operational vessels.[40] Yet whether this is a defence review by stealth is not clear. The government has remained committed to a fifty-ship Navy, and some orders for new ships have been placed. Perhaps the problems with the Navy reflect the strains in the defence budget as a whole, rather than any sinister attempts to change the nature of the force posture of the British armed forces.

A different approach to the reformist strategy would be to cut Trident and withdraw from the strategic nuclear role. All the opposition parties opposed the procurement of Trident at the 1983 and 1987 General Elections on the grounds of cost. Indeed, in 1987 the Labour Party argued for the cancellation of Trident increasingly in terms of its effect on the defence budget, rather than in terms of the morality of withdrawing Britain from its strategic nuclear role as it did in the 1983 General Election. Labour calculated in 1987 that, if then present trends continued, the non-nuclear defence budget would have to be cut by 20 per cent by the 1990s because of the combination of level funding and the purchase of Trident.[41] In contrast, Labour estimated that had Trident been cancelled in 1987 (along with the out-of area role) savings of 15 per cent of the defence budget would have been made by 1991.[42] However, the massive Conservative victory in the 1987 general election has made the option of cancelling Trident on cost grounds redundant. By 1991, the bulk of the expenditure on Trident will have been committed. One submarine hull will be completed, a second will be almost complete, and a third hull will have been laid. Cancellation of Trident at this point would probably release only some £1.5 billion. The changed circumstances have been recognised by the opposition parties, who no longer consider the cancellation of Trident on economic grounds to be a viable political argument.[43] As Martin O'Neill, Labour's Defence spokesperson has commented, 'Frankly, there is not much that can be done about the Trident programme, because it is so far down the road. By the next general election, I believe that it will be about 70 per cent complete.'[44]

If Britain does not renounce one of its commitments, then it could redefine the role of its forces in one of those commitments. This was the proposal put forward in the 1981 defence review. *The Way*

Forward was based on the argument that while it was important that the UK maintained its maritime role in the Eastern Atlantic, the means to fulfil that role did not require a surface fleet of the size and shape then possessed. Instead, the plan was to substitute a combination of maritime patrol aircraft and submarines for frigates and destroyers on anti-submarine warfare operations. The resources thereby released were to be used to bolster Britain's other commitments while not reducing the effectiveness of the patrol in the Eastern Atlantic. Such a widespread reordering of Britain's defensive abilities in the Eastern Atlantic is unlikely because of the political battles fought over the Navy in 1981 and 1982. However, some movement in this direction may prove possible, particularly in terms of adjusting the balance between increasingly expensive weapons platforms and relatively inexpensive weapons systems.

A third reformist strategy would focus on the possibility of redefining the role of the British forces in Germany. Former Commander-in-Chief of the UK Land Forces, General Sir Frank Kitson, has argued for 'a major reassessment of tri-service defence commitments within the next few years'.[45] Kitson's solution was to redefine the Army's role in Germany, by moving the BAOR northwards to the Baltic approaches command, north of the Elbe. Defending this area would be much cheaper than defence in the North German Plain, because the terrain in the Baltic command is much less suited to armour. At the same time, the Army could merge the BAOR with the UK Mobile Force, which is already earmarked for the Baltic. The new command would enable additional funds to be saved. The major difficulty with such a plan is the replacement of the BAOR in northern Germany. It is unclear who would take over this responsibility. The Federal Republic already faces severe personnel constraints in the 1990s. France, for political reasons, will want to continue to provide the strategic reserve rather than be moved forward wholesale. And concern has been expressed over the continuation of the present American force levels, let alone an increase in their number.

There is a minority opinion that would reject both the managerial and the reformist positions. Instead, the argument would be for a radical change in defence plans, away from current structures and postures, and towards an all-defensive defence including, for example, the development of militia. Arguments in favour of defensive defence might be advanced by the difficulties over the tension between commitments and resources. These arguments, however, suggest a radical restructuring of the NATO Alliance and Britain's role within it. The desires to move towards defensive defence are therefore motivated by strategy and morality, not by economics. As such, arguments behind a move to a defensive posture are distinct from the difficulties over reconciling the tension between commitments and resources.

The arms control impact

The pressures for a defence review are great, and emanate from many sources. It is not only the government's political opponents and critics who seek such a review. The editors of the *Daily Telegraph* have argued that 'The case is certainly strengthening, as this newspaper has consistently argued, for a thorough-going defence review.'[46] Christopher Coker, in his paper 'Less Important than Opulence', argue for a defence review,[47] as did Leon Brittan who also made the case for a cut in the size of the Navy.[48] Even *The Economist* joined the chorus, arguing in 1988 that 'the logic underlying the Nott cuts remains inescapable.'[49] As the *Financial Times* noted, 'Something, somewhere is going to give. Almost the only hope, it seems, is that Mr Gorbachev will feel the pinch even tighter than we do.'[50]

Yet the political pressures on the government to avoid such a defence review are almost equally great. No minister wants to suffer the political fate of John Nott, who was pilloried and isolated in Parliament and the party, before resigning from politics. Moreover, a cutback in defence would allow the government's political adversaries to argue that the Trident purchase has led to cuts in conventional defence, as they had predicted for a decade. Thus, for personal and party political reasons, as much as for strategic or military rationales, defence ministers and the government would be likely to put off a defence review for as long as is practicable. The sensible solution would clearly be to have a defence review every four or five years. This would allow change to be planned for and would provide definite opportunities for developing a defensive posture along strategic lines. This could be done as part of a regular NATO-wide process, thus allowing a degree of co-ordination as well as political solidarity. Although regular defence reviews have been suggested, no concrete proposals have, as yet, been made.

How long, then, can a defence review be delayed under the managerial strategy? This depends in part on government priorities and the performance of the British economy. Six months before the Reagan-Gorbachev Washington summit and the signing of the INF Treaty, David Watt noted in *The Times* that 'To hear ministers talking with real, though wistful enthusiasm of East–West detente is to realise that they are looking for a miraculous escape from what could well turn out to be a fatal political trap.'[51] Were East–West relations to be characterised by detente, the pressures on the defence budget might be reduced. For example, there would be less urgency about expensive modernisations. A substantial arms control agreement, however, might produce significant cuts and hence real savings. This could relieve much of the pressure and allow a defence review to be delayed almost indefinitely.

The conclusion of successful arms control agreements incorporating significant disarmament measures,[52] would be of benefit to both reformers and managers, but much more so for the latter. For the reformers, arms control cum disarmament could provide the incentive for the full defence review that they seek. Yet it could also put severe constraints on the reformist programme. Were an arms control agreement to stipulate fixed force levels for individual nations, then in the aftermath of that agreement, room for major reform could be reduced to almost zero. This implies that the process of reform must occur before the signing of an agreement; indeed, preferably at the stage of preparing a negotiating position. Yet the Conventional Forces in Europe talks have already begun; and in any case, such a process would allow Britain's NATO allies a major say in the nature of the reform of the UK's defence posture. The British defence posture would in these circumstances emerge from the NATO bureaucracy bearing the hallmarks of international bureaucratic politics, and the label of being made by an international committee. If the reformist argument carries any intellectual weight, it is that such reform should be carried out by British strategists, showing due concern for the impact upon allies and adversaries, and based on strategic analysis rather than historical accident. For the reformists, therefore, the conclusion of successful arms control negotiations may prove to be a mixed blessing.

For proponents of the managerial approach, however, the conclusion of such arms control agreements seem to hold out the possibility of avoiding a defence review. Cuts would occur multilaterally, not unilaterally, and the personal and party political disadvantages of the defence review would be turned into the triumphs of successful international statesmanship. However, the successful conclusion of arms control agreements that lessen the pressures for the technological improvement of equipment, or lead to reductions in the numbers of specific items, would be of limited benefit to the managerial approach for two reasons. First, the very process of negotiation creates its own pressures for force enhancements to provide stronger bargaining positions. This consideration formed at least part of the rationale for deploying ground-launched cruise and Pershing missiles in 1979, and it was also one of the incentives behind the discussion of a follow-on system for Lance. Second, while a conventional arms control agreement is likely to set limits on particular force levels, it would not stop the movement towards more expensive generations of weaponry. If such a deal meant that Britain would buy say 190 instead of 260 European Fighter Aircraft, it would represent a significant saving; but at an estimated £25 million a copy, it still represents a major investment in replacing F4 Phantoms at £10 million a copy.

At any rate, it is not clear that a conventional arms control agreement would result in significant reductions on the British side.[53] The Bush CFE proposals would lead to significant reductions in US and Soviet troops in central Europe, but would represent only a small saving for the UK. A further limitation on force reduction is that certain force structures require a minimum level of provision. A certain number of troops are required to make Forward Defence credible, regardless of how small Warsaw Pact forces become. Due to the necessity of refits, there are a minimum number of submarines required for a nation always to have one SSBN on station. Finally, the successful implementation of an arms control agreement may be many years away. This would still leave the managerial approach facing the question of how best to manage the defence budget in the interim.

The successful conclusion of an arms control agreement would therefore seem to have less impact upon the future of Britain's defence budget than is often implicitly assumed. While there are some incentives for managers and reformers to engage in the arms control process in order to ameliorate the tensions which exist between defence commitments and ability to fund them, Britain's scope for progress in such a process is limited. The East–West arms

control agenda is controlled by the US in the West, and any negotiations would have to be conducted within an Alliance framework.
Although other NATO nations share similar problems to Britain,
there are very different emphases. In other words, Britain's concerns
– whether managerial or reformist – are unlikely to shape the arms
control agenda but are likely to be shaped by them.

Conclusion

The conventional wisdom that arms control will assist the UK in
adjusting its defence commitments to its available resources demonstrates the dominance of the managerial approach in the political
agenda, and particularly in government policy, regarding defence
and arms control issues. For the managers, arms control and disarmament are seen as the only way of avoiding another unilateral
reduction in Britain's prestige and position in the world. A disarmament agreement would bring about deterrence at lower levels,
but lower levels for all; Britain's relative position would remain
unchanged. For the reformers, arms control might have some benefit
for the defence budget, but the two are largely unrelated. For the
reformers a defence review is a necessary part of the process of
coming to grips with the inevitable: a further descent from power, as
measured in military terms. For the reformers, arms control is
unlikely to solve Britain's defence budget problems because it is a
process that will continue to be driven by strategy and politics rather
than economics. While arms control offers the promise of an escape
from existing resource-commitments dilemmas, it is a promise that is
unlikely to be turned into reality, or which may create a different set
of resource-commitment dilemmas. The solution to the dilemmas, as
on all other occasions since 1945, will have to come from within the
UK.

When discussing the future shape of the British defence budget, the
force of underlying assumptions means that it is not a debate about
economics. Instead, it is a debate about political vision, about how
Britain sees its role in the international system and how necessary a
high level of military provision is to that vision. Whether a decline in
military power is inevitable and what the consequences of this may
be for Britain's place in the international system is open to question.
The advocates of management and reform within the defence debate
provide different answers to this question. For the reformers, on the

one hand, a decline in military provision is both inevitable and desirable as part of the process of Britain's reconciling itself to the roles and responsibilities of a medium-sized power and the changes in Europe. Realism and vision, in this view, are required for the nation to adjust to these new realities and to prevent decline from becoming a rout. The managers, on the other hand, reject both the need for reform and the assumptions on which it is based. The approach denies the inevitability of a retraction of defence commitments and international status. They argue that because the world is a changing place it would be foolish to accept decline unless or until it is absolutely necessary. The paradox is that only the course of future of East–West relations, which are largely beyond the direct control of the UK, will demonstrate which view prevails.

Notes

1 F. S. Northedge, *Descent from Power*, George Allen and Unwin, London, 1974.

2 *Statement on the Defence Estimates 1988*, Cm 344–I, HMSO, London, 1988, para. 119, p.4.

3 Britain also has a fifth – though very much smaller – role in terms of out-of-area capabilities.

4 *Statement on the Defence Estimates 1987*, Cm 101–I, HMSO, London, 1987, para. 603, p. 52.

5 House of Commons Defence Committee 'Proceedings and Minutes of Evidence', *Statement on the Defence Estimates*, Session 1985/86, p.xvii.

6 Nick Butler, Len Scott, David Ward and Jonathan Worthington, 'Working for Common Security', *Fabian Tract No.533*, The Fabian Society, London, January 1989, p. 22.

7 An increase of £150 million in 1989/90, £600 million in 1990/91 and £910 million in 1991/92 was announced. Mark Urban, 'Three year deal pleases Younger', *The Independent*, 27 November 1988.

8 See C. McInnes, 'The U.K. Trident programme: problems and prospects', paper presented to the PSA Conference, 7–9 April 1987, p. 7.

9 See T. Taylor, 'Managing defence procurement', paper presented to the PSA Conference, 7–9 April 1987, p. 2.

10 Secretary of State for Defence George Younger has stated that 'it is certainly true that the Trident programme is not as expensive as the Tornado programme ...'. *Hansard*, 28 June 1988, col. 182.

11 Mark Urban, 'Navy at "minimum destroyer strength" ' *The Independent*, 26 October 1988.

12 Letter to *The Times*, 5 March 1987.

13 Mark Urban, 'Soaring bill for air weapons stockpile', *The Independent*, 10 December 1988.

14 Secretary of State for Defence George Younger, *Hansard*, 29

November 1989, col. 562.

15　J. Alford, 'Alternatives for British defence policies in the 1990s within NATO's integrated defences' in John Roper and Karl Kaiser (eds), *Anglo–German Defence Co-operation*, Jane's Publishing for the Royal Institute of International Affairs and Forschungsinstitut der Deutschen Gesellschaft für Auswartige Politik, London, 1988.

16　*Statement on the Defence Estimates 1988*, para. 503, p.47.

17　See *The Independent*, 26 February 1987.

18　Mark Urban, 'Defence: Tory promises that cannot be kept', *The Independent*, 26 February 1987.

19　See Taylor, *op. cit.*, p. 7.

20　*ibid.*

21　See *Statement on the Defence Estimates 1987*, para. 503, p. 44.

22　*ibid.*, pp. 45–6 and 54–5.

23　*Statement on the Defence Estimates 1988*, para. 510, p. 49.

24　See Stuart Croft, 'The Westland Helicopter Crisis: Implications for the British Defence Industry', *Defense Analysis*, III, 1987.

25　See *Statement on the Defence Estimates 1988*, Table 8, p. 47.

26　See Taylor, *op. cit.*, p. 9.

27　This, of course, minimises the significance of the argument that it is important to preserve British research and development capabilities and the ability to produce complete weapons systems rather than components alone. Michael Heseltine made much of this in his evidence to the House of Commons Defence Committee enquiry into Westland Helicopters. He argued that it would be 'totally unacceptable as a judgement, both in the strategic concept that you should never allow the strategic control over your essential defence requirements to be outside your hands, and, secondly, because the acceleration of the brain drain, the loss of jobs, the destruction of the high technology base and the civil implications would be wholly unacceptable.' House of Commons Defence Committee Session 1985–86, 'The Defence Implications of the Future of Westland plc', Minutes of Evidence and Appendices HC 169, HMSO, 1986, p. 204.

28　David Greenwood, 'Defence' in P. Cocklan (ed), *Public Expenditure Policy*, MacMillan, London, 1985, p. 117.

29　John Baylis ' "Greenwoodery" and British Defence Policy', *International Affairs*, LXII, 1986, p. 457.

30　Jonathan Alford writes, '[Salami slicing] is one future I would prefer to avoid and would take almost any other road to avoid'. See Alford, *op. cit.*

31　R. Smith, 'The Case for a British Defence Review', *ADIU Report*, VII, March–April 1985, p. 4.

32　G. Kennedy, 'Managing the Defence Budget', *The Royal Bank of Scotland Review*, June 1986, cited in Taylor, *op. cit.*, p. 10.

33　Mark Urban, 'Three year deal pleases Younger', *The Independent*, 27 November 1988.

34　M. Chichester and J. Wilkinson, *British Defence: A Blueprint for Reform*, Brassey's, London, 1987.

35　D. Greenwood 'Nott's Way Forward', *Defence Attaché*, IV, 1981, p. 15.

36   Letter to the *Daily Telegraph*, 6 October 1988.

37   See Alford, *op. cit.*

38   See Sixth Report from the Defence Committee of Session 1987–88 on the Future Size and Role of the Royal Navy's Surface Fleet, HC 309. See also the government's reply, Cm. 443.

39   Captain Richard Sharpe, 'Foreword' in *Jane's Fighting Ships 1988–9*, Jane's Publishing Company, London, 1988.

40   Mark Urban, '50 ship fleet based on "unrealistic statistics" ', *The Independent*, 10 June 1988.

41   *Modern Britain in a Modern World*, 'The Power to Defend our Country', The Labour Party, London, 10 December 1986.

42   See 'Defence and Arms Control at the 1986 Party Conferences', *ADIU Report*, VIII, November–December 1986, p. 13.

43   For an example of the change of view in the Labour Party see, Butler, Scott, Ward and Worthington, *op.cit.*, p. 19.

44   Martin O'Neill, 'Royal Navy: Debate on Motion for Adjournment', *Hansard*, 28 February 1989, col. 179. During the same debate, the Defence spokesperson of the Social and Liberal Democrats, Menzies Campbell, when asked by Jonathan Sayeed whether his party would pledge themselves to maintaining Trident into the future, answered 'Yes. I hope that a monosyllabic answer does not take the hon. Gentleman unawares', *ibid.*, col. 214. This view was confirmed at the 1989 SLD Party Conference in Brighton.

45   Sir Frank Kitson, *Warfare as a Whole*, Faber and Faber, London, 1987.

46   Editorial, *Daily Telegraph*, 24 June 1988.

47   Christopher Coker, 'Less Important than Opulence', Institute for European and Strategic Studies, London, Summer 1988.

48   Leon Brittan, 'Defence and arms control in a changing era', *PSI Discussion Paper 21*, Policy Studies Institute, London, 1988.

49   'Nott's question remains', *The Economist*, 21 May 1988.

50   Edward Mortimer, 'A potential vote-loser for the Tories', *Financial Times*, 12 July 1988.

51   David Watt, 'Defence: the great retreat', *The Times*, 10 May 1987.

52   When arms control is talked of in this sense, it is usually arms control of the 1980s-type, rather than the 1970s. In the 1970s, arms control lead to a build-up of forces at higher, although arguably more stable levels. In the 1980s, arms control has aimed at bringing about stability at lower levels of weaponry: for example, the INF Treaty, the START proposals, and the purpose of the Conventional Forces in Europe negotiations. Arms control thus does not inherently lead to agreements on disarmament. Further, certain forms of arms control – such as confidence-building measures – would not lead to any savings at all.

53   See *Statement on the Defence Estimates 1988*, Figure 15, p. 61.

Part II:

Arms control issue areas

Nuclear arms control and the UK

Introduction

Successive British governments – both Conservative and Labour – have professed their faith in the value of the process of multilateral nuclear arms control ever since that process began in the 1960s. This position was consistently reiterated by the Thatcher government during the breakdown in the British defence consensus in the early 1980s. Despite this, there have never been any arms control negotiations that have included the British minimum nuclear deterrent. The UK, like the Soviet Union, has historically reacted to an agenda set by the US in the nuclear arms control process. But unlike the Soviet Union, this situation has historically proved beneficial to Britain. The Soviet Union has accepted the American distinction between theatre and strategic weapons, even though some of the former are capable of striking the Soviet homeland and none the American. For the UK, this distinction has allowed the British deterrent to be kept out of arms control negotiations.[1] When the superpowers discussed strategic systems during the SALT process in the 1970s, the British force was defined as 'theatre'. During the 1980s, with movement towards a zero–zero INF agreement in theatre systems, the same British system – Polaris – has been recast as 'strategic'.[2]

The nuclear arms control process has, therefore, apparently historically worked in Britain's interests. In this process, the UK seems to have three strategic objectives. First, Britain has sought to maintain its position as one of the few nuclear powers in the world. The methods for pursuing this have been the promotion of both the Test Ban Treaty and the Non-Proliferation Treaty. The British government has also refused to allow its minimum deterrent to face any threat of obsolescence: hence the Chevaline programme, and the decision to buy first the Trident C4 and then the D5 system. Consequently, Britain has proved unwilling to move towards a Comprehensive Test Ban Treaty. The British have argued that such a Treaty could not be verified. In reality, such a Treaty could threaten the future viability of the British minimum deterrent.[3] Second, the UK has sought to keep its deterrent out of arms control negotiations. The official line has been that this is because the aggregate of superpower nuclear weaponry far outnumbers the British. A more compelling explanation, however, is that the British minimum deterrent is precisely that – a minimum. It would be difficult for the UK to enter into any agreement which reduces the British force without making the deterrent incredible and therefore worthless. This, of course, is premised on the Moscow criterion.[4] A lesser criteria for the British deterrent would diminish this pressure. But at present, the alternatives at the strategic nuclear level appear to be no arms control or effective disarmament.[5] Third, Britain has sought to have its interests protected and its view of the important elements of nuclear stability and deterrence considered in the superpower arms control negotiations that have taken place. Since the politics of the Cold War have meant that the British have been unable to exert influence over the Soviet Union, the British have sought to achieve this by concentrating on and exerting influence in the 'special relationship' with the US.[6]

Since the UK has not participated in the major strategic nuclear arms control negotiations, the British have had to react to that process and attempt to influence it at arms length. For Britain, arms control proposals seem to be considered according to four tactical criteria which are related to the three arms control objectives that Britain has pursued. First, the UK must assess how the changes brought about by arms control will affect the international environment. Specifically, this relates to whether the changes will allow the US to fulfil its Alliance obligations, particularly in terms of extended deterrence. The maintenance of credible extended deterrence is a key interest for Britain. Second, the British government must assess the impact of nuclear arms control initiatives in terms of the cost of their implementation and the continued maintenance of its minimum deterrent. Third, if the 'special relationship' is deemed to be important, the British need to consider whether the initiatives will enhance or reduce the influence of the UK in Washington. Since they do not directly participate in negotiations, this is seen as an important means of promoting British interests in East–West strategic relations. Fourth, the UK will have to react to proposals in such a way as to maintain Alliance cohesion and prevent the Soviet Union from exacerbating Alliance tensions. Since the British believe that nuclear weapons should deter all war in Europe, this is of over-riding importance in the nuclear field.

Despite being largely on the outside of the negotiations, the UK has been broadly successful in achieving its aims in the nuclear arms control process, at least until 1985. Britain viewed the SALT agreements favourably, especially the ABM Treaty. And Britain supported the American move in the early 1980s which effectively blocked progress towards an INF agreement with the zero–zero proposal which, it was initially felt, the Soviet Union could not accept. There are two possible explanations for this success. It is possible that the British were merely the fortunate beneficiaries of a community of interests between themselves and the US, in which the US controlled the arms control agenda. The other explanation is that this success demonstrates the effectiveness of the 'special relationship' with the US. Since the British are unable to exert real influence in Moscow, influence in Washington has traditionally been viewed as a vital means of enhancing British and European security. The 'special relationship' is deemed to be important in terms of access to intelligence, technology, but most importantly influence in Washington. Particularly in British government circles, this latter explanation has seemed to be more persuasive than arguing that the British have been fortunate beneficiaries of an independent process.

This explanation, however, has been called into question by developments in the 1980s. These events, particularly since the end of 1985, point to an assessment that the 'special relationship' has in some important senses broken down. Since the mid-1980s, the nuclear arms control process has ceased to work to Britain's advantage. There have been two significant related developments in that process in this period which have changed the political environment. First, the US has proved less willing to consider European, including British, concerns. Examples of this were the events at the Reykjavik superpower summit, and the progress towards the conclusion of the INF Treaty. After Reykjavik, British officials were shocked to learn how close the superpowers had come to a deal on which the Europeans had not been consulted. And the INF Treaty resulted in the abolition of a class of weapons, despite a clear British preference for retaining limited numbers of ground launched cruise and Pershing missiles. Both these events have taken place in an atmosphere where nuclear weapons have increasingly been delegitimised. Second, in parallel with the events in Washington, the Soviet Union has begun to have a major impact on the nuclear arms control agenda. Since the British have relied on their influence in Washington and the ability of the US to set the arms control agenda to further British interests, this is a most unwelcome development from the British point of view. To examine whether the 'special relationship' has broken down in the nuclear arms control field, the three major areas of nuclear arms control – space, strategic and theatre systems – and their impact on the UK will be analysed.

Space weapons

The debate over space weapons has proved to be a difficult one for the UK. The four tactical criteria which were outlined above, when applied to space weapons, prove to be in conflict. The first criteria was an evaluation of the impact of certain arms control measures on the strategic environment. As Sir Geoffrey Howe made clear in a speech to RUSI in 1985, the British government consider strategic defences to be potentially destabilising.[7] The British government have never been supporters of the SDI concept as expressed in its original 'astrodome' concept, and have managed to minimise their support to arguments that research is necessary because of the danger of a Soviet break-out from the ABM Treaty. And it is that Treaty that makes the whole issue more complicated. Not only are space weapons seen as destabilising, but any American attempt to undermine the ABM Treaty will be seen by Britain as threatening the whole process of superpower arms control. The UK supports that process as a means of enhancing strategic stability.[8] In terms of assessing the impact of space weapons on the strategic environment, therefore, the British would seem to be against the deployment, as opposed to research into, SDI, and in favour of the ABM Treaty as traditionally understood. It is for these reasons that the British government did not support the Reagan administration's attempts to reinterpret the ABM Treaty. This seemed to place the UK in some senses in an 'unholy alliance' with the Soviet Union against the proposals and prescriptions of the Reagan administration. However, this opposition to US policy was obscured by the official British line that the ABM Treaty is a bilateral Treaty to which Britain is not a party, and therefore does not have to pronounce on the subject.

These strategic considerations are reinforced by the second criteria – an assessment of the effect on the British deterrent. The further development of strategic defences in the Soviet Union in response to SDI or the abrogation of the ABM Treaty would be highly problematic for the UK. The last time that the development of extensive Soviet ballistic missile defences were a concern, the British developed the Chevaline warhead as a means of overcoming such defences, at a cost of some £1 billion. The development of extensive Soviet strategic defences would affect the credibility of the Trident D5 system before the end of its life by undermining its ability to effectively target Moscow. This could produce an incentive to increase the number of warheads on each missile to guarantee overcoming defences, which could undermine efforts to de-MIRV in a post-START strategic environment. Allied to improvement in Soviet strategic defences, the credibility of the UK deterrent would be further undermined by Soviet ASW improvements. Any improvements in Soviet ASW techniques over the next twenty-five years would be that much more important and threatening, and would increase the incentives to maximise the number of boats on station. Consequently the possibility of moving to a three boat force, either through arms control or due to defence costs would be lessened. The combination of such factors puts real constraints on the UK's entering into the arms control process in the nuclear field.

Thus a strategic and national assessment would seem to indicate that the deployment of space-based defence systems would be against Britain's interests. Hence the UK would be expected to support a restrictive superpower arms control agreement in this area. However, the other two considerations mitigate the level of British opposition. Given the American commitment to SDI, outright British hostility would present the Soviet Union with a perfect opportunity for wedge-driving in the Alliance. The British government, unlike the French but like the West German government, has thus felt constrained from making its opinion known in public. On top of this, the UK has sought to maintain its 'special relationship' with the US. Both of these requirements have resulted in limited expressions of British support for SDI as expressed in the annual *Statement on the Defence Estimates.*[9] It may be argued that the 'special relationship' is the best conduit for the British to outline their reservations over American strategic policy, to the US. But, it is impossible to quantify, or to evaluate its utility. In order to work within the 'special relationship', it is necessary to lobby privately while in public supporting the project in question. If this mechanism for moderating policy is unsuccessful, however, the political costs of coming out against American deployment of strategic defences at a later stage, having given it support for a number of years, may well be too great.

The British, who felt compelled to engage in the SDI project for national reasons as well as for the advantages of Alliance cohesion, can tentatively point to the possibility of a new 'twintrack policy' developing with regard to SDI. This would legitimise the UK approach by arguing that it is in favour of pursuing a system from a position of strength in order to force an arms control agreement from the Soviet Union. This tactic, it is publicly claimed, successfully brought concessions from the Soviet Union over INF systems, leading to an INF Treaty that abolished four Soviet warheads for each American one. This approach would sit well with the Prime Minister's oft repeated claim that: 'It is absolutely vital that we negotiate from a basis of strength because that tactic got the inter-mediate nuclear weapons treaty.'[10]

It is also possible that some sort of consensus may develop around deployment of Senator Sam Nunn's Accidental Launch Protection System (ALPS). It would be difficult for Britain to oppose deployment along these lines. Such deployment – limited in scope, excluding space weapons, and achieved in agreement with the Soviet Union within a modified ABM Treaty – may well be an acceptable long-term compromise position, not only in Washington but also for the superpowers. But an increase in the number of ABM launchers allowed under the ABM Treaty to say, 400, while providing very limited defences for the superpowers against each other's arsenals, would greatly complicate British nuclear planning.[11]

Alternatively, the British can hope that under President Bush the SDI programme will disappear as an issue, either through under-funding or a shift in the administration's strategic policies. Yet before a START agreement can be finalised, some decisions will have to be taken about the future of SDI. And the Bush administration has major political incentives to not upset the right-wing in American politics by reaffirming and tightening ABM Treaty limitations. Therefore, strategic defences are likely to remain on the arms control agenda and continue to pose a serious dilemma for Britain's strategic deterrent and nuclear arms control policy.

Strategic nuclear weaponry

In the strategic nuclear arms control process, the agenda for the 1990s agenda will focus on deep cuts in the superpowers strategic nuclear arsenals rather than planned force increases. This largely reflects both American concerns and the American ability to set the arms control agenda. For the Reagan administration arms control of the SALT variety, the attainment of mutually agreed force increases, was discredited. The strategic nuclear arms control process was to be firmly separated from the political goals of detente that were dominant in the 1970s and focused on strategic goals. With its roots in the late 1970s concern with the 'window of vulnerability', the aim of the Reagan administration was to eliminate the threat posed to the US by the Soviet land based ICBM force. This explains the importance of radical arms control proposals in this field, in the 1980s. The essence of the original American START proposals was the reduction of ballistic missile forces by 50 per cent. But SDI has also been seen as a means of reducing the Soviet ICBM threat. When Reagan spoke in his SDI speech of March 1983 about making 'Nuclear weapons impotent and obsolete', what he referred to in practical terms in the rest of his speech were Soviet ballistic missiles.[12] For the Reagan administration, SDI and radical arms control were both means of reducing this threat. This focus on Soviet hard target kill capability will almost certainly be continued under the Bush administration, particularly given the influence of National Security Advisor, Brent Scowcroft. It is within the confines of this new strategic arms control agenda that UK strategic arms control policy will have to develop. More importantly, it is likely that these fundamental changes in the agenda of the strategic nuclear arms control process will work against British interests.

The Reagan administration's strategic desire did not become coherent and realistic until the end of 1985. It was not until the 1985 Geneva Summit that Reagan obtained a verbal agreement with Gorbachev to seek 50 per cent cuts in strategic weapons. This was taken further at the Reykjavik Summit in October 1986, when both leaders agreed to move towards the elimination of all ballistic missiles within ten years. The President explained that all strategic weapons 'would be reduced by 50 per cent in the first five years. During the next five years we would continue by eliminating all remaining offensive ballistic nuclear missiles.'[13] Movement in this direction has so far been delayed by a series of factors: debate regarding its merits within the US strategic and defence community; the hostile reaction of the allies, in particular of the UK; the difficulties inherent in negotiating and verifying such an agreement (such as what to do with sea-launched cruise missiles, and whether to prohibit the deployment of mobile ICBMs); and by Soviet insistence on constraining SDI to the laboratory. The progress towards a START Treaty will therefore depend on overcoming these obstacles.

It might seem that the UK could draw some hope from these difficulties. The focus on cuts, the political importance of SDI, along with the downgrading of political imperatives to reach agreements and the American renunciation of the SALT II guidelines may all combine to make the attainment of formal agreements in the strategic nuclear arms control process more unlikely. In the START arena, the US may be unwilling to compromise on strategic issues for the purpose of achieving an agreement. But rather than reinforcing a status quo, in which Britain's strategic deterrent force can happily exist, the likely effect of reducing constraints on the strategic arms race is a lessening of strategic stability. And of course, an added concern for the British in such an environment would be Soviet improvements in their ballistic missile defence capability.

The greatest danger for the British, however, is precisely the opposite: that the superpowers will reach an agreement on deep cuts and will continue the process with little regard for European concerns. In terms of the four British criteria for assessing nuclear arms control proposals, such developments could well appear to be disadvantageous. In assessing the impact on the strategic environment, the UK is unlikely to seek a process of large reductions in the Soviet's ICBM force if those reductions are to be reciprocal. Some argue that this would lead to the 'Return to the Bomber Age' and there are grave doubts as to whether it would add anything to strategic stability.[14] More importantly, American ICBMs are deemed to be crucial for extended deterrence and a strategic arms control agreement entailing substantial deep cuts could be seen by some as decoupling America from Europe. This is a recurring fear, expressed often during both SALT negotiations, and during the INF Treaty negotiations.

In terms of the second criteria, the impact of the costs on Britain, once again such an agreement looks unfavourable. A large cut in the superpower arsenals of between 30 and 50 per cent[15] would inevitably bring the future of the British deterrent into question both internationally and domestically.[16] This would be particularly so, at a time when the British would be completing the purchase of a vast increase in firepower. Concern over the future of the Trident purchase may increase in these circumstances, since obtaining the missile technology depends on the US. This would cause particular problems if the Soviet Union made the limitation of the Anglo–American Trident deal a condition for a major American–Soviet treaty.

The British will want to resist these pressures to reduce the Trident purchase for two reasons. First, as already noted, the British deterrent is a minimum one, and there is virtually no scope for significant reductions (as long as the Moscow Criterion remains). Second, even a major reduction in the superpower arsenals of the magnitude of 50 per cent would still not be sufficient to increase the significance of the British deterrent in strategic terms, although it clearly would in political terms.[17] The difficulty is that the British government has promised to include its own forces in nuclear arms control negotiations 'in the light of the reduced threat'[18] if there are major superpower reductions. It does not seem excessive to say, therefore, that deep cuts, although arguably in the American strategic interest, may not work in the political interest of the UK if Britain's bluff in the arms control arena is called.

Yet there are several constraints on British opposition to a deep cuts regime. The UK, along with the other West European countries, seeks to maintain the situation whereby the US continues to share in the risks of the European members of NATO. In such circumstances, to oppose the Americans seeking changes in the strategic environment that will apparently improve American security – whether deep cuts or SDI – may well increase the US's unilateralist tendencies. Such tendencies were illustrated in January 1988 with the publication of *Discriminate Deterrence*.[19] Although not a government document, *Discriminate Deterrence* demonstrated an important strand in American strategic thought. The Report focused in the main on global Soviet–American competition rather than the European theatre, and called for the adoption of what some might consider to be nuclear war-fighting strategies. The further development of American unilateralist tendencies would not enhance the effectiveness of the 'special relationship'. Indeed, it could well lead to a qualitative change in the nature of that relationship. On top of this, such a situation would present the Soviet Union with opportunities for wedge-driving. Finally, it is unclear how the British government can mount any sort of opposition to disarmament of almost any reciprocal kind, without suffering a major domestic political backlash.

The UK, therefore, faces problems with the current strategic arms control agenda. But it is the nature of the agenda that presents the British with problems, rather than the specific turn of events within the negotiations. That agenda presents twin dangers: either the superpowers might fail to reach an agreement or that they might succeed. But it is the latter which causes the most concern: the implementation of superpower deep cuts and the continuation of that process would clearly place the British government in the most difficult of positions. The implementation of such a regime would continually raise questions regarding Britain's participation in the next round of strategic arms control.

The public presentation of the government's current views on these dilemmas is that:

> ... if Soviet and US strategic arsenals were to be very significantly reduced, and if no significant changes occurred in Soviet defensive capabilities, Britain would want to review her position and to consider how best she could contribute to arms control in the light of the reduced threat.[20]

The clear implication of this logic is that the British possess a deterrent to *deter* a Soviet ballistic missile nuclear attack. Thus, the reduction or elimination of Soviet ballistic missiles will lead to a reduced Soviet threat. Of course such a position is untenable. The British deterrent is not only focused against nuclear attack but is linked into the deterrence of all war in Europe. The difficulties apparent in the above quotation demonstrate the grave problems that the British have in reacting to the new American agenda, for the British deterrent has little strategic utility – its deterrent effect is political in nature. This political nature of the British independent deterrent is lost in the new strategic rhetoric of the arms control process. As long as the Soviet Union possesses even the conventional capability to damage Western Europe, the British government will want to maintain its nuclear deterrent. As the Prime Minister has said, 'We want a war-free Europe, and we need to keep nuclear weapons to achieve that.'[21] How that will be achieved politically, in the context of a process of deep cuts, is unclear.

The most effective argument would seem to be to suggest that many other agreements need to be reached before Britain can integrate Polaris/Trident into the START process. This is the line that George Younger, then Secretary of Defence, began to take:

> We have always made it clear that if, in the future, there is a major change in the line-up of the super-powers, if there is a 50 per cent START reduction, if the conventional imbalances can be substantially reduced, and if there is a world wide ban on chemical weapons, we shall be prepared to see whether we can make a further contribution in respect of our deterrent.[22]

Yet problems abound with this approach. The link between negotiations over Trident and a world-wide chemical weapons ban is tenuous at best. Why should the world-wide abolition of chemical weapons make it acceptable for Britain to enter the START process? It would be a new rationale for Trident to argue that it deters a Soviet chemical attack. And why should the integration of the British Trident system have to wait until the achievement of conventional parity? While George Younger has argued that conventional parity and flexible response are compatible, it is not clear why conventional parity should change the strategic environment to the degree that Trident may be integrated into the START process.[23]

In reality, of course, this approach does not have the purpose of integrating the UK deterrent into the START process; instead, the aim is to place diplomatic barricades on the road to the integration of Trident into that process. But this approach will become increasingly difficult for any British government to maintain, given that the new arms control agenda is structured in such a way as to repeatedly ask the question, 'when will the British Trident be incorporated into the START process?'

Theatre nuclear forces

It is as a result of the INF Agreement that the changes in the nature of the nuclear arms control process have become most clear for the British. If the UK faces a series of problems in the field of space and strategic nuclear arms control, it has faced enormous difficulties over arms control affecting theatre systems. These difficulties are apparent in its policies regarding the 'double zero' INF proposal and its reactions to the possibility of a 'third zero', removing short range, battlefield nuclear weapons.

In 1981 when the Zero Option was proposed by the US, it was supported by Britain. The reason for that support was that the proposal placed the Soviet Union diplomatically on the defensive, demonstrated Alliance unity, and showed that the arms control element of the 1979 Dual Track decision was being treated 'seriously'. Above all, the British knew that it was a proposal that the Soviet Union would be unable to accept. In the mid-1980s, the apparent political viability of the various zeros demonstrated the newfound Soviet willingness to set the arms control agenda. Zero–zero, once unacceptable to the Soviet Union, was put back onto the agenda by the Soviets themselves. To an American President apparently more interested in disarmament than traditional notions of deploying the necessary weapons and ensuring certain linkages to enhance European security, and with the demands for a foreign policy success following the Irangate affair, such an agenda was most welcome.

The British government has been able to claim that Soviet willingness to make concessions in the INF field was due to the Dual Track decision of 1979 and 'negotiating from strength.' Yet one of the major reasons for the deployment of American cruise and Pershing II missiles in Europe was to further European–American coupling. Response to the Soviet SS-20s was always a secondary consideration. As a Foreign and Commonwealth Briefing Paper argued:

While the INF Treaty by itself could be accepted or even welcomed, NATO military planners were quick to point out that INF had been brought to Europe not solely or even principally as a direct counterweight to the Soviet SS20s, but as a political guarantee by the US to Western Europe.[24]

Central to this coupling and deterrence in Europe is the NATO strategy of Flexible Response, which Britain has long supported. The problem is that the Double Zero Option incorporated into the INF Agreement seems to weaken coupling, while the Treble Zero could be seen by many to effectively destroy the credibility of Flexible Response. The British position is therefore enormously difficult: to support the INF Treaty while opposing the logic of the agenda that the Treaty has set in motion. As George Younger has argued, 'none of us wishes to see a third zero in nuclear weapons in

Europe.'[25] Britain's position, as was evident at the 1989 NATO Summit, is that further progress in this category would lead to the 'denuclearisation of Europe'.

But as was equally evident in the run up to the 1989 NATO Summit, Britain faces problems in airing its difficulties with theatre nuclear arms control in public as this is seen as undermining Alliance cohesion. This initially led to a recourse to exerting its influence via the 'special relationship'. The Camp David meeting between Reagan and Thatcher in November 1986 stressed that 'reductions in nuclear weapons would increase the importance of eliminating conventional disparities' and that 'nuclear weapons could not be dealt with in isolation, given the need for a stable balance at all times'.[26] Britain's unease regarding the theatre nuclear arms control process manifested itself in arguments that the completion of conventional force reductions were a prerequisite for initiating talks on a third zero. A significantly modified version of this was adopted as NATO policy at the 1989 Summit.

But it is not clear whether this new agenda will help Britain. What would happen to the nuclear threshold if conventional parity were achieved? The British government believes that nuclear weapons should deter all war. But it could be argued that conventional parity would raise the nuclear threshold to the extent that Europe would be made safe for at least a limited conventional war, such as the 'Hamburg snatch', or aggression against Berlin, Norway or Turkey. More significantly, a reduced perception of a Soviet threat in the West and Soviet dominance in the East could lead to the re-emergence of national tensions within Europe. Many of these stresses – between Germans and Poles, Hungarians and Romanians, Serbs and Slovenes – could lead to conflict with a high nuclear threshold and no local or military deterrent. Of course the possibility of such conflicts adversely affecting East–West relations is high. The British should therefore be wary of a process that leads to conventional parity. This is certainly the case because such a balance would inevitably create enormous public pressure on NATO to remove all theatre nuclear systems. In such a context, the current attitude of the Thatcher government, regarding the necessity for nuclear weapons in Europe would seem incredible. In addition, it would be argued that the changes wrought and promised by Mikhail Gorbachev in the Soviet Union makes such conservatism seriously misplaced. But for British strategists in the government, the focus cannot solely be on the reforms of one General Secretary of the Soviet Communist Party. The Prime Minister has explained that while welcoming reforms in the Soviet Union:

> ... it is only on the basis of a sure defence and a sure deterrence that we can encourage openly the reforms that are taking place. We know that it is not easy. If they fell apart, if trouble is caused in the satellite countries, or if the Soviets return to a much more Stalinist figure, we know that, whatever happens, our defence continues to be sure because we take the necessary decisions in time ... lead times for modern equipment are very long, and one mistake now in refusing to make decisions could undermine the defence of the whole country. That is our fully consistent position.[27]

The logical implication of this point of view is that the possibility of the Soviet Union seeking to gain unilateral advantages over the West through arms control proposals must be taken seriously. The British desire to begin conventional arms control talks before negotiations over the 'third zero', relate to such concerns, particularly as they affect 'the denuclearisation of Europe'. Certain aspects of the third zero do look attractive: trading 88 Lance missiles for some 1400 Soviet counterparts, for example. But since the government believes that nuclear weapons deter all war, the danger is not knowing where this process would lead. For this reason, the British want to modernise theatre nuclear systems.

However, given the current concern over these forces, particularly in Germany, and the progress made in the superpower relationship, it is not clear how these forces can be modernised without an arms control offer, a new dual track policy. This is particularly relevant, given the British presentation of the INF Treaty as a success for NATO's 1979 Twin Track decision. Modernisation – and the successful conclusion of a conventional arms control agreement – thus have the seeds of the third zero sowed within it. The concentration on the conventional aspect of arms control is unlikely to lessen the pressure for further nuclear disarmament, despite Britian's hopes.

In this environment, the British are disadvantaged in two ways. First, the arms control agenda is increasingly being set where the British have very little influence, in Moscow, rather than Washington. Such a situation may continue under President Bush, particularly if the aftermath of the Senate's refusal to ratify the nomination of John Tower as Defence Secretary is a more assertive Congress in defence issues, circumscribing the power of the President. Throughout 1989 senior members of Congress have expressed dissatisfaction with the Bush administration's handling of opportunities presented by Gorbachev. This process, at least in part, explains the effort that the British government has made to improve and deepen relations with the Soviet Union since Gorbachev's accession to power. This improvement in relations was symbolised by Thatcher's visit to Moscow in the spring of 1987 (the first British Prime Ministerial visit since 1975), the Thatcher–Gorbachev meeting before the November Washington Summit, Gorbachev's visit to London in 1989 and Thatcher's stop-over in Moscow later that year. Second, the arms control agenda now favours disarmament rather than the management of existing armament levels. This also reduces British influence in Washington, for they have grave reservations about the utility of such a process. Hence there appears to be something of a breakdown in the consensus between London and Washington. On top of this, British influence in Washington is lessened since disarmament is almost by definition a global rather than regional occupation. This is clearly evident in the final INF Treaty which initially focused on regional concerns but came to incorporate global coverage.

In theatre nuclear arms control, the British government is not animated by a vision of how European security might evolve most beneficially, but rather by a desire to maintain the way that European security has traditionally looked. In theatre nuclear arms control, an area in which the British have far more influence than in the space or strategic talks, and the area in which the agenda is most fluid, British influence is apparently being used to call a halt to the dynamic of regional nuclear arms control. In this endeavour, the British are very vulnerable to being swept away with the tide, as other nations attempt to create an evolving security framework for Europe.

Conclusion

The central aspects of British nuclear arms control policy has been the pursuit of the three strategic objectives discussed above: the maintenance of Britain's position as a nuclear weapons state; ensuring that its strategic deterrent stays outside of nuclear arms control negotiations; and that its views on nuclear stability are influential in

US and NATO arms control proposals. For the most part, this has entailed keeping a low profile. This is very evident in the successive British *Statements on the Defence Estimates*, which provide a summary of the state of Soviet–American arms control negotiations from a NATO standpoint rather than a picture of the British view of those negotiations.[28] There are several reasons for Britain's arms control profile. First, the UK does not have to enunciate its positions in great detail and in a blaze of publicity, since it does not take part directly in any of the nuclear arms control fora. Second, the British seek to present an image of a united Alliance. Since there are very major disagreements on these issues within NATO, it is deemed best not to debate them in public. However, it is also evident that the Thatcher government is willing to argue very strongly and potentially risk Alliance unity if it feels that its views on the necessity for certain nuclear deployments are not being duly heeded by other members of the Alliance. Finally, a British low profile acts as a pre-condition for the operation of the 'special relationship'. But what is the current state of this 'special relationship' in the nuclear arms control process?

In the three major areas of nuclear arms control British and American interests, as currently defined, appear to differ. Over ballistic missile defence and the reinterpretation of the ABM Treaty, the British position has effectively come closer to that of the Soviet Union than to that of the US. Given the political pressure on President Bush from the right-wing, this situation may not change dramatically, although, as London clearly hopes, there may be less public prominence. In the debate over theatre systems, the British apparently fear a superpower condominium agreeing to disarmament measures that may not be in the security interests of Britain and Europe as traditionally understood. Over strategic systems, there appears to be a drift towards a fear of Soviet–American agreement regardless of European interests. What this demonstrates is the pragmatic nature of the British assessment of nuclear arms control. In the field of space weapons, the British favour a very restrictive agreement, supporting the ABM Treaty as traditionally interpreted. Over strategic systems, they seem to favour a limited agreement that strengthens the strategic arms control process and enhances both strategic stability and extended deterrence. And in theatre nuclear systems, it is clear that the UK does not favour any further agreement.

For the UK, it must be the 'special relationship' that is the key to influencing the nuclear arms control process. But if the UK holds dissenting views to the US, and the US continues to pursue its own line or increasingly focuses on Bonn, it is not clear that the 'special relationship' can successfully operate in Britain's interests. It may be that the US is willing to consider the view of the UK and take counsel from the British when there is some measure of consensus between the two governments. In such a situation, there could be discussions over the nature of the implementation of particular common goals. But in the 1990s, it is not clear that the US would be able to seriously consider British prescriptions in areas in which the British do not share a common view of the goals of the nuclear arms control process.

This leaves open the question of whether the 'special relationship' has really been effective historically: it may be that the British were merely fortuitous beneficiaries of sharing a common view with Washington. More importantly, it may be increasingly difficult to recreate and maintain a consensus of view between London and Washington in the 1990s. In such circumstances, the only remaining task for the British is one of damage limitation, which in the 1980s seemed to be the primary utility of the Camp David meetings between President Reagan and Prime Minister Thatcher. In this, the maintenance of British access to the American Trident system is the most crucial element.

Yet in government circles, policy is still framed in terms of the 'special relationship', in the traditional manner in which Britain believes it exerted influence over the East–West nuclear arms control process. But the breakdown in the strategic consensus between Britain and the US must call the effectiveness of the 'special relationship' in the nuclear arms control arena into question. Bipartisanship, whether in the domestic or international context, depends on the existence of a basic consensus. Whatever its past, the future of the 'special relationship' depends crucially on the re-establishment of a basic consensus between the UK and the US over the nature of Western security and the purposes of nuclear arms control. It is this that would seem to be a key goal for the British government in its relations with the Bush administration.

Notes

1   This tension between the theatre and strategic categorisations of the British force has always been inherent in the Anglo–American nuclear relationship. It was most explicit in the Nassau Agreement of 1962, when the US agreed to sell Polaris to Britain. Since that agreement, the British force has been formally committed to NATO: it has been assumed that SACEUR has targeted the British force against fixed target sets in Eastern Europe and the western military districts of the Soviet Union. For SACEUR, therefore, the British force has a theatre role. But, the British force therefore also has a strategic role. In the Nassau agreement, Prime Minister Macmillan reserved the right to use the British deterrent when 'supreme national interests are at stake ...' See President John F.Kennedy and Prime Minister Harold Macmillan, 'The Nassau Agreement: Statement on Nuclear Defence Systems – 21 December 1962' reprinted in Andrew Pierre, *Nuclear Politics: The British Experience with an Independent Strategic Force*, Oxford University Press, London:, 1972, pp. 346–7. Thus, it is not clear that SACEUR can, in reality, rely on the British to meet NATO targets. As Peter Malone notes, nuclear weapons are unlikely to be used except when 'supreme national interests are at stake'. See Peter Malone, *The British Nuclear Deterrent*, Croom Helm and St. Martin's Press, London and New York, 1984, pp. 92–3.

2   Prime Minister Sir Alec Douglas-Home's claim that Britain's nuclear force would provide a ticket of admission to the top table has not held true. As Lawrence Freedman has noted, SALT 'was the first major arms control activity from which Britain had been excluded ....' See Lawrence Freedman, *Britain and Nuclear Weapons*, Macmillan for RIIA, London, 1980, p. 96. However, it is more likely the case that in the 1970s and 1980s, the British have preferred to be excluded from the top table in order to protect their nuclear force.

3   For a discussion of the tensions within the British position on the CTBT see the chapter by Wyn Rees, John Simpson and Darryl Howlett in this volume.

4   British targeting is premised on being 'capable of posing a credible threat to key aspects of Soviet state power .. to maintain our ability to inflict, if necessary, an unacceptable level of damage on those targets likely to be most valued by Soviet leaders', *Statement on the Defence Estimates 1987*, p. 39. This is taken to mean an ability to destroy the Soviet leadership in Moscow, since the Soviet Union is seen as a highly centralised totalitarian state. Whereas the French may be content, to use de Gaulle's phraseology, with a capability to 'tear an arm and a leg off the bear', the British want to be able to 'tear off the bear's head'. But of course the British have the capability to attack targets other than just Moscow. See Lawrence Freedman, 'British Nuclear Targeting', *Defense Analysis*, I, 1985.

5   Of course, in a post-START strategic environment where warheads are deemed to be more important than launchers, the Trident system may offer other alternatives.

6   For analyses of the rationales for the British nuclear force, see

Lawrence Freedman, *Britain and Nuclear Weapons*, especially pp. 127–41, and Peter Malone, *The British Nuclear Deterrent*.

7   Sir Geoffrey Howe, 'Defence and Security in the Nuclear Age: The British View', speech to RUSI on 15 March 1985, *British Information Service*, Washington DC, 1985.

8   That process is also important to the British government in enhancing the legitimacy of British possession of nuclear weapons to a domestic audience to whom the Soviet threat is not always seen to be as dangerous as the threat of nuclear war.

9   The limited nature of British support for SDI was demonstrated in the 1986 *Statement*. 'The British Government supports the SDI research programme. It is essential to Western security that the Soviet Union should not gain a decisive unilateral advantage in any particular capability' (p. 5). No assessment was made of the strategic value of SDI, and this was only mentioned in passing by Sir Geoffrey Howe in his 1985 speech to RUSI. British support was even more limited in the 1987 *Statement*. Noting NATO discussions concerning the debate over the reinterpretation of the ABM Treaty and calls by some leading Americans for early deployment of strategic defences by the US, the *Statement* noted that 'Such a decision would have important implications for the consideration of the future place of ballistic missile defences in the strategic relationship, for arms control, *and for the conduct of British participation in SDI research*' [emphasis added], p. 10.

10   Prime Minister Margaret Thatcher, *Hansard*, 4 March 1988, col. 1282. The then Defence Secretary George Younger put this point of view even more starkly: 'if the dual track decision had not been the policy of this Government, there would have been no INF Treaty, and no reduction of nuclear weapons of this sort ...', *Hansard*, 26 January 1988, col. 156. Such claims prompted Sean Hughes, a Labour Party Defence spokesperson, to accuse the Government of having 'developed a singular capacity for claiming the success achieved by others. It is like the self-decorated south American dictators who luxuriate in the reflected splendour of their national team's World Cup success – but even they do not say that they scored the goals.' See 'The Army: Debate on motion for Adjournment', *Hansard*, 26 January 1988, col. 253.

11   For a further analysis of this, see Stuart Croft, 'The Impact of Strategic Defences on European–American Relations in the 1990s', *Adelphi Paper No.238*, International Institute for Strategic Studies, London, 1989.

12   This referred to SLBMs as well as ICBMs. Part of the rationale for the American Maritime Strategy is the elimination of Soviet SSBNs.

13   'Text of President's Speech on Iceland Summit', *Congressional Quarterly*, 18 October 1986, p. 2610.

14   See Lawrence Freedman, 'Return to the Bomber Age?', *Council for Arms Control Bulletin*, No. 30, January 1987.

15   Current talks may lead to less than 50 per cent cuts because of counting rules relating to bombers. See Michèle A. Flournoy, 'A Rocky START: Optimism and Obstacles on the Road to Reductions', *Arms Control Today*, October 1987, pp. 7–13.

16   Particularly if there is interest in a START II. See Malcolm Chalmers, 'START and Britain's nuclear force', *ADIU Report*, X, March–April 1988. The Labour Party has increasingly looked to the possibility of START II negotiations as a way of integrating the British nuclear force into arms control negotiations.

17   The British government argues that 'Some have argued that the British Government is planning an excessive increase in the number of warheads compared with Polaris, at a time when the superpowers are discussing 50% reductions in their strategic arsenals. In fact we have made it clear that each British Trident boat will carry no more than a maximum of 128 warheads – far less than the full capacity of D5; this represents an increase of up to 2½ times the payload of the Polaris boats, when they entered service in the 1960s each carrying 48 warheads ... Even after the 50% decrease in superpower arsenals discussed at Reykjavik, Trident would represent a smaller proportion of Soviet strategic warheads than did Polaris in 1970.' *Statement on the Defence Estimates 1987*, p. 41.

18   *ibid.*, 1987, p. 9.

19   *Discriminate Deterrence*, Report of the Commission On Integrated Long-Term Strategy, 12 January 1988.

20   'Defence Policies for Britain: Conservative', *Council for Arms Control Bulletin*, No. 32, Foreign and Commonwealth Office, May 1987, p. 5.

21   Prime Minister Margaret Thatcher, 'NATO Summit (Brussels)', *Hansard*, 4 March 1988, col. 1294.

22   George Younger, *Hansard*, 7 March 1989, col. 744.

23   George Younger argued, in response to the question, does the Government believe that conventional parity is compatible with flexible response: 'Yes, it is a very compatible aim that we should get conventional weapons on each side down to parity or much nearer parity, while the whole question of the flexible response enables us to have a variable range of different types of major weapon to respond to whatever threat comes.' *Hansard*, 26 July 1988, col. 245.

24   *Briefing Paper 210*, Foreign & Commonwealth Office, London, 1988, p. 1.

25   *Hansard*, 7 March 1989, col. 742.

26   *Statement on the Defence Estimates 1987*, p. 8.

27   Prime Minister Margaret Thatcher, 'NATO Summit (Brussels)', *Hansard*, 4 March 1988, cols. 1290–1. For a further examination of different views on this subject, see Stuart Croft, 'Will Gorbachev End the Cold War?', *The Council for Arms Control Bulletin*, No. 40, October 1988.

28   See, for example, *Statement on the Defence Estimates 1987*, pp. 7–8.

Conventional arms control, theatre nuclear weapons and European security

Introduction

The declared objective of the UK's arms control policy is 'the search for balanced and verifiable arms control agreements, which provide for security at lower levels of weapons...'.[1] It is a policy which is framed in the multilateral context of the NATO Alliance and has, in practice, traditionally been reactive and sympathetic to the arms control policy of the US. In examining the manner in which this policy is being pursued in the post-INF world, it is possible to discern a distinctly British approach towards conventional arms control, theatre nuclear weapons and European security. However, it is an open question as to whether Britain's traditional approach to such issues is viable in the face of the new political and strategic opportunities and challenges of the 1990s.

Strategic assumptions of British security policy

It is within the framework of the Atlantic Alliance that Britain seeks to lessen the risk and cost of confrontation with the Warsaw Pact through arms control. However, while being prepared to embrace arms control as a means of easing tensions between the blocs and achieving a greater degree of security at a lower level of arms, the UK does not consider it desirable to pursue either arms control or disarmament policies which seek to transcend the security system which has formed the basis of Western security in the post-war era or which would undermine the strategy of Flexible Response which underpins it. Rather, Britain believes that the preservation of the status quo in Europe is the best way of preserving peace, and to this end resists any attempts to restructure the framework of post-war European security.

These goals manifest themselves in policies which are opposed to the denuclearisation of Europe, the decoupling of the US commitment to Europe, and indeed to any radical disarmament or arms control measures which, by either desire or effect, would alter the post-war boundaries of Europe, particularly with regard to the reunification of Germany. These concerns make the UK profoundly cautious and conservative in its approach to conventional arms control. While recognising that the post-war structure of European security is not ideal, it is the British view that this security framework is sufficiently robust, in contrast to a future of uncertainties, to be worth preserving.

Fundamentally, Britain's concern to preserve a status quo which includes American nuclear forces in Europe is rooted in the orthodox view that the superior numbers of Warsaw Pact conventional forces leave NATO little choice but to rely on the threat of nuclear war to deter Soviet aggression. Further, it is the British view that even with a conventional balance on the continent, nuclear weapons in Europe would still be necessary in order to put at risk the Soviet homeland. The rationale for nuclear weapons and the role of the US in European security are inextricably linked. It is the commitment of the US to the defence of Europe, and the commitment of nuclear weapons by America as part of that defence, which Britain sees as essential to European security.

While the UK has developed its conventional force posture, together with its arms control position, in concert with its NATO allies, these policies, agreed through inter-allied consultation, have also served Britain's strategic interests. This is in part due to the harmony of attitudes and interests which exists between the UK and the US but it also reflects the deftness with which Britain has ensured that its security concerns are reflected in the positions finally adopted by NATO. However, in context of a post-INF world, the strains and contradictions in British and Alliance perspectives on conventional arms control and European security are becoming evident.

The new detente: The post-INF world

The celebration by the NATO allies of the signing of the INF Treaty at the Brussels summit in March 1988 was wrought with irony given that the arms control track of the NATO INF deployment decision was never meant to be taken seriously. The double-zero option was proposed precisely because the US missiles were not meant to be bargaining chips. Rather they were considered a necessary modernisation of a military capability, coupling nuclear and conventional forces and providing NATO with further options to ensure its ability to implement Flexible Response. In the light of the fears of super-power condominium and decoupling which exercised Chancellor Schmidt in 1977, they were also considered necessary for political cohesion within the Alliance and as a symbol of the continued US commitment to Europe. The elimination of these weapons with little reference or regard for the European allies has simply served to exacerbate those concerns which the systems were initially envisaged to counter.

Whatever the intentions, the elimination of a whole category of nuclear weapons from the European theatre has had the effect of focusing attention on the relationship between the nuclear and con-ventional components of Flexible Response. In doing this, the some-what metaphysical relationship between these two elements of NATO's security policy has been damaged in both image and substance. The delicate and purposely ill-defined relationship in the European theatre between a conventional defence which is good enough to forestall the early use of nuclear weapons but not compre-hensive enough to make a protracted conventional war in Europe imaginable, and nuclear weapons, which are sufficient to provide a credible linkage to the US strategic arsenal but insufficient to pre-clude that necessity, has been opened up for minute scrutiny by the events of the late 1980s.[2]

The effect of the INF Agreement is a post-INF world characterised by a military and, more importantly, political debate on short-range nuclear weapons, their relationship with the conventional balance in Europe and the future of extended deterrence. The task of dealing with these challenges is made more difficult by the political momentum generated by the INF agreement. The destruction for the first time of a whole category of nuclear weapons has given a boost to the arms control process and generated interest in other areas where progress in East–West relations can be made. This momentum, most evident in the foreign policy of the Soviet Union under President Gorbachev, has created an agenda of change in the European secu-rity environment precisely at a time when NATO had sought to consolidate and reinforce its strategy of Flexible Response.

Building on the momentum created in the arms control process by the INF Treaty and in preparation for the new set of conventional arms control negotiations with the West, President Gorbachev announced his intention to address Western concerns with the state of the conventional military balance. He signalled the start of this process in December 1988 by announcing to the UN General Assembly his plans to cut Soviet conventional forces unilaterally and to restructure the military posture of the Warsaw Pact to one which is 'clearly defensive'. These reductions, amounting to a cut of 12 per cent of the total strength of the Soviet armed forces, would be carried out over a two year period beginning in April 1989 to be completed by the end of 1990. Following the lead given by Gorbachev's UN speech, other Warsaw Pact countries announced unilateral cuts in both their conventional armaments and in their military budgets, in order to restructure their armies in 'even more of a strictly defensive nature' than before.[3]

The reaction of the British government to Gorbachev's UN announcement was extremely cautious, particularly when compared with those of its allies. While welcoming the proposed arms reductions, the Prime Minister was quick to point out that despite these cuts there would 'still be a major asymmetry in the Soviet Union's favour.'[4] The Foreign Secretary warned that a sense of perspective was necessary in evaluating the significance of Mr Gorbachev's announcements: 'We must not confuse hopes or even expectations with reality'.[5] The British government also sought to counterbalance Gorbachev's diplomatic initiatives by constant references to the nature of Soviet society, to human rights abuses, the role of the KGB, the Berlin Wall and even the durability of Gorbachev's leadership.[6]

While the cuts announced throughout the Warsaw Pact represent real reductions in military capability and should ease NATO's concern over surprise attack, the Prime Minister was correct in pointing out that they do not significantly alter the ability of the Soviet Union to mount a major offensive operation against Western Europe with forces substantially superior to those of NATO.[7] However, the political dynamic of the Gorbachev proposals is more important than the net military effect of the reductions themselves. While part of the motivation for the reduction and restructuring of the Warsaw Pact's armed forces is undoubtedly rooted in economic considerations, this does not detract from the fact that these moves are both militarily and politically significant for European security. The realisation of the need to remove and restructure Soviet forces away from a posture

which is offensive at the 'military-technical' level, in order to assuage
the fears of the West, is illustrative of both a sensitivity to NATO's
position and of a seriousness of intent in lowering the military
confrontation in Europe.[8] It is for this reason that the conventional
arms control negotiations underway in Vienna have become a
central focus for the future of European security.

Conventional arms control: The CFE negotiations

The negotiations on conventional arms control established in Vienna
in March 1989 are being conducted under the auspices of the Conference on Security and Co-operation in Europe. At NATO's
suggestion, two parallel sets of talks have been set up to deal with
different aspects of European security, a formula which also allows
peculiar French and American concerns to be accommodated. The
mandate for the larger set of negotiations, based on the CSCE
framework, is to address confidence and security building measures,
while the other forum has the task of dealing with the more substantive area of reducing conventional forces in Europe.

The former body is a continuation of the work done in Stockholm
in September 1986 by the Conference on Disarmament in Europe
(CDE) where substantial improvements were made on the modest
confidence building measures contained in the Helsinki Final Act of
1975. Britain is particularly keen to promote this type of arms
control agreement and 'played a significant role' in developing
NATO's proposals in the CDE which formed the basis of the
Stockholm package.[9] British security policy-makers consider confidence building measures an attractive policy instrument because
they address serious security concerns, such as surprise attack, without presenting any challenges to the UK's strategic interests and
NATO's strategy of Flexible Response or threatening to fundamentally alter the framework of European security. The aim of this
body, which is comprised of the thirty-five states of Europe, is to
expand on the achievements already made by the CSCE in reducing
the risks of war by creating more openness, confidence and predictability of military activity in the whole of Europe.

The other body, consisting of the twenty-three member states of
the Warsaw Pact and NATO Alliance, aims to deal with the more
substantive questions of force reductions under the title of the Conventional Forces in Europe (CFE). The Soviets suggested that these

negotiations should move beyond the Mutual and Balanced Force Reduction (MBFR) Talk's concentration on central Europe, focusing instead on the area from the Atlantic to the Urals (ATTU). While there is to be no linkage between these two sets of negotiations in their day-to-day business, an undertaking has been made whereby progress in CFE will be reported to all thirty-five CSCE states at periodic intervals.[10] This arrangement was agreed in order to prevent progress in the confidence-building talks being held back by difficulties in CFE and also to prevent an agreement between the two blocs being slowed down by objections from the neutral or non-aligned states of the CSCE.[11]

The insistence of the US that progress in the separate fora should not be disrupted by the other illustrates a sensitivity to the difficulties involved in conducting arms control negotiations in this area.[12] As the MBFR experience graphically demonstrates, reaching a conventional arms control agreement is extremely problematic. Basic obstacles to an agreement include such problems as the complexity of dealing with multiple negotiating partners; disparate security concerns both within and between each alliance, including what consequences conventional force reductions in Europe might have; and assessing the conventional military balance and verifying any force reductions that might result from a treaty.[13]

CFE: The focus on 'offensive forces'

While many of the difficulties associated with negotiations on conventional arms control remain, several developments in this area have significantly increased the prospects of an agreement being reached. Not least of these developments is the establishment, within the mandate for the Vienna talks, that the primary aim of the negotiations, in the initial stages at least, is the reduction of offensive forces capable of surprise attack. This approach, while addressing those capabilities considered most threatening to the stability of peace in Europe, also has several practical advantages as a focus for arms control. By focusing on reducing offensive forces rather than redressing the alleged NATO/Warsaw Pact imbalance *per se* it is possible to avoid the type of disagreement on this subject which hampered the MBFR talks. Instead of exchanging data on the size of the respective arsenals at the outset of the talks, the negotiators will concentrate their efforts on setting common force ceilings and establishing a strict verification regime to ensure compliance. Prospects for agreement on the traditionally problematic area of verification of a conventional arms control agreement have been greatly advanced by the precedents set by both the INF Treaty and the Stockholm CDE agreements. The establishment in these agreements of the right to mandatory on site inspection is a significant and necessary development in this area. The task of verifying a CFE treaty is also aided by the decision by both sides to focus on military equipment, rather than manpower, as the primary unit of account.

The acceptance by the Soviet Union that asymmetrical reductions by 'the side that is ahead' in a given category of weapons, together with the agreement to focus these cuts on offensive forces, represents a major achievement towards the goal of a conventional arms control agreement.[14] Agreeing precisely what is meant by the term 'offensive forces', however, remains to be established. The initial statement issued by NATO in December 1988made clear that as far as the Alliance was concerned:

The major threat to stability in Europe comes from those systems which are capable of mounting large-scale offensive operations and of *seizing and holding territory*. These are above all, main battle tanks, artillery and armoured troop carriers.[15]

For this reason NATO opened the CFE talks in March 1989 with a proposal for substantial cuts in these systems amounting to reductions of 50 per cent in the total number of tanks and artillery in this region. NATO also proposed that no one country ought to have more than 30 per cent of the forces within the overall limits. The intent of this proposal is substantial reductions in the amount of armour fielded by the Soviet Union. In practice, this would mean cuts of about two-thirds in Soviet tanks and artillery and well over half in its armoured personnel carriers.[16] In addition to limitations on the number of forces permitted by each alliance and each alliance member, NATO also proposed restrictions on the deployment of these forces and a series of geographic sub-limits in order to prevent undue concentrations of forces. Sir Geoffrey Howe explained that such a measure would ensure that military forces were spread evenly throughout the continent and would avoid creating zones of unequal security in Europe.[17]

The Warsaw Pact's proposals reflect a different orientation. It has expressed the desire for the creation of a special disarmament zone, probably 100–150 km wide, along the line of contact between the two alliances. Such a scheme is unacceptable to NATO, however, as its implementation would undermine the Alliance's ability to implement its policy of forward defence and thus violate NATO's pledge to defend all areas of its territory without exposing any member to an unequal degree of risk.[18] Furthermore, while accepting the focus on 'offensive forces', the guiding principal for the Warsaw Pact in the CFE talks is the dictum that 'the side that is ahead' in any given weapon category must reduce its forces, in the first instance, to the level of the lowest side. So, although the Soviet Union accepts the need for asymmetrical reductions in its tank armies, it has made it clear that it expects cuts of a similar nature in areas where NATO has an advantage. Specifically the Soviet Union favoured the inclusion of tactical airpower, troop levels and naval forces as well as the simultaneous discussion of nuclear weapons which they insist are inextricably linked to the conventional balance.

While NATO disputed its alleged superiority in these forces, their offensive nature and their relevance for conventional arms control, it was clear that it was being perceived as dragging its feet over conventional arms control. In an effort to regain the initiative in the arms control process and partially accommodate the security concerns of the Soviet Union, NATO modified its initial proposals to the CFE talks in Vienna to include troop levels, combat aircraft and attack helicopters, while insisting on the explicit exclusion of naval forces from the CFE mandate.[19] These proposals were followed by President Bush's proposals for a reduction of manpower for both US and Soviet forces stationed in central Europe to a common ceiling of 195,000 and for a reduction in combat helicopters and land-based combat aircraft by 15 per cent below NATO's current levels in the Atlantic to the Urals area.

The Bush proposals have both advantages and disadvantages for the Alliance. If accepted, the cuts proposed in President Bush's initiative would result in the removal of 110,000 US troops and 375,000 Soviet troops from Europe. Such a reduction, amounting to a cut of 70 per cent of the US's current manpower, would leave NATO with a numerical superiority in troop numbers at current levels without meeting the Soviet Union's goal of cutting NATO military personnel by a million men. However, the decision by NATO to accept the bilateral levels announced by President Bush masks a wider concern as to how the reductions in NATO forces brought about by CFE will be allocated and affect burden-sharing. Clearly an across the board percentage cut, while easiest to implement, would be the least effective use of CFE reductions. Instead the opportunity should be used to define role specialisation by national forces within the Alliance. Such a policy would not mark a new departure for NATO members, but would amount to an acceleration of an existing process, in part brought about by the unilateral abandonment of some roles and missions by individual members in the face of economic and political pressures. The difficulty with absorbing the CFE reductions in this way is that they would not result in an even distribution of defence cuts and would probably leave those most concerned with the preservation of the status quo shouldering a higher proportion of the defensive burden of the central front.

For example, implementation of the Bush proposals would proportionally increase the percentage of burden borne by the British Army of the Rhine (BAOR) in defence of the Central Front. While Britain is not keen to take on a larger proportion of the defence of the central front, this consideration would have to be set against its desire to maintain the status quo in European security. However, the wisdom of Britain following such a policy of buttressing the status quo by maintaining large force levels on the central front, while simultaneously running down its naval strength in the Eastern Atlantic, may not represent the most rational role specialisation of the UK's forces within NATO. Certainly, the logic in favour of depleting Britain's maritime capabilities in favour of preserving the continental commitment is far less obvious now than it was in the early 1980s. And it is a question which needs to be considered not only within the context of the CFE negotiations but more importantly within the context of a UK Defence Review.

The most significant and potentially problematic aspect of the Bush proposals is the decision to include airpower in the first phase of the CFE talks. This marks a significant departure from the Alliance's traditional policy with regard to this category of forces.[20] NATO has consistently denied the equation put forward by the Warsaw Pact that the Alliance's superiority in air power gives NATO an offensive capability akin to the Warsaw Pact's advantage in tanks.[21] While the Alliance has always accepted that the main purpose of its air forces is to offset the superiority in Soviet armour, it does not accept that these forces are offensive or that asymmetrical reductions should automatically follow. The fundamental difference between ground and air forces, NATO argues, is that ground forces pose the offensive threat of overrunning, while air forces do not. Therefore, 'NATO air power as a whole should be seen as defensive, in the sense that its job is either to kill offensive Soviet tanks or to destroy Soviet air power (which exists to hinder the killing of Soviet tanks).'[22] It is for this reason that the Alliance's position on the CFE talks emphasises a focus on those forces which are capable of 'seizing and holding territory.'[23]

Significantly, President Bush's decision to include airpower in the CFE negotiations and to recognise the importance of these forces in the central region not only amounts to a departure from NATO's own conception of 'offensive' but also rejects the distinction made by the Soviet Union between 'offensive' and 'defensive' in their definition of combat aircraft. In this way the impasse between the two different conceptions of the role of airpower in Europe may be overcome by seeing this category of forces as significant to, but separate from, the reduction of land forces. Furthermore, the NATO definition of 'combat aircraft' eliminates the opportunity for the Soviet Union to exclude its own 'air defence aircraft' while including NATO carrier-based aircraft.[24] Whether this classification, together with that on combat helicopters, will be acceptable to the Soviet Union as yet remains to be seen, but the acceptance by NATO of the principle of including aircraft in the CFE talks must be considered a breakthrough from the Soviet perspective.

The Soviet Union, however, is not the only state which is concerned to discover precisely what forces are to be covered by the reductions in air power announced by President Bush in his March 1989 proposal. Whether these reductions are to be borne by the US Air Force alone, perhaps encompassing the withdrawal of US F-16s from Spain, or whether and on what basis these reductions are to be spread throughout the Alliance, remains to be established. The condition in the Bush proposal that all aircraft withdrawn from the ATTU area must be destroyed renders this type of arms reduction less palatable than other forms of arms cuts, especially to those NATO countries which have recently undergone vastly expensive modernisation programmes for their air forces.

CFE: linkages between conventional and nuclear forces

Sensitivities to reductions in air power are most acute when consideration is given to those aircraft which combine their conventional interdiction role with that of theatre nuclear strike. The difficulty presented by dual capable systems, a category of weapons which also includes artillery pieces, is that negotiations on their conventional capabilities inevitably encroaches, either implicitly or explicitly, upon the nuclear roles of these forces. The position which Britain and NATO have adopted on this subject is that they are prepared to discuss dual capable systems in the conventional arms control negotiations, but only in their capacity as conventional weapons. For this reason, US Secretary of State James Baker made it clear that British and French nuclear strike aircraft would not be included in the reduction proposals. Nevertheless, Britain and France persisted in their reluctance to include aircraft in the conventional arms control negotiations up until President Bush announced his initiative. They remain highly sceptical of this approach precisely because of their desire to maintain the distinction between negotiations on nuclear and conventional forces.

This policy is part of the UK's attempt, supported by the US within NATO, to avoid the inclusion of any discussion of nuclear systems in the conventional arms control talks, which in turn is based on the belief that nuclear arms control should remain separate and subordinate in priority to chemical and conventional arms control. Indeed, the initial NATO position on CFE negotiations represented a deliberate and explicit refusal by the Alliance to contemplate an arms control agreement for the European theatre encompassing both conventional and nuclear elements. However, opposition from the Federal Republic of Germany to the introduction of a follow on to the Lance missile without simultaneous negotiation for a partial reduction of this category of missiles to a lower but equal level has lead to a change in NATO's official position on this firm distinction between nuclear and conventional negotiations. As a consequence, the Alliance adopted a form of words at its May 1989 summit which effectively resolved this difference of opinion, by delaying the decision on Lance modernisation until 1992.[25] A commitment by NATO to enter into negotiations with the Soviet Union on short-range missiles at the same time as these systems are due to be modernised was balanced in this inter-alliance agreement by the decision not to begin negotiations until the results of the CFE talks 'have been implemented'. Furthermore, any reductions in Soviet and American land-based nuclear missile forces would only be 'partial' and would not lead to the total elimination of this category of weapons. This allowed both Britain and the Federal Republic to argue that the Alliance had adopted their position. For its part, Britain insists that this compromise in NATO's official language does not amount to a significant change in NATO's policy of separating conventional and nuclear arms control. Whether Britain's deliberate attempt at avoiding the restructuring of European security along the lines of further denuclearisation will succeed remains to be seen.

Fundamental to Britain's position within this debate on NATO strategy is its rejection of the idea of a pan European 'security partnership' which has been advocated by the German left and encouraged by the Soviet Union. To this end Britain was instrumental in initiating an attempt within NATO to buttress the Alliance's traditional approach to security with the introduction of new nuclear weapons. Specifically, Britain advocated the modernisation of Europe's short-range nuclear forces (SNF) in the form of new artillery shells, a replacement for the Lance missile and new air-launched stand-off missiles. Britain has pushed this modernisation to the top of the Alliance agenda in response to several concerns. First is the unease with which the German Christian Democrats view the nuclear balance in Europe following the INF treaty. The inequality of nuclear risk following the removal of all but the short-range systems is a situation which the German right is unhappy with and eager to rectify. Britain has been most vociferous in its insistence, within NATO, that this should be done by sharing the nuclear risks within the Alliance with new longer range weapons rather than by the removal of the SNF altogether. A second concern behind the adoption of this position is the fear that unless the existing nuclear forces in Europe are modernised, functional disarmament will occur by the gradual obsolescence of these systems. The third concern is the desire to push through the nuclear modernisation process before any further momentum builds up for an arms control agreement on these systems, either on their own, or as part of a package involving conventional arms control.

The importance of this latter concern, held by Britain and the US within NATO, has had a substantial influence in shaping the Alliance's security policy, including conventional arms control. It has resulted in NATO's stated desire to see the conclusion of both chemical and conventional arms control agreements before any nuclear arms control below the strategic level was undertaken.

Behind Britain and NATO's policy is the desire to slow down the momentum in the arms control process and thus prevent any further nuclear arms control at the European level. By focusing on conventional arms control, attention is focused on the asymmetries in conventional force postures which favour the East. More importantly, as a stalling tactic they focus on an area where negotiations have traditionally been long and unfruitful. This is not to say that the UK and NATO position is one which is not serious about conventional arms control or indeed about future nuclear arms control. Rather, this approach is intended to prevent any further movement down what former Secretary of State George Schultz described as the 'slippery slope' of denuclearisation. Specifically, this position on the priority of any further arms control negotiations is intended to prevent the agreement of the 'third zero' eliminating nuclear missiles with ranges less than 500km, and to ensure that these systems are maintained and modernised. Support for this position in London is unequivocal. As a 'senior British official' argued:

There is no good answer, militarily, as to why these missiles are important. You can do the same job with air-launched weapons. The gut answer why we want to keep them is because they are seen as the thin edge of the wedge. If you believe in nuclear deterrence you have to draw the line somewhere.[26]

Associated with this desire to maintain nuclear weapons in Europe as part of NATO's force posture is the belief, supported by both Britain and France, that nuclear weapons would still be necessary even if a balance in conventional weapons could be achieved. This position is based on the concern that Europe must not be made safe for conventional war while the superpowers are left invulnerable by virtue of being mutually deterred by nuclear weapons. It was for these reasons that the British government insisted on the inclusion of the following paragraph in the March 1988 communique following the Brussels summit.

The relationship between nuclear and conventional forces is complex. The existence of a conventional imbalance in favour of the Warsaw Pact is not the only reason for the presence of nuclear weapons in Europe. The countries of the Alliance are, and will remain, under the threat of Soviet nuclear forces of varying ranges. Although conventional parity would bring important benefits for stability, only the nuclear element can confront a potential aggressor with an unacceptable risk: therefore, for the foreseeable future deterrence will continue to require an adequate mix of nuclear as well as conventional forces.[27]

The INF experience, however, set a precedent in the arms control process which remains a problem for the approach which Britain persuaded NATO to adopt in order to stem the tide of denuclearisation. The 1979 'dual track' decision promised to accompany the deployment of its Pershing II and GLCMs with a diplomatic effort to remove the Soviet equivalents of these forces. It is in large part this 'successful' formula which forms the basis of the compromise deal reached over the Lance modernisation issue by the Alliance in its March 1989 summit. Despite acclamations by the Prime Minister that this formula represented the prevalence of the British position within NATO, in reality British concerns that any negotiations would lead ultimately to a 'third zero' were subordinated to the need for Alliance unity without persuading the UK of the merits of this approach. The very basis of the compromise, the belief espoused by Hans Dietrich Genscher that negotiations could be limited to agreeing equal but lower levels of short-range missiles, is rejected by Britain. A 'senior British source' expressed precisely these doubts, stating 'Why should the Russians accept anything greater than zero and so legitimise through treaty the presence of American nuclear missiles in Europe? We fell into that trap once before "with the INF Treaty": we cannot afford to again.'[28]

For these reasons Britain remains strenuously committed to its policy of advocating the separation of conventional and nuclear arms control negotiations until at least the first phase of the process is completed and only then may the partial reductions of land-based nuclear missiles to an equal level be contemplated. Moreover, with the likelihood that the conventional imbalance will be reduced by asymmetrical reductions, there is a growing realisation of the need to move away from the simplistic and misleading rationale that NATO's nuclear weapons are necessary to offset the WTO's conventional superiority. This realisation is evident in The Alliance Comprehensive Concept which explicitly divorces the nuclear rationale from the conventional imbalance. It states quite plainly: 'The Allies' sub-strategic nuclear forces are not designed to compensate for conventional imbalances'.[29]

More importantly, the British position on the need to replace Lance missiles is concerned with the viability of NATO's strategy of flexible response. As one British source put it: 'If we have no land-based nuclear systems in Europe, I do not see how we can claim to have flexible response.'[30] However, the British position is based on a static conception of what flexible response is and what it requires: in this case the most up to date nuclear weapons in every category despite the prevailing political climate. Support for this position in NATO, however, is limited. On his fact finding tour of Europe in February 1989 Secretary of State Baker was informed that at least half the NATO members – West Germany, Italy, Spain, Belgium, Denmark, Norway, Greece and Iceland – were opposed to an immediate decision on the modernisation of short-range nuclear weapons to replace the Lance.[31] Significantly, within Europe only France fully supports the British position, and this stance is due to concern that negotiations on SNF would eventually suck French nuclear weapons into this process.[32] It is in part this concern over national nuclear forces being inextricably drawn into European arms control processes which underpins British policy.

This division of opinion within the Alliance on the 'modernisation' of short-range nuclear forces, together with the peculiar sensitivity of this issue within the Federal Republic, presents NATO with the prospect of a Euromissile deployment plan as potentially contentious as the last. The linkage made between conventional and nuclear arms control by President Gorbachev presents the Alliance with the prospect of progress on conventional forces being impaired as a result of NATO's commitment to maintain and modernise those systems which the Soviets, together with large sections of German public opinion, want to eliminate. This would have very damaging consequences on Alliance unity where a consensus on the position adopted by NATO on this issue is lacking. In terms of public perceptions of NATO policy this would be disastrous. The Soviet Union would be seen to be arguing for reductions in nuclear and conventional weapons while NATO was engaging in the deployment of new and more modern nuclear weapons.

Thus Britain's insistence on negotiating conventional arms control as a completely separate and prior concern to nuclear arms control and its eagerness to effect the modernisation of Europe's SNF may prove counterproductive. Its strategic goals of maintaining the status quo in Europe, avoiding decoupling and preventing the process of denuclearisation may ultimately not be served by this policy. The conservative stance proposed by the UK, and adopted by NATO, may well precipitate precisely the opposite results to those intended. If in 1992 the Federal Republic refuses to accept the deployment of new SNF in response to NATO unwillingness to contemplate the negotiation away of these systems, then the position of the US forces in Europe will once more be brought into serious question. The sloganised argument 'no nukes no troops' may well be rehearsed in a new era of Atlantic relations. The consequences of this debate, and its effect on European security, will surely undermine the status quo which Britain seeks to preserve.

Britain's pursuit of its security objectives need not necessarily lead in this direction. Nor need the consideration of a degree of nuclear arms control as part of a conventional arms control package lead to an unending process of denuclearisation. A less rigid approach embracing an arms control package on favourable terms might avoid a rift within the Alliance by taking account of those concerns expressed in the Federal Republic, much of NATO Europe and indeed the US. Indeed, embracing an arms control package of this nature may be the best option available to Britain for securing these strategic goals.

An arms control package which included the simultaneous reduction of certain categories of nuclear weapons and Soviet armour is an approach which would address the Soviet Union's linkage between tactical nuclear weapons and asymmetrical reductions in its tank armies. Such a deal could also have several advantages for NATO. The Alliance could use the opportunity to move away from its threatened early use of battlefield nuclear weapons. These systems, comprising short-range tactical ballistic missiles and nuclear artillery are inherently escalatory, requiring an early decision for their use in order to avoid being overrun. These weapons are very unpopular with the forces who operate them: they believe that no such decision would be taken and that the weapons therefore lack any credibility. NATO's ability to maintain effective command and control of these forces in a crisis is also open to question.[33] Indeed, General Galvin's plan to remove 2,900 short-range nuclear warheads such as artillery shells and free-fall bombs, in exchange for a longer-range replacement for the Lance missile, recognises the limited value of these systems even if it does not recognise the political unacceptability of a Lance replacement. The general principle he espouses, however, that of replacing short-range nuclear systems with longer-range weapons is a valid one and has its logical conclusion in a move to a greater reliance on long-range systems such as airpower.

The total removal of these systems in exchange for their Soviet counterparts represents a favourable exchange in itself. NATO would be trading 88 Lance launchers for the Warsaw Pact's 1,400 SS-21s, Frogs and Scuds. This deal would also remove the growing threat of pre-emptive attack on NATO forces by conventionally armed tactical ballistic missiles.[34] Indeed, unless the threat presented by tactical ballistic missiles is seriously addressed by arms control, then air assets in particular become increasingly vulnerable. It is for this reason that it is important to address the short-range ballistic missile threat in conjunction with, or prior to, negotiations on tactical airpower. This approach would also be in accord with the desire, strongly advocated by Britain and France within NATO and enshrined in *The Alliance's Comprehensive Concept*, to see changes in the Warsaw Pact's posture before any discussion on aircraft is undertaken.[35]

The removal of short-range nuclear forces by NATO, however, should only be contemplated as part of an agreement substantially reducing the Warsaw Pact's capability for launching surprise attack and for initiating large-scale offensive action, a process already agreed as the basis of CFE. While the precise details of such a comprehensive agreement would have to be worked out in negotiations within NATO and between the two alliances, the scope for mutual reductions in offensive systems would have been substantially overcome by the Alliance's willingness to address the nuclear question.

Such a deal would not amount to a realisation of Britain's worst fears of denuclearisation leaving NATO Europe, or indeed the Federal Republic, nuclear free. Rather, it would shift NATO's reliance away from unstable and unpopular short-range systems in favour of nuclear weapons based on more survivable and flexible platforms. Specifically, several hundred sea launched cruise missiles could be dedicated to NATO's supreme European Command and an additional 55 to 60 F-111s could be deployed in Britain armed with stand off missiles. There is evidence that Britain has already agreed in principal to the deployment of additional F-111s.[36] In addition to this, some 72 F-15E aircraft may be deployed in Europe in the 1990s.[37] The deployment of these American forces to Europe would also enhance the US's ability to strike the Soviet homeland from Europe, thus acting to reinforce the credibility of extended deterrence. A move by NATO to such systems would also have the benefit of not being totally reliant on American nuclear weapons, since the French ASMP and new RAF stand off missile for the

Tornado would also constitute part of this force. More importantly, as Freedman notes, these systems would be important politically 'in demonstrating a European readiness to take on nuclear responsibilities and contribute to all levels of flexible response, so as to influence American attitudes towards NATO.'[38] In addition, the deployment of these systems would reinforce the 'second centre of decision making' rationale for independent nuclear forces at a critical point on the escalation ladder.

Conclusion

For the first time in the post-war period, an arms control agreement substantially reducing the largest concentration of military forces in history and the threat to peace which they presented now seems likely. President Gorbachev has demonstrated his commitment to 'New Thinking' in Soviet defence policy by announcing substantial unilateral force reductions, and in the realm of arms control agreeing to asymmetrical cuts in offensive forces and accepting the need for intrusive verification. In response NATO has set out its security priorities and negotiations have begun on the basis of agreed mandates in two separate arms control fora in Vienna.

Significant differences exist within the NATO Alliance, however, as to how best to proceed with the arms control negotiations. These differences over how rapidly the negotiations should progress and what forces should be included are based on conflicting conceptions of where these negotiations should lead. Central to this debate within the Alliance is the conservative position adopted and advocated by Britain of resisting the momentum within the arms control process for moving beyond the existing framework of European security. Rather than embracing the opportunities presented by the New Detente and the CFE process for transcending the security structures and political geography of Europe, Britain remains committed to preserving and protecting the status quo.

The conservative position which Britain has adopted in its approach to the negotiations on Conventional Forces in Europe may actually prove counterproductive to the realisation of its broader strategic goals. Adopting such policies in order to maintain the status quo in European security is no longer a viable policy as a response to the bold initiatives and substantive changes brought about by President Gorbachev. A more fruitful course of action for both British,

Alliance and European security, therefore, would be to adopt policies in the arms control process which would be both conciliatory to the concerns and anxieties of the other allies, and in fitting with the new opportunities and challenges presented by the Soviet Union.

The British position, which has also been adopted by NATO, of making further nuclear arms control dependent on progress on conventional arms control, is one which creates an artificial distinction and an artificial barrier to further arms control in Europe. NATO's refusal to make nuclear concessions in order to agree a more favourable and stable conventional balance, however, may come back to haunt the Alliance in the 1990s when its continuing efforts to modernise these nuclear forces run into considerable opposition. NATO's failure to act positively in response to the apparently attractive arms control initiatives of Mr Gorbachev may place unbearable strain on the delicate political balance in German security policy or indeed in the evolving Atlantic relationship.

British efforts to maintain the status quo in the European security environment may also effect the allocation of force reductions following the negotiations of a CFE agreement. In its efforts to mitigate the effects of force reductions on the central front, Britain may well find itself accepting commitments which amount to an increase in the disproportionately large share of NATO's defence burden which it bares. Such an attempt to single-handedly stem the prevailing trend in alliance thinking would constitute both an unrealistic commitment of British defence resources and one which did not take account of Britain's strengths as a navel power in NATO's attempt to effect a greater degree of role specialisation. More fundamentally, however, the implementation of policies designed to limit the effects of change on both NATO strategy and European security may well be, and be seen to be, counterproductive both in terms of Alliance unity and in harnessing the winds of change to the collective advantage of all concerned.

The risks involved for British and European security of such a conservative stance in arms control are too great and the opportunities are so momentous that the continuation of this policy approach can no longer be justified. A new, more imaginative approach to providing Britain's security objectives is needed. Fundamentally, such an approach requires the serious discussion of

European security, including both nuclear and conventional armaments within the Alliance, but also with the Soviet Union. Specifically, Britain must embrace the idea of moving towards a greater
reliance on long-range nuclear platforms, such as airpower, for the
maintenance of deterrence within Europe, while simultaneously conducting negotiations with the Soviet Union on short-range nuclear
systems. In 1984 Mrs Thatcher said that she could 'do business' with
Mr Gorbachev. The time is now right for that business to begin.

Notes

1 *Statement On The Defence Estimates 1987*, Command 101-1,
HMSO, London, p. 7.
2 See Robert D. Blackwill, 'Conceptual Problems of Conventional Arms
Control', *International Security*, XII, 1988.
3 See Rupert Cornwell, 'Gorbachev spells out 14% cut in defence
spending', *The Independent*, 19 January 1989; Mark Urban, 'Kremlin
streamlines a rusty fortress', *The Independent*, 26 January 1989 and '5,300
new tanks scrapped', *The Independent*, 22 March 1989 and Patricia
Clough, 'Honecker announces defence reduction', *The Independent*, 24
January 1989.
4 The Prime Minister, Margaret Thatcher, speaking in the House of
Commons, 8 December 1988. See 'Thatcher is cautious on Gorbachev arms
offer', *Guardian*, 9 December 1988.
5 See John Eisenhammer and Rupert Cornwell, 'West gives cautious
welcome to Warsaw Pact force details', *The Independent*, 31 January 1989.
6 See Patrick Wintour, 'Howe wary on Soviet arms cuts', *Guardian*, 12
December 1988; John Eisenhammer and Rupert Cornwell, 'West gives
cautious welcome to Warsaw Pact force details', *The Independent*, 31
January 1989; John Bulloch, 'West Berlin Wall has to go', *The Independent*,
18 January 1989. Britain was also the first signatory to invoke the Vienna
accords on human rights agreed in January 1989 as part of the Conference
on Security and Co-operation in Europe (CSCE) and was one of the last to
agree to a human rights conference in Moscow in 1990. See John Bulloch,
'UK steps up human rights protest', *The Independent*, 23 February 1989.
7 See Lawrence Freedman, 'Gorbachev forces Nato's hand', *The Independent*, 16 December 1988.
8 The Soviet Union makes a distinction in its military doctrine between
the 'socio-political' aspect, which it describes as defensive, and the 'military
technical' aspect, which is configured to conduct all-out offensive operations. See Roy Allison, 'Current Soviet Thinking on Conventional Arms
Control in Europe', *The Journal of Arms Control and Disarmament*, IX,
September 1988.
9 See *The UK Role in Arms Control*, p. 14.
10 See Stephen J. Ledogar, 'A New Beginning for Arms Control', *International Herald Tribune*, 7 March 1989.

11   See Joseph Fitchett, 'Arms Talks: Hopes For Easing Tension', *International Herald Tribune*, 10 March 1989.

12   *ibid.*

13   See Robert D. Blackwill, *op.cit.*

14   See Jack Snyder, 'Limiting Offensive Conventional Forces: Soviet Proposals and Western Options', *International Security*, XII, Spring 1988.

15   *Conventional Arms Control: Statement Issued by the North Atlantic Council Meeting in Ministerial Session at NATO Headquarters, Brussels,* (8–9 December 1988). Press Communiqué M-3 (88)75. Emphasis added.

16   See Robert Mauthner and Judy Dempsey, 'Western alliance takes aim at East bloc tanks and artillery', *Financial Times*, 7 March 1989.

17   *ibid.*

18   See Robert Mauthner, 'Vienna arms talks launched on a wave of hope and confidence', *Financial Times*, 10 March 1989.

19   *ibid.* See also Don Oberdorfer, 'Soviets Offer Cuts in Vienna', *The International Herald Tribune*, 7 March 1989.

20   There are a number of conceptual problems which make it difficult to reach a conventional arms control agreement involving air power. First, is the problem presented by the mobility of air power. An agreement limited to the region between the Atlantic and the Urals, for example, would face the prospect of rapid circumvention in a time of crisis by virtue of the speed by which aircraft could return to the area. Second, trying to agree global limits of aircraft in an attempt to overcome this problem threatens to upset the airpower balance in other regions such as in Asia and the Third World. Third, establishing a conventional arms control regime for air power would face the difficulty of adequately addressing the 'emerging technologies' which most concern the Soviet Union. These technologies include high accuracy precision guided munitions, are very small, numerous, easy to conceal, and in some instances consist merely of 'strap on' additions to existing equipment and are very difficult to monitor and verify. See Snyder, *op.cit.*, p.74.

21   While the Warsaw Pact has a numerical superiority in most categories of air power, it is generally considered that NATO's qualitative superiority gives it an advantage in this area.

22   Snyder, *op. cit.*, p. 69.

23   *Conventional Arms Control*, p. 1.

24   The definition proposed by NATO states that 'a combat aircraft is a fixed-wing or swing-wing aircraft permanently land-based of a type initially constructed or later converted to drop bombs, deliver air-to-air missiles, fire guns/cannons, or employ any other weapons of destruction.' *Negotiations on Conventional Armed Forces in Europe*, Vienna 13 July 1989, p. 6.

25   Specifically *The Alliance's Comprehensive Concept* states that: 'With special reference to the Western proposals on CFE tabled at Vienna, enhanced by the proposals by the United States at the May 1989 summit, the allies concerned proceed on the understanding that negotiated reductions leading to a level below the existing level of their SNF missiles will not be carried out until the results of these negotiations have been implemented. Reductions of Warsaw Pact SNF systems should be carried out before that

date ... [and further] ... The question concerning the introduction and deployment of a follow-on system for the Lance will be dealt with in 1992 in the light of overall security developments.'

26   John Eisenhammer, 'NATO party for inflexible friends', *The Independent*, 17 May 1989.

27   *Conventional Arms Control: The Way Ahead*, Press Communiqué, Mi (88) 12., p. 2.

28   See John Eisenhammer, 'East bloc offers talks on missiles', *The Independent*, 13 April 1989.

29   *The Alliance's Comprehensive Concept*, May 1989, No. 27, p. 6.

30   *ibid*.

31   See Patrick Marnham, 'French to attend Nato summit', *The Independent*, 18 February 1989.

32   John Eisenhammer, 'East bloc offers talks on missiles', *The Independent*, 13 April 1989.

33   See Jeremy Leggett, 'Nato's fragile structures may disintegrate in the fog of war', *The Independent*, 27 April 1988.

34   Developments in missile guidance and conventional munitions make the use of tactical ballistic missiles with non-nuclear warheads an increasingly important threat against a whole range of targets in Europe. See Donald L. Hafner and John Roper (eds.), *ATBMs and Western Security: Missile Defenses For Europe*, RIAA, London, 1988. In particular see the chapter by Dennis M. Gormley, 'The Soviet Threat: New and Enduring Dimensions'.

35   See Joseph Fitchett, 'NATO Will Offer Further Cuts At Conventional Arms Talks', *International Herald Tribune*, 3 April 1989.

36   See Mark Urban, '50 US nuclear jets for Britain', *The Independent*, 29 June 1988, in which he states that fifty additional F111s will be deployed in the UK in 1989 or 1990. See also Hans Binnendijk, *op. cit*. Although these initial reports were denied by the Ministry of Defence, funds for basing these systems in the UK were apparently included in Pentagon budgetary documents in 1989. See Mark Urban, 'US "to step up" nuclear bomber base', *The Independent*, 12 April 1989.

37   See Hans Binnendijk, 'NATO's Nuclear Modernization dilemma', *Survival*, XXXI, March/April 1989, pp. 137–55.

38   See Lawrence Freedman, 'Britain's other nuclear forces', *The Independent*, 21 January 1988.

British nuclear non-proliferation policy

Introduction

A national policy consists of a set of attitudes, objectives and actions of a government or regime towards an issue area linked together within an historical context. British nuclear non-proliferation policy can be usefully analysed and understood in these terms. The *attitudes* are the views held in the UK of the nature of the international political environment, the role of nuclear weapons and nuclear energy within it and the significance of the possession of such weapons by Britain and other states. The *objectives* are what successive UK governments have both said they were attempting to achieve and can be retrospectively judged to have been attempting to achieve in this area. The *actions* are those activities undertaken by the governments of the UK in respect of its own nuclear activities, its nuclear exports, international organisations connected with nuclear energy and states which threaten to acquire nuclear weapons. All these have been subject to change over the fifty years of nuclear energy related activity in the UK, and no doubt will continue to be so in future.

Britain's attitudes towards nuclear weapons and the objectives of nuclear non-proliferation policy

Since 1945, successive UK governments have adopted the position that the country must possess nuclear weapons for its own security. Initially this was because they were the 'most modern weapons', but as the military nuclear programme moved from development to stockpiling in the late 1950s complex rationales concerning its role in sustaining both the US commitment to Europe and extended deterrence were developed. In 1958 the UK entered into an agreement with the US for the transfer between the two countries of weapons design information, fissile material, weapon components and a submarine propulsion reactor.[1] Such an agreement had been sought since 1946 and once it was made it became the cornerstone of Britain's nuclear weapons policy. Successive British governments since 1958 have therefore taken the attitude that Britain would not enter into any nuclear non-proliferation commitment that would place in jeopardy any part of this agreement. Thus in one respect the essence of British non-proliferation policy can be summed up in the phrase 'keep your dirty hands off our bomb'!

Once it became a full thermonuclear weapon state, Britain's leaders were anxious to bolt the door against further nuclear powers appearing, or at the very least slow that development. This motivation was displayed in three sets of attitudes. First, the UK accepted and actively assisted the US policy of making arrangements with the NATO allies to enable them to deliver US owned nuclear weapons with their own systems in the event of a Soviet invasion: the 'key to the cupboard' arrangements. This policy sought to dissuade additional European states from seeking to produce their own nuclear weapons. With the exception of France, it can be argued that this policy has been remarkably successful. Proliferation has been avoided by pseudo-dissemination, which it is vigorously argued is legally non-dissemination.

Second, British leaders recognised that if the development of strategic weapons could be halted at the point reached by 1958, and a nuclear freeze engineered, it could sustain a relationship of near nuclear equality with the USSR and the US indefinitely. If it could not do this it would become increasingly expensive for Britain to compete with the superpowers as anti-ballistic missile systems made their operational debut. The choice would then lie between delivery systems which were not technically credible, and increased reliance upon US technology to ensure that British nuclear weapons could penetrate to their targets. The British government, therefore, fought hard to achieve both a Comprehensive Test Ban and a fissile material cut-off in the period through to 1964. This campaign combined both popular aspirations to escape from the nuclear nightmare and hard-headed calculations about British national interests. This included a belief that the appearance of additional nuclear weapon states would be detrimental to British and international security: more would not be better, even if the more included France. What Britain was not prepared to do, however, was sacrifice its own nuclear capability in order to persuade France to give up its military nuclear programme.

In part, this reluctance to sacrifice British nuclear capability for non-proliferation objectives reflected a belief that non-proliferation policy could not be separated from the disarmament of the existing nuclear weapon states. The latter was seen to be the only way to prevent further proliferation, and was based on a belief that disarmament was still technically possible, as all fissile materials that had been produced could still be accounted for. By the mid-1960s, however, it had become increasingly clear that neither a fissile material cut-off nor a comprehensive testing ban were likely to be implemented. The search for the comprehensive ban had been largely abandoned in favour of a partial test ban treaty, signed by the US, the Soviet Union and the UK in August 1963. At about the same time it had been reluctantly accepted that fissile material limitations were no longer the crucial element in determining the size of stockpiles. There was just too much uranium available by then in the possession of nuclear weapon states. In addition, with the arrival of thermonuclear weapons and the cancellation of the plans of the US and Britain in the late 1950s for the deployment of thousands of tactical nuclear weapons and anti-aircraft and ABM warheads, the idea of such limitations to constrain the arsenals of the nuclear weapon states was largely abandoned.

In the mid and late 1960s a significant change thus started to appear in British attitudes towards nuclear non-proliferation. The idea that the disarmament of the nuclear weapon states was the only feasible policy to persuade other states to abandon plans to possess nuclear weapons was undermined by the twin beliefs that such disarmament was now no longer technically possible, and that nuclear proliferation was inevitable, though it could be slowed down. A major reason for this inevitability was the spread of 'peaceful' nuclear technology, and the resultant quantities of fissile materials that fell into the statistical category of 'material unaccounted for'(MUF). This rather negative attitude towards the possibilities of controlling and safeguarding civil technology was in part a product of the cut-throat commercial battle taking place between American and British nuclear power reactor manufacturers, and in part because the British nuclear power stations then under construction were derived from reactors used to produce military plutonium. By contrast, the American reactors were derived from naval propulsion designs. Thus to the UK (and the USSR) there were no intrinsic differences at that time between civil and military reactors: they could only be differentiated by the way they were operated, in particular the frequency with which they were refuelled.

Throughout the latter part of the 1960s, therefore, British attitudes towards international nuclear non-proliferation developments could best be described as rather less than enthusiastic. This is not because they were seen as contrary to Britain's security and general foreign policy interests, but because they were regarded as both unlikely to have much practical impact and because they were seen as a covert attempt by the US to undermine British commercial policy. Unlike the US, the UK had few bilateral safeguards agreements that it wished to transfer to the International Atomic Energy Agency (IAEA), and its nuclear export policy was proving to be a disaster. Moreover, the Non-Proliferation Treaty negotiations were largely being orchestrated by the US and USSR and the UK was concerned to prevent any resultant treaty affecting its nuclear weapon relationship with the US. At the same time a major disagreement had developed between the US and the UK over the utility of placing enriched uranium of US origin, which had been shipped to the UK for use in its civil reactors, together with other UK civil facilities, under IAEA safeguards. This disagreement was not only a product of different attitudes towards safeguards in nuclear weapon states, it was also a product of the way the US Congress was attempting to impose its version of American non-proliferation policy upon the British government.

By the early 1970s, however, the NPT was both ratified and in operation; a majority of states had accepted IAEA full-scope safeguards; the prospects for British reactor sales were bleak; and the disagreements with the US over safeguarding civil plants had been largely resolved, not least by Britain's entry into the EEC which itself meant acceptance of such safeguards under EURATOM. As a result of these developments, the British attitude changed to being much more supportive of active non-proliferation policies and much closer to American perspectives over this issue. This was confirmed by the active role played by the UK in convening the initial meeting of the nuclear technology suppliers group in London in the immediate aftermath of the Indian nuclear explosion in 1974. The idea behind the 'London suppliers group' was to place some restrictions on the supply of technology which could be used to make materials for weapons, especially to those states which seemed likely to be next in line to acquire them. It was argued that there was no contradiction between the proposition that Britain needed nuclear weapons for its own security and the proposition that India or Pakistan did not. At the same time the argument was made that since British enrichment, fuel fabrication and reprocessing activities were all under EURA-TOM/IAEA safeguards, non-proliferation considerations should not be allowed to interfere with domestic commercial developments such as the construction of the THORP reprocessing plant for enriched fuel at Sellafield. This in turn led to considerable disagreements with the non-proliferation policy of the Carter administration and its attempts to ban the reprocessing and use of plutonium by both domestic legislation and international negotiations such as the INFCE.

British attitudes towards nuclear non-proliferation are now highly supportive of the IAEA, the NPT and the other less formal elements of the regime. But this is a product of the general harmony of interests between the non-proliferation regime and Britain's international security concerns outside of Europe. Where Britain's own national security interests are concerned, however, or where commercial interests intrude, there can be less certainty that this general proposition will hold. In Moscow in April 1987, Mrs Thatcher's speech argued that the UK had an absolute need for nuclear weapons because it had to confront a large nuclear armed state like the USSR.[2] Thus, at the national level, Britain's justification for its possession of nuclear weapons constitutes, in effect, a nuclear proliferation charter.

One final aspect of British attitudes towards non-proliferation is that while international measures to monitor the use of nuclear technology and deny materials and technology to potential proliferators are seen as a necessary component of the non-proliferation regime, it is accepted that these may slow down proliferation but will not prevent it. Thus nuclear proliferation is seen as essentially a political activity which has to be tackled in a broad political context on a case by case basis. At this point it may become indistinguishable from general policy towards the state concerned and its security problems. In short, the non-proliferation problem resides in specific states, not the non-proliferation regime, and policies have to be shaped accordingly.

The implementation of nuclear non-proliferation policy

British nuclear non-proliferation policy is manifested in a wide range of activities, some of which have clear connections with the area of concern, while other are more contestable. These include, inter alia, policy towards the NPT; policy towards the IAEA; nuclear export policies; policies over civil and militarynuclear activities in Britain; policy towards a comprehensive test ban treaty; policy towards nuclear free zones, and regional policies.

The Non-Proliferation Treaty

This is regarded as the cornerstone of the non-proliferation regime, if only because its adherents have made a legally binding political commitment not to acquire nuclear weapons. The treaty itself has no executive body attached to it, and as a consequence attention is focused on the five-yearly review conferences and, increasingly, the issues which surround the extension of the treaty beyond 1995.[3] Attention therefore rises to a peak during the review conference period and then declines. British policy on the Treaty is to support it, to take the line that its nuclear activities do not detract from it, and to assist in measures to improve technical assistance to developing states.

The IAEA

Britain provides one of the Governors for the IAEA[4] and the External Affairs director is also usually British. The UK has been generally supportive of the organisation, acting, for example, as a trial horse for safeguards on reprocessing and centrifuge enrichment plants. It seeks to prevent politicisation of the organisation's activities, and would not necessarily support the US in any dispute involving Israel or South Africa. As a member of EURATOM, IAEA safeguards are not now directly applicable to Britain. They operate indirectly through the EURATOM safeguards system.

Nuclear export policies

Britain attempts to control the export of nuclear related materials and technology through domestic customs regulations and export controls. Exporters have to apply for a licence and the transaction has to be approved by an interdepartmental committee including the FCO, DTI and the MoD. A key criterion in all these decisions is the reliability of the recipient state. The issue is held to be one of problem states, and not problem technologies, and while the UK is unlikely to trade with certain states it may regard as politically suspect, it wishes to hinder the development of the international nuclear industry as little as possible. This policy is expressed in the Callaghan guidelines of 1976.[5] The major problem with the operational aspects of this policy is either that important items will not be specified on customs lists, or that items will be exported clandestinely. There is some evidence that both may have occurred in the case of the Pakistani enrichment plant.

On the whole, there have been few instances during the 1980s where Britain's commercial interests have clashed with its non-proliferation policies. It has not been a major exporter of nuclear technology, a market which in any event has been virtually non-existent since the late 1970s, and the reprocessing and enrichment activities of British Nuclear Fuels have been concerned almost exclusively with work for advanced industrial states, rather than the 'problem states'.[6] It is clear, however, that this situation is unlikely to persist, and at least two major issues in this area are already visible.

The first concerns the transfer of nuclear submarine reactor technology to non-nuclear weapon states. This issue arose as a consequence of the Canadian Defence White Paper of June 1987, in which it was stated that Canada was to procure a fleet of ten to twelve nuclear submarines during the remainder of the decade. Whilst a decision has been taken to drop these plans,[7] had a British design been chosen, arrangements would probably have had to be made to remove the material to fuel each submarine from IAEA safeguards in Canada, to enrich it in the UK and US to weapon grade, fabricate it into reactor cores in the UK and then return it to safeguards once it has been discharged from the reactor. This procedure would have been very troublesome both because it threatened to involve a non-nuclear weapon state in the handling of weapon grade nuclear material outside of IAEA safeguards, and because it could have opened up possibilities for other non-proscribed military uses of either weapon grade materials or of the technology to produce them. Since the NPT deals only with weapons, it does not specifically debar these other military uses.[8]

The second issue is that the UK is embarking on a programme for the construction of a new generation of power reactors. Present plans include the commissioning of four pressurised water reactors

(PWRs) by the year 2000, the first of which is under construction at Sizewell in Kent.[9] The move to construct PWRs in Britain came about partly in the belief that experience in the design and construction of this reactor type would allow the creation of a competitive export capability in this area. This, in turn, will enable export sales to be sought, with consequent choices in the future over whether to export the technology to certain states. How far these policies will be affected by the privatisation of the electricity industry is unclear.

The delineation of civil and military activities

A major issue with regard to the NPT has been the controversy over Article VI of the Treaty. The NPT has been seen by many developing states as a nuclear weapon state disarmament treaty, while the nuclear weapon states themselves have seen it as only applying to the non-nuclear weapon states. As a consequence, the NPT has been used by domestic groups opposed to Britain's possession of nuclear weapons to argue that Britain is not fulfilling its commitments under the Treaty, because it is not only retaining its own nuclear arms, it is actually increasing them.[10] This argument – that in all respects Britain must act as though it was a non-nuclear weapon state – affects two further areas of activity: safeguards, and the delineation between military and civil nuclear activities.

The arguments over safeguards upon UK domestic activities revolve around two conflicting propositions. The first is that it is pointless applying safeguards to nuclear weapon states as they already have the bomb. The second is that expanding safeguards to all activities in a nuclear weapon state is a direct method of forcing progress towards its nuclear disarmament. In practice the British government started from the first proposition, arguing it was a waste of scarce IAEA inspectors and resources to operate safeguards in nuclear weapon states. It then gradually accepted that the 'equality of misery' principle required that inspection was necessary in order to remove arguments that its absence placed nuclear weapon states at a commercial advantage. Entry into the EEC changed the legal position with respect to ownership. All nuclear material in the UK is now technically owned by the Commission and assumed to be used for peaceful purposes under EURATOM safeguards, unless a nuclear weapon state chooses to expressly remove it from such safeguards.

In practice, the inventories of UK military material have not been declared to the EEC, but all uranium ore entering the country is now subject to EURATOM safeguards. As a consequence it will be necessary at some point in the future to start removing some of this material from these safeguards in order to continue to operate the unsafeguarded military reactors at Calder Hall and Chapel Cross. Those groups in the UK who are anxious to constrain British nuclear activities argue that these unsafeguarded military facilities should be placed under the EURATOM safeguard regime.

The controversy over the delineation between civil and military activities has also fuelled a desire to directly constrain UK military activities, but has its roots in the period from 1958 to 1970 when UK governments saw little point in separating military from civil activities. It had been appreciated at an early stage in the planning of Britain's first nuclear power programme that the reactors being built for the civil electricity boards could be used to produce weapon grade plutonium, and would produce this material in the normal course of their start up operations. Agreement was then reached with the US to exchange American weapon grade enriched uranium for plutonium produced in the CEGB and SSEB reactors. Both supplies were to be used for military purposes, and this exchange was implemented through to early 1970.

In order to meet the needs of the military production programme, a large reprocessing plant (B205) was completed at Sellafield in 1964, the same year in which the production of military grade plutonium in the UKAEA's eight Calder Hall type reactors officially ceased. Subsequently, all the used fuel from both unsafeguarded (military) reactors and safeguarded (civil) ones was reprocessed together. Decisions on how much to place in the unsafeguarded military store at Sellafield were reached on the basis of calculations of how much plutonium came from the two sources. Thus plutonium from the CEGB civil reactors undoubtedly was deposited in the military store. Moreover, no attempt was made to account for the isotopic composition of the material to either the IAEA or EURATOM. Accusations were levelled at the British government that it was separating out weapon grade plutonium arising from the civil programme and swapping it for less militarily useful plutonium in the military store at Sellafield. EURATOM then demanded the ability to monitor the flow of safeguarded material passing through the B205 plant. This was opposed initially by the British government as such measurements would also indicate military flows through the plant. In 1987, this was resolved by a decision to process material of civil origin in separate batches from that of military origin. The unintended effect of this, however, is that the military reactors can now be operated in a manner which would produce weapon grade plutonium without this being detectable by the general public and Parliament.

At the 1985 NPT review conference, a strong recommendation was put forward by a group of states favouring nuclear disarmament that the military and civil fuel cycles in nuclear weapon states should be separated as far as possible.[11] Unfortunately, for Britain to do this would require extensive building of additional, costly fuel reprocessing facilities, as well as fuel fabrication plants. These costs would rise even further if the plan involved having the military and civil cycles physically separate. This issue seems likely to be a running sore between the government and its domestic anti-nuclear opponents through to the end of the century, though the degree to which the issue actually has an international impact must be open to doubt.

A comprehensive nuclear testing ban
A Comprehensive Test Ban Treaty is seen as symbolically important for the NPT for two reasons: it is mentioned in the preamble to the Treaty[12] and it would mean that the nuclear weapon states would have restrictions placed upon them to counter-balance those imposed on the non-nuclear weapon states by the NPT. For the last eight years, however, the US has taken the position that it did not want to see a CTBT concluded, and the negotiations on the subject which recommenced in 1977 have been stalled since 1980.

These negotiations are the only ones on superpower nuclear matters to which the UK is a party.[13] The US has argued that it needs to maintain its nuclear deterrent indefinitely, and testing is needed to maintain the reliability of its stockpile,[14] as well as explore new types of weapon to be used in the SDI. Britain took the view that a treaty is still not possible because verification capabilities in respect of such a ban are inadequate, though it recently moved to adopt the US position on this issue. There is little doubt, however, that if the US was to decide to sign such a treaty, the UK would have to follow its example. It also appears that in such a situation the UK nuclear force would be much more at risk, if unreliability were to manifest itself, than that of the US or the Soviet Union, as Britain has only one strategic design in the nuclear stockpile at any given time, in contrast to the several possessed by the superpowers.

If it appeared likely that the US and the Soviet Union were to agree further constraints on weapon testing,[15] such as, for example, an annual quota of tests and a lowering of the current 150 kt yield ceiling, the UK would have to go along with these constraints as it uses testing facilities in the US. However, it is not clear how such a quota would be shared between the US and the UK. Such limitations, even were they to be negotiated, are unlikely to be satisfactory to those NPT states who seek a total ban in order to choke off fresh weapon programmes. They would certainly not resolve the debate over the implementation of Article VI of the NPT.

Nuclear free zones
There are currently three of these zones: in Antarctica, South America and the South Pacific. The Antarctica one is non-controversial, though it is shortly to come up for renewal.

The Latin American Treaty of Tlatelolco of 1967 is more controversial because of the British role in the Falklands War. The UK has signed the two relevant protocols to this Treaty. It also argues that it abided by its commitments under these protocols throughout the war, and did not introduce nuclear weapons into the area. The Argentineans argue that nuclear weapons were on ships of the Task Force, and that this was a breach of the Treaty, as was the use of nuclear powered submarines. They also argue that the continued British presence on the islands undermines the Treaty, even though Argentina itself has not ratified it.

The South Pacific Nuclear Free Zone (The Treaty of Raratonga) is of more recent origin (1985), and covers large sea areas in the South Pacific. Among the motivations for this treaty was the French nuclear testing programme at Muroroa Atoll, which is within the Zone, and the desire of governments to prevent nuclear armed warships docking in their territory. The Treaty does not directly affect Britain, though it might pose problems for its warships on their infrequent visits to the area if there are demands for assurances that they are not carrying nuclear weapons. However, perhaps out of a desire to show solidarity with France, Britain has decided not to ratify the relevant protocols attached to the Treaty,[16] much to the disgust of its Commonwealth partners Australia and New Zealand.

Regional policies

The central concern of the UK government in the area of non-proliferation is to deal with proliferation threats by timely political pressures on the states concerned, as well as by attempts to resolve regional disputes. The major regional threat at the moment is the one bequeathed by Britain upon the world: the India–Pakistan situation. However, British influence here is limited, as the US has most influence on Pakistan and the Soviet Union on India. Both Israel and South Africa are seen to be stabilised situations, though they will both continue to figure heavily in the politics of both the IAEA and the NPT Review conferences. In Latin America, the problem appears to be more the effects of the British presence in the Falklands upon Argentinean activities than any stimulus provided by Argentinean/Brazilian rivalry. In all these situations, the influence of the UK appears very limited.

Conclusions: the scope for action

As this examination of the implementation of British non-proliferation policy indicates, a major problem in delineating the lines of that policy is its fragmented nature. This relates both to how nuclear activities are structured, and to the policy-making machinery in each of these areas of nuclear activity. Thus the close historical, and actual, links between the civil and military aspects of nuclear energy in Britain; the apparent withdrawal of publicly owned bodies from nuclear activities; and the uneasy overlap between public and privately owned firms, which will be accentuated by the privatisation of the electricity industry, mean that the structure of the domestic industry is itself fragmented. This fragmentation is reinforced by a policy-making system which is very fluid and based on the concept of a lead department in the issue area under consideration. Hence there is no one centralised department responsible for the whole, discreet area of non-proliferation, split as these issues are between the domestic and external, civil and military, and public and private realm, within each of which issues are likely to be decided on criteria other than rather peripheral concerns with nuclear non-proliferation.

Moreover, non-proliferation policy in Britain has been closely linked to the desire to protect its own nuclear weapon status: in any conflict between the two, nuclear non-proliferation policy is likely to come a poor second. Its implementation covers such a wide range of activities that it can easily come into conflict with commercial policy.

The lack of competitive products has in the past limited this problem, though in the future there may be major difficulties over the sale of nuclear submarines and power reactors. At the same time non-proliferation policy is likely to become entangled with arguments over the need to separate military from civil activities in Britain. Yet in the last resort British policy can be summed up in those immortal words: 'do as I say, not as I do'.

Notes

1 For fuller details of these arrangements see John Simpson, *The Independent Nuclear State: The US, Britain and the Military Atom*, Macmillan, London, 1983, especially pp. 129–41.

2 *The Economist*, 4 April 1987.

3 For a discussion of these issues see David Fischer, 'The 1995 Nuclear Non Proliferation Extension conference: issues and prospects' in John Simpson (ed.), *Nuclear Non Proliferation: An Agenda for the 1990's*, Cambridge University Press, Cambridge, 1987.

4 The current incumbent is also an under secretary at the Department of Energy.

5 In 1976 Mr James Callaghan, then Foreign Secretary, stated:
'When considering the export of nuclear equipment, material or technology we shall study each case on its merits. Our first consideration will always be the provisions of the Non-Proliferation Treaty, the Euratom Treaty, and whether or not the prospective customer has concluded a safeguards agreement with the International Atomic Energy Agency.

Our detailed requirements will include the application of IAEA safeguards or comparable safeguards which are verified by the IAEA to exported nuclear material or equipment; an assurance that whatever we export will not be used to manufacture nuclear explosives for any purposes; an assurance that our exports will be adequately protected against the possibility of theft or sabotage; and assurances that if the equipment or material that we export is re-exported, then the new purchaser will be required to give the same assurances on safeguards, non-explosive use and physical protection as were given by the original customer.

We shall also study with particular care proposals for the export of sensitive equipment or technology. By sensitive I mean equipment or technology which could lead to the construction of Uranium enrichment plants, reprocessing plants or heavy water production plants. In general we shall exercise constraint in the export of such plants or their technology, and we are at present contributing to the IAEA's study of the feasibility of including such plants in regional fuel centres in the future. When we decide to export them we shall, of course, require assurances that any sensitive plants using transferred technology, now or in the future, will be subject to IAEA safeguards. We shall also need to be consulted before our customers can re-export any sensitive nuclear materials or sensitive equipment or

technology to a third country.'
Hansard, House of Commons Debates, Vol. 980, written parliamentary answer to Mr Carter, 31 March 1976, Cols. 514–16.

6   BNFL treats fuel from the FRG, Spain, Switzerland, Italy, Sweden, The Netherlands and Japan. See Jane Bird, 'Britain seeks nuclear waste from abroad', *The Sunday Times*, 14 May 1989. It also, for example, exports Uranium Hexafluoride to the Soviet Union. See Kevin Brown, 'Moscow imports N-fuels from the UK', *Financial Times*, 2 November 1988.

7   Mark Milner and Clyde Sanger, 'Budget sinks £3.5bn deal', *Guardian*, 28 April 1989.

8   John Simpson and Ben Sanders, 'Nuclear Submarines: Cause for concern', *PPNN Occasional Paper 2*, Centre for International Policy Studies, University of Southampton, 1988.

9   Consent is being sought for a PWR at Hinkley Point in Somerset, and additional sites under consideration for new nuclear stations are Winfrith, Dungeness, Sizewell ('C'), Trawsfynydd, Wylfa and Druridge. 'Sizewell: the beginning, not the end', *ATOM*, No. 374, December 1987, p. 9.

10   For an assessment of the extent to which the UK has fulfilled its obligations under Article VI, see Dan Keohane, 'Britain's performance in implementing Article VI of the NPT' in Ian Bellany, Coit Blacker and Joseph Gallacher (eds.), *The Nuclear Non Proliferation Treaty*, Frank Cass, London, 1985.

11   Harald Mueller and David Fischer, 'Non Proliferation beyond the 1985 Review', *CEPS Papers*, No. 26, 1985, p. 22.

12   The UK, US and Soviet Union are also committed to concluding a CTBT under the terms of the 1963 Partial Test Ban Treaty. An amendment conference to the PTBT will be held in 1990, in which it is proposed that the PTBT be amended to incorporate a definite, agreed and staged timetable for the introduction of a comprehensive nuclear weapons test ban. The chances of success for this amendment are only slim given the power of veto of each depository state, one of whom – the US – has already rejected the concept of a comprehensive ban on nuclear testing whilst it continues to rely on nuclear deterrent forces for its security.

13   For a fuller discussion of UK policy on a comprehensive test ban, see the chapter by Wyn Rees, John Simpson and Darryl Howlett in this volume.

14   'US policy on Nuclear Testing', *Arms Control Update*, No. 9, US Arms Control and Disarmament Agency, Washington DC, October 1988, p. 6.

15   Neither the Threshold Test Ban Treaty, which limits explosions to 150 Kilotons, signed in 1974, nor the Peaceful Nuclear Explosions Treaty, signed in 1976, have ever been ratified due to US insistence on verification provisions satisfactory to it. In September 1987, the US and the Soviet Union agreed to provide for negotiations to limit, but not ban, nuclear tests in stages. The effect of this agreement has been widely viewed as postponing the possibility of a total ban on tests for decades. The first stage is the attempt to agree verification protocols to the above two treaties, with stage two to involve the negotiation of intermediate limits on testing, leading to a complete ban only as part of a larger disarmament process to reduce and

eliminate nuclear weapons. Notably, the UK was not a party to this agreement. See William Epstein, 'UN presses Superpowers on test ban', *Bulletin of the Atomic Scientists*, March 1988, p. 7.

16   Protocols 1 and 2 have been signed by two nuclear weapon states, China and the Soviet Union. The Soviet Union, by decree of 29 January 1988, has ratified both Protocols. The other three nuclear weapon states, France, the UK, and the US have shown no interest as yet of signing any of the protocols. See, P. Papadimitopoulos, 'The Rarotonga Treaty: A regional approach to non-proliferation in the South Pacific', *IAEA Bulletin*, January 1988.

Britain and the Comprehensive Test Ban Treaty

Introduction

The negotiations to achieve a Comprehensive Test Ban Treaty (CTBT) are unique in two respects: they have been going on for over thirty years, making them the longest standing item on the global nuclear arms limitation agenda; and they have been conducted on a trilateral basis between the US, the Soviet Union and the UK, rather than the more usual US–Soviet Union bilateral basis. As a consequence these negotiations have a rich history, marked by elements both of continuity and change in the British approach towards them. Active negotiations, however, have been restricted to two short periods in these three decades: the first between 1958 and 1962 (during the Macmillan government), which culminated in the decision to settle for the Partial Test Ban Treaty (PTBT) of August 1963; the second between 1977 and 1980 (during the Callaghan and first Thatcher government), when a treaty text was partially completed, but which then was adjourned *sine die* following the problems which beset the end of the Carter administration and the negative attitude taken towards it by the successor Reagan one.

To the extent that there has been a distinctive British 'approach' during the CTBT negotiations, four underlying themes stand out: the UK's concern over verification of a CTBT; the desire to use a CTBT to sustain the British military and political position in the international system; the desire of the British nuclear weapons establishment to test in order to sustain the UK's nuclear capability; and finally, the problems associated with developing an independent position on the CTBT because of the UK's alliance with the US. This chapter will discuss these four themes, especially as they have affected British policy during the two active negotiating periods outlined above. It will also discuss the position currently taken by the

British government and assess how trends and developments are likely to affect the UK's CTBT policy in the future.

The UK and the first phase of active CTBT negotiations, 1958–63

A variety of factors influenced the attitude of British policy-makers towards arms control policy in the period preceding the trilateral negotiations of 1958. The UK still saw itself as an actor of considerable influence on the world stage, yet was having to come to terms with a reduced power base in the post-war period. By the early 1950s, resources were found to be inadequate to fund the level of conventional military rearmament thought to be necessary after the Korean War. The possession of nuclear weapons was seen both as the only means of deterring nuclear aggression against the UK and as a way of reducing the size and costs of conventional forces. These ideas were publicly expressed in the Defence White Paper of 1957 which both announced the end of National Service and emphasised the importance of the independent nuclear deterrent.[1]

The premium set upon the maintenance of a deterrent force was evident in the UK's nuclear weapons programme of the 1950s. At the time the UK exploded its first thermonuclear device at Christmas Island, a nuclear armed cruise-missile for the V-Bomber force and a Medium Range Ballistic Missile, Blue Streak, were also under development. It was felt that such capabilities would close the gap between the UK and the superpowers and sustain the UK in a position of influence in the international system. One fear of British policy-makers was that a nuclear arms limitation agreement might be reached between the superpowers that would effectively freeze the UK into a position of permanent inferiority. In June 1957, President Eisenhower had stated that the US was willing to participate in a testing ban and in the same month Harold Stassen, Special Assistant to the President on Disarmament, proposed an end to the production of fissile material.[2] The Macmillan government felt that if the Soviet Union agreed to this, the UK would have to go along with it. But such a superpower accord would have left the UK in a very weak position, as at that point the UK only had a stockpile of some tens of relatively small yield fissile weapons. The UK needed fissile material to enlarge this stockpile and needed time to prove its thermonuclear and light-weight tactical weapon designs before any moratorium on testing was agreed.[3]

A second factor which shaped British attitudes to a test ban was the nature of the UK's relationship with the US. The UK was seeking closer security co-operation with the US in order to alleviate the pressure on its domestic economy.[4] This took the form of seeking co-ordination of conventional defence planing in theatres around the world and in attempting to secure assistance with the UK nuclear weapons programme. The British were finding it difficult to keep up with the technological advances in the nuclear field after independently acquiring a nuclear capability. The US could offer help in warhead designs, rocket motor engineering for missiles and in submarine reactor technology. The price, however, was that the UK would be increasingly dependent upon US assistance in the nuclear field, which in turn would create pressure to accept American initiatives in arms limitation negotiations, despite any reservations British governments might have about them.

A third factor which influenced UK policy in the 1950s was the question of whether a CTBT (in the context of General and Complete Disarmament) would enhance the UK's long-term security prospects. The UK's attitude towards a CTBT was shaped primarily by its view of the Soviet Union. UK policy-makers remained deeply suspicious of Soviet intentions in the CTBT negotiations at a time when Cold War rivalries were at their most intense, a view epitomised by the British Prime Minister himself, Harold Macmillan.[5]

The UK's CTBT policy in 1957 was thus determined by several considerations, of which the effect that such a testing ban would have on the British nuclear deterrent capability was paramount. However, when the Conference on the Discontinuance of Nuclear Weapons Tests (CDNWT) was convened in October 1958, the same month that a nuclear testing moratorium came into effect, the British government was satisfied that a CTBT would no longer have a detrimental affect on its own nuclear weapons programme. Two events created this change. The most important of the two was the amendment by Congress of the 1954 Atomic Energy Act in June 1958. This lead to a bilateral agreement being signed in Washington in July 1958 that allowed the US administration to transfer to the UK information on nuclear weapon design, development and fabrication.[6] The immediate needs of the UK nuclear weapon programme were satisfied by this means, which also ensured that it was no longer vulnerable to either the moratorium on testing called for by the Soviet Union in March 1958, nor a cut-off of fissile material. The second event was a report in August 1958 by an eight nation Conference of Experts that had been asked to look into the complex question of verification for a Test Ban.[7] They concluded, on the basis of the 'Rainier' test explosion in the US in the previous year, that underground testing could be monitored effectively and that a CTBT could be adequately verified.[8]

The British delegation to the Test Ban Conference was headed by Ambassador David Ormsby-Gore and his Deputy, Sir Michael Wright: its negotiating position was carefully co-ordinated with the US.[9] The British provided a number of supporting technical papers on seismology, especially research reports on cruciform arrays of seismographs that could improve the detection capabilities of individual countries without recourse to intrusive inspections.[10] A call was made for the acceptance of on-site inspections (OSI) and the implementation of the recommendation of the Conference of Experts that approximately 170 land-based control posts be established to monitor seismic activity. This was a pattern that was repeated in subsequent periods of CTBT negotiation as the UK continued to contribute heavily in the area of working papers on various aspects of seismology and verification.

Nevertheless, the issue of verification proved to be the stumbling block for the first Conference. For while the UK and the US favoured a verification system involving a comprehensive global network of seismic monitoring stations and effective procedures for OSI, the Soviet Union argued for a verification system which was less grandiose and far less intrusive. The principal verification issues which divided the negotiating parties were twofold: how to discriminate between naturally occurring seismic events, such as earthquakes, and a low-yield nuclear test; and how to detect and confirm clandestine testing.[11] The Soviet Union initially wanted to restrict those staffing the seismic monitoring posts to nationals of the country in which they were based. Any other nationals who were present were not to take part in the technical operation of the post. This was unacceptable to the UK (and the US), and the Soviet Union then agreed that additional foreign observers could staff the control posts and take part in their operation.[12]

Over OSI, the Soviet position was to restrict the numbers of foreign nationals in inspection teams to a minimum. The UK considered this to be unacceptable 'self-inspection'.[13] The Soviet Union also insisted on a right of veto over such inspections, which it considered a cloak for military intelligence gathering. The UK wanted each state to 'have the right of a limited number of inspections each year which could not be challenged by the other side.'[14] The reason for this demand was spelled out at the time by Selwyn Lloyd, the then Secretary of State for Foreign Affairs:

The veto is of special importance in relation to underground tests, because to detect whether or not there has been an underground test it is vital to have an on-site inspection. Rather different considerations apply to tests in the atmosphere. The Soviet position up to now has been that there must be unanimity that there is something to be investigated – in other words, that an event has taken place which could have been a nuclear explosion. Secondly, they claim that there must also be unanimity before an inspection group can be dispatched to the site of the suspected incident. On both those points we feel that we cannot accept a veto.[15]

Although both the UK and the US were in agreement that OSI was an essential component of any future test ban treaty, the two countries differed over the exact numbers of annual inspections that would be permitted. The US wanted a very rigorous inspection programme involving the possibility of many visits whereas, as noted above, the UK position was that a much more limited number would be acceptable. Two British experts, William Penney and Solly Zuckerman, were dispatched to Washington to try and convince American officials that a test ban could be verified in this way.[16]

But further research in the US into the monitoring requirements of a test ban had lead to a hardening of the American negotiating stance. Data from their 'Hardtack' nuclear test, conducted in October 1958, suggested that the Conference of Experts had been too optimistic in their evaluation of seismic monitoring capabilities, especially their ability to distinguish between naturally occurring earth tremors and those that were man-made. The Soviet delegation refused to acknowledge the validity of the new data, regarding it as a political ploy, and called on the US to return to their former position.

By February 1960, the UK and the US had resolved their differences and tabled a new set of proposals for a treaty. These included several innovations, particularly that underground tests which had a seismic magnitude greater than 4.75 on the Richter scale (about 50 kilotons) were to be banned. In effect, the US and the UK were proposing a testing yield limitation rather than a testing ban. This was a significant departure from the previous position of demanding a complete ban with extensive OSI. It reflected both the inability of all sides to agree on a definition of a nuclear test, and therefore what would be banned under a CTBT, and a recognition by the Western states that a comprehensive ban was not necessarily going to bring them major strategic advantages in relation to the Soviet Union.

Initially the Soviet Union was prepared to accept the basis of the proposal, but still wanted a ban on all underground tests of any magnitude on the Richter scale and on all space tests.[17] A new complication entered the picture in February 1960, however, when France detonated its first nuclear device in North Africa. Efforts were then made to get France to enter discussions on testing, a proposal which was greeted with hostility in Paris where it was regarded as a means of preventing France acquiring an operational warhead. A summit involving France, the UK, the US and the Soviet Union was held in Paris on 16 May 1960. Initially the meeting had been called in an attempt to settle some of the outstanding nuclear testing issues but the shooting down of an American U-2 reconnaissance plane over the Soviet Union on 2 May soured the political climate and the summit failed to produce any results. After this incident the Soviet Union rejected proposals involving OSI, and the CTBT negotiations became stalemated.

As the prospects for a CTBT receded, attention reluctantly moved to the option of negotiating a more limited agreement. At the same time, Macmillan urged the new US President, Kennedy, to make one last effort to secure a comprehensive agreement and to tackle the French problem by offering to transfer to France the nuclear weapon information its government needed. However, it was already clear that while the British saw national benefits flowing from such a test ban agreement, the Americans were now much less enthusiastic than in 1958. Indeed, it was only Macmillan's pressure upon the US that sustained some momentum behind the negotiations after May 1960.

In April 1961, the UK and the US tabled a joint text of a possible test ban treaty. The draft contained a threshold for underground tests and refinements to the control and inspection system, with some elements of OSI. The Soviet Union opposed OSI on principle but was prepared to offer a quota of three inspections a year. The UK and the US proposed an annual quota of between twelve and twenty inspections.[18] The Soviet Union then broke the testing moratorium at the end of August 1961, and the US recommenced testing soon after. Negotiations on a treaty continued, however, and in

September 1961 another joint proposal was tabled by the UK and the US involving a ban limited to atmospheric tests only, to be verified by national technical means (NTM) rather than OSI. This was rejected by the Soviet Union, which at this point was still insisting on a CTBT.[19]

With negotiations between the three nuclear weapon states stalemated, attention moved to the newly established Eighteen Nation Conference on Disarmament (ENDC). In the ENDC several further draft treaties were tabled, but the size of any OSI quota remained a crucial difference between the approaches of the original trilateral negotiating parties. Following the Cuban Missile Crisis in October 1962, it became clear that the Soviet Union and the US were now both prepared to accept a more limited test ban treaty. By 5 August 1963 the text of the Partial Test Ban Treaty (PTBT) had been agreed and was signed in Moscow by the Foreign Ministers of the UK, the US and the Soviet Union. The PTBT[20] banned all nuclear tests except those taking place underground. Verification was to be by NTM, thus overcoming the difficulties associated with OSI.

The aftermath of the PTBT: the UK and a CTBT

The signing of the PTBT was seen as a positive move by the UK, but attitudes towards a CTBT remained somewhat ambiguous because of the tension between three sets of concerns. The first was the question of where nuclear weapons technology would progress in the future and how this would affect the UK's security position. The UK still feared being left behind in the technological arms race which was beginning to develop between the US and the Soviet Union, particularly in the development of nuclear equipped ballistic missile defence systems. To some extent, this fear had been lessened by the December 1962 Nassau Agreement under which the UK purchased the Polaris Submarine Launched Ballistic Missile (SLBM) system from the US. It was further reduced by the realisation that by limiting nuclear testing to underground locations, the PTBT had made it highly unlikely that nuclear armed ABM systems would ever be deployed in large numbers by the Soviet Union. By preventing the systems being tested in the environment in which they had to operate, namely the upper atmosphere and outer space, their effectiveness and reliability could not be accurately calculated. This made it unlikely that governments would make the huge investments necessary for the systems to be deployed operationally. This in turn allowed the UK to deploy a minimal Polaris deterrent force, as it was not necessary to contemplate overwhelming a Soviet national ABM defence system by swamping it with large numbers of missiles. Thus from a security standpoint, given a strong belief in nuclear deterrence, strong support for the PTBT but not a CTBT appeared to be the optimum position.

A second British concern was over the global proliferation of nuclear weapons technology and the challenge to international security and the UK's contemporary global commitments and international position which such dissemination posed. A CTBT was seen to be significant in this context, as such a treaty might prevent additional nuclear weapon states from overtly establishing their technical credentials.

The third concern related to the question of how effective were seismic and other surveillance means in verifying compliance with a possible CTBT, or more specifically in detecting USSR clandestine testing. The key problem here was not the positive question of interpreting the seismic data obtained by the surveillance systems, but the belief that other intelligence means had demonstrated that nuclear tests had been carried out by the USSR which had not been detected by the existing seismic surveillance systems.

By the mid-1960s, the implications of these three concerns pushed UK policy in different directions. On the one hand, the concerns over horizontal nuclear proliferation pointed strongly towards the value for the UK of a CTBT. On the other hand, national security and verification considerations suggested that sustaining the PTBT and not moving towards a CTBT might be the better option.

Once the PTBT had been signed, the US proceeded to conduct a full underground testing programme throughout the rest of the 1960s, with an average of nearly forty explosions per year. The British programme in Nevada was much more modest.[21] British scientists at the Aldermaston Atomic Weapons Research Establishment were working on a warhead for the Polaris A3 missile, using a US design as a guide.[22] Only two British tests were carried out at the Nevada range in 1964 and 1965, before the Wilson government announced a unilateral moratorium on all British nuclear testing, following its decision not to develop any more nuclear warhead designs.[23] Despite this political decision that the UK did not need to engage in further tests, no attempt was made to have the CTBT

negotiations restarted. Instead, political attention was focused first
on the negotiation of the Non-Proliferation Treaty (NPT) and later
the bilateral strategic arms talks. The latter in particular had one
significant impact on British security policy in the mid-1970s: it was
made clear to the British government that any attempt to activate the
Polaris sales agreement to obtain the Poseidon missile as a mid-life
replacement for the Polaris system would not be welcomed by the US
as it would add yet another complication to the SALT 2 negotiations.
Thus any modernisation of the British Polaris system would have to
be done by using the existing missile and fitting a new warhead to it.

Concerns about the degree to which the UK nuclear force was
dependant upon US assistance, and the willingness of the US to offer
that assistance in future, were aggravated by the Eurocentric
approach of the Heath government in the early 1970s. The Heath
government made little effort to cultivate the UK's nuclear relationship with the US. It was not until the Heath government was
nearing the end of its period in office that decisions were taken to
resume nuclear testing in Nevada and to press ahead with modernisation plans for Polaris. The Labour government of Wilson, which
took office in early 1974, soon found itself faced with a situation
where the unilateral action of a US President, anxious to hang on to
office, had constrained its potential freedom to conduct nuclear tests
by concluding a bilateral Threshold Test Ban Treaty (TTBT) with the
Soviet Union which limited underground nuclear explosions to 150
kilotons. This agreement was allied to a treaty on Peaceful Nuclear
Explosions (PNEs) which was eventually signed in 1976.[24]

The CTBT and the Callaghan years

The second round of active CTBT negotiations was triggered by the
election of President Carter in the US. For the Carter administration,
arms limitation negotiations were a high priority and a CTBT consequently became a major policy commitment. After an initial bilateral
meeting between the US and the Soviet Union on the issue, the UK,
then under the Callaghan government, was invited to participate in a
Trilateral Conference on the subject in Geneva in October 1977. The
results of this meeting were then reported to the Conference of the
Committee on Disarmament, the United Nations forerunner of the
Conference on Disarmament.

Two problem areas dominated the negotiations and the internal national discussions supporting them: verification of a CTBT and the impact such a treaty would have on the reliability of nuclear stockpiles. In the area of verification, which formed the core of the negotiations, at issue was not so much the form and content of the CTBT but of the ancillary document, the Separate Verification Agreement (SVA), that would govern the verification system exclusive to the nuclear weapon states.[25] Prospects for an agreement on this appeared favourable as improvements in seismic detection techniques offered some hope that OSI would be of less significance than in the earlier negotiations. Furthermore, the bilateral PNE Treaty had involved the Soviet Union agreeing to a limited form of OSI and it was thought that this might provide the basis for an agreement.

Nevertheless, the US feared that a potential to cheat still existed if weapons were exploded in porous rock which would reduce the seismic signal, or by 'decoupling' an explosion by conducting it in an over-sized cavity.[26] To safeguard against these possibilities, the US demanded stringent verification provisions. It was agreed that ten tamper-proof remote seismic stations would be established on the territories of both the Soviet Union and the US, to monitor all earth movements.[27] These 'black boxes' could then relay data to the other nuclear weapon states, to supplement an International Data Exchange which would disseminate globally information gathered from other seismic sources. In addition, the US and the Soviet Union would use their national satellite capabilities to monitor compliance with the treaty and an understanding was reached in principle that OSI of the sites of suspect events would be implemented on a voluntary, rather than mandatory, basis.

Initially the trilateral negotiations appeared to be moving rapidly toward a successful conclusion. John Edmonds, the British Ambassador to the negotiations, has stated that an agreement had been reached with the Soviets 'on the greater part of a draft CTB Treaty.'[28] Herbert York, the chief negotiator on the American side, has also argued that by January 1979 the basic framework for an agreement was in place.[29] This positive assessment was based on four elements: that remote seismic stations, transmitting data back to the other nuclear weapon states, would be established in the territories of the three negotiating parties; in cases of a suspicious seismological event provision was to be made for OSI; the treaty itself was to be of a fixed duration of three to five years and a conference would be convened at the end of the period to decide whether it would be extended (which might depend on the positions of China and France at that time); and that peaceful nuclear explosions would be banned.[30]

This seemed to be the foundation for a workable agreement and David Owen, the British Foreign Secretary of the period, has similarly since stated that a treaty was within the grasp of the three states.[31] However, a basic difference of approach remained over whether the verification system was to be designed to provide assurance that the treaty was being complied with, or was to be based on the assumption that somebody would cheat unless all breaches could be detected with near certainty. The Soviet Union then made a demand that the UK should also have ten national remote seismic stations on its territory (the same number as both the US and Soviet Union were to have). The rationale for this puzzled both the UK and the US, and was interpreted by some as a bid to remove the UK from the negotiations. The Soviet Union further suggested that the ten stations should be sited at Eskdalemuir, Scotland; Aldabra Island; Brunei, Borneo; Tarawa Island; Pitcairn Island; Malden Island; Port Stanley, Falkland Islands; Egmont Island; Belize; and Hong Kong,[32] which further confused the British delegation, as some were no longer British sovereign territory.

In January 1979 the British cabinet rejected the Soviet proposal for the UK to have ten such stations, as well as their locations, on the grounds both of cost and irrelevancy, given that the British tests were known to be conducted in Nevada. In response the UK proposed that only one station at Eskdalemuir be based on British territory and the ratio for stations be 10–10–1, not 10–10–10. The Soviet Union would not accept such a minimal figure on the part of the UK and the negotiations became stalled on this issue.

While the trilateral discussions on verification had been proceeding, considerable debate had been taking place between the US and British nuclear weapon and political establishments over whether a CTBT was actually desirable and in their mutual political and security interests. The UK weapon designers had discovered to their dismay that the nuclear device they had exploded in 1974, which ended the nine year unilateral testing moratorium, had not functioned as had been expected. As a result it had been necessary to conduct a series of further tests before the design for the new warhead to go into the Polaris mid-life modernisation system, Chevaline, could be validated.[33] This led many of those working on this programme to the view that any further testing ban was likely to lead to similar problems in sustaining knowledge of nuclear weapons. This would in turn rule out the design and deployment of any new weapon designs, such as those that might be needed for a Polaris replacement programme or the modernisation of the British stockpile of gravity bombs.

Concerns over the future reliability of the British nuclear stockpile were heightened by studies undertaken to pinpoint areas where unreliability might occur and what could be done to tackle it in the absence of nuclear testing. In the main the concern was over metallurgical problems in the fissile core of weapons. Two solutions were investigated: re-manufacturing the weapon; and manufacturing an American design which could act as a substitute in the UK. The first was found to be inadequate as the British weapon specifications and manufacturing techniques had not been recorded in sufficient detail to give confidence that the re-manufactured weapon was identical to the original. The second was rejected when it was discovered that British manufacturing facilities, among other things, were not capable of reproducing the American weapon design in a manner which would assure that it was a replica of the original. There were various reasons for these concerns and the subsequent lack of solutions: the UK having manufactured its weapon grade plutonium through to 1964 to a different isotopic composition to that used by the US; the consequent uncertainties over its impact upon the existing British designs as its isotopic composition changed with age; and the effect of using it in a replica of an American design without any proof via testing. They were also restricted in having only one British weapon design in service, which meant that if that design was to become technically suspect the UK's deterrent capability would be thrown into doubt. By comparision, the other nuclear states, which had a number of different warheads in service, did not face the same problem.

These concerns and the subsequent lack of solutions resulted form several factors. The fundamental difficulty was that through to 1964 the UK manufactured its weapon grade plutonium to a different isotopic composition to that used by the US. This in turn meant that there were uncertainties over the impact upon existing British designs of the differing rates of change in isotopic composition as the fissile material aged. There was also the added difficulty of using it in a replica of an American design without any assurance of its reliability via testing.[34] The pressure that was placed on the Carter administration by those lobby groups in the US who regarded nuclear testing as essential to sustain US nuclear deterrent capabilities helps to account for the decision to reduce progressively the proposed duration of the draft agreement to five years and then to three years, and then to give negotiation and ratification of a SALT II agreement priority over a CTBT.

Although a draft text of a CTBT was in existence by the end of the second active period of trilateral negotiations, it merely served to highlight the sticking points over verification and duration on which the sides were far apart. Before the conference could be reconvened to attempt to narrow the differences and further elaborate the verification system, it fell victim to the general decline in East–West relations that occurred at the end of the Carter administration with the failure of Congress to ratify SALT II and the invasion of Afghanistan in 1979. Although a report was made to the United Nations Committee on Disarmament in Geneva in June 1980 stating that significant progress had been made in the search for a CTBT, the political momentum had by then been lost and the trilateral forum was never reconvened once the Reagan administration, which was openly hostile to any imminent CTBT, achieved power.

British policy towards these negotiations had thus been confronted with a basic dilemma: between giving priority to the national security requirements alluded to above; or foregoing such considerations by giving precedence to other national objectives, such as enhancing nuclear non-proliferation strategies and constraining further technological advancements. This basic dilemma is illustrated by a statement made by the then British Foreign Secretary David Owen, which continues to be salient:

What one is after in a comprehensive test ban is to try to persuade those countries which are on the threshold of becoming nuclear states not to cross that threshold. They wish to be convinced that the nuclear weapon states are themselves contributing to disarmament and that it is not merely a one-way process. We should not always ask the non-nuclear weapon states to exercise restraint while we, the nuclear weapons states, continue to test an increasingly sophisticated range of weapon systems.[35]

British attitudes towards a test ban: the Thatcher years

The UK, under Prime Minister Thatcher, has stated that a CTBT is a long-term goal but that present conditions do not favour a treaty. Over the last decade, the UK has placed less emphasis on the desirability of arms control for the positive influence it might exert on East–West relations and voiced more concern for the possible security risks involved. The justifications for the UK's hesitant approach are those that have been consistently in the background of British policy towards a test ban since the 1950s: the need for an effective verification system; the desire to maintain the UK's international position; the necessity of nuclear testing; and the considerations stemming from the UK's alliance with the US.

In particular, the Thatcher government has made it clear that it believes that nuclear deterrence, especially an independent British deterrent force, will remain the guarantor of security. This of necessity requires continuing nuclear tests. David Mellor, explaining the UK's policy to Parliament in June 1988, said:

For the foreseeable future the UK's security will depend, in part, on the possession of nuclear weapons. That will mean a continuing requirement to conduct underground nuclear tests to ensure that our nuclear weapons remain effective and up to date ...[36]

In addition, new weapon designs are being developed for the UK inventory and this requires continued testing. These include the warhead for the UK's Trident D-5 missiles, though this has already been proven, and for the Tactical Air-to-Surface Missile (TASM) that will replace the gravity bombs. All of these nuclear warhead programmes, and the dependencies upon the US created by the Trident programme, have encouraged the UK to co-ordinate its arms control position with the US.

Until very recently, the UK has rested its case for not proceeding with CTBT negotiations on the grounds that such a treaty could not be adequately verified. The UK argues that it does not have sufficient confidence in existing monitoring capabilities to sign such a treaty.[37] The UK's position has been that seismic signals from explosions can be confused with earthquakes and that low-yield nuclear detonations are indistinguishable from large conventional explosions. Soviet officials by contrast have consistently maintained that a treaty would be verifiable. Scientific opinion varies on this. Charles Archambeau has argued that a network of seismic arrays on the territory of the Soviet Union could be expected to detect explosions down to a very low level but could not detect all tests.[38] The key issue then becomes whether very low yield tests would have any value and thus be worth risking. At this point it is clear that verification has become a political rather than a technical issue. This was recognised in 1988 when the UK moved its position on a CTBT towards that already taken by the US, by making it clear that the main reason for not proceeding with a CTBT were its own security interests.

Although the UK has only committed itself to seek a CTBT in the long term, there are a number of pressures on the British government to move forward more quickly in this area. These pressures originate from two sources: first, existing treaty commitments to progress on a test ban, such as those contained in the NPT; and second, encouragement from other disarmament agencies. In the first category, vociferous calls by the non-nuclear weapon states (NNWS) in the NPT for advancement on the CTBT have been mounting and adding to further tensions over the treaty. The UK has also announced that the requisite number of signatories to the PTBT have requested an amendment conference to demand progress towards a CTBT. In the second category, other disarmament agencies around the world have sought to encourage further nuclear testing restrictions from the UK and the other nuclear weapon states (NWS); most notably the Third United Nations Special Session on Disarmament in 1987 and the Forty Nation Conference on Disarmament in Geneva. It is clear that the NNWS have no intention of letting the UK, and the other NWS, neglect what they perceive to be their treaty obligations.

There has also been activity between the US and the Soviet Union in connection with a test ban which has taken place without the apparent participation of the UK. In August 1985, the newly-appointed leader of the Soviet Union, Mikhail Gorbachev, announced that his country would observe a nuclear test moratorium and he called on the US and the UK to follow suit. The Reagan administration declared that such a moratorium would be unverifiable and resisted the Soviet initiative. The US was supported in the response by the Thatcher government and in the absence of any Western response to the initiative, the Soviet Union resumed testing in February 1987.

Bilateral talks on testing had started in 1986, however, with the US arguing for an incremental approach of proving the technology to verify the yields of tests by non-intrusive means, and then amending the TTBT to reduce yields. In August 1988, Joint Verification Experiments (JVEs) were conducted at Semipalatinsk in the Soviet

Union and at Nevada in the US. These experiments were designed to compare and improve verification techniques in order to build up the confidence necessary for the US Congress to ratify the 1974 Treaty and move to lower threshold figures. Some progress was achieved in this area, but not enough for the Reagan administration to recommend to Congress that the TTBT and the PNET be ratified.

For the Bush administration, the primary focus has been to emphasise the need for an agreement on conventional forces in Europe before moving on to further nuclear arms control. In this context a CTBT will undoubtedly receive a low priority on the arms control agenda. This is a situation which the UK government is quite happy to live with, as it will allow UK nuclear security concerns to be fully safeguarded.

Summary and conclusions: the British approach to a CTBT

The negotiations to achieve a CTBT, like all nuclear arms control talks, have depended for their success on the existence of mutual agreement between the superpowers on its desirability. While the UK has remained at the margins of the negotiations between the superpowers on reducing nuclear missile delivery systems, it has taken a direct role in the negotiations on a CTBT by virtue of its status as a nuclear weapon state. In theory, the UK could pursue three possible options in CTBT negotiations: refusing to go along with a US–Soviet agreement and seeking to block it; allying its position with one of the two superpowers; or attempting to act as a mediator and 'Honest Broker'. In practice, however, its public position during the periods of negotiation has been a combination of the second and third of these options: to attempt to facilitate a successful outcome of the talks while remaining firmly allied to the US negotiating position towards them.

In the Macmillan period, during the first period of active trilateral negotiations, the UK sought to achieve a CTBT because it was seen as a means of consolidating its international position, both with regard to the superpowers and potential proliferators. There was little recognition at that time of its impact upon the reliability of the British nuclear stockpile, which was in any event being continuously re-manufactured. A CTBT would have had the effect of maintaining the UK's position as a major power within the international system: politically via its role in negotiating an agreement and militarily by ensuring that it was not outpaced by the US and the Soviet Union in technological developments. In addition, the singularity with which the UK argued for a treaty, even when the initial US enthusiasm had waned, was a direct result of Macmillan's commitment to the project once he had been assured that it would not deny the UK's access to US nuclear technology.

Support for a CTBT has varied widely among later British governments, depending upon the state of British plans for nuclear modernisation and confidence in the reliability of the British nuclear stockpile. During the Callaghan government, the UK was again involved in active test ban negotiations. The UK's support was predicated then, not on an assessment that a test ban would pose no serious threat to its nuclear deterrent, but on a political judgement that the wider international advantages that would flow from it were worth any perceived risks to British security.

Under the Thatcher government there has been an almost open hostility towards the idea of a test ban, couched in terms of such a treaty being a 'long-term objective'. The prospects of signing a CTBT in the near future remains remote as long as the UK and the US take the view that 'we still lack the technical confidence to ensure that nuclear test at a militarily significant level could be detected and identified'.[39] But above all, a nuclear disarmed world is now regarded as a remote possibility and the necessity to sustain those national deterrent forces now in existence is openly acknowledged in this context as a top priority.

The tensions between national security policy, non-proliferation policy, Alliance considerations and verification requirements, which have underpinned much of the British approach to the CTBT negotiations, still persist. As British policy has evolved, the tendency has increasingly been to give priority to safeguarding the ability to test to ensure the credibility of the UK's nuclear deterrent force and not to hide behind verification arguments as a justification for not favouring an immediate CTBT. At some point in the future, however, the need to take technical risks with the nuclear deterrent force to gain non-proliferation benefits may once more have to be faced and the British government will then have to decide where its long-term security interests lie. The UK increasingly has an incentive to restrict new technical developments to a minimum, such as third generation nuclear systems, and to prevent the further spread of nuclear weapons around the globe. These issues will undoubtedly become more acute in the 1990s. Faced with such an international environment, a CTBT may yet provide a viable policy option for the UK.

Notes

1   H. Macmillan, *Riding the Storm, 1956–1959*, Macmillan, London, 1971, p. 300.

2   The challenge to British strategic programmes of a fissile cut-off had been foreseen the previous year in a Joint Chiefs of Staff document, 'From our point of view this is a dangerous situation as it might well prevent our achieving an adequate stockpile of hydrogen bombs, for whereas the Americans have a stockpile of material from which they could continue to make bombs, we have not.' DEFE 5 (66) COS (56) 101, 8 March 1956.

3   DEFE 4/105 JP (58) 26 (Final), 6 March 1958.

4   For a more detailed study see W. Rees, 'Brothers in Arms: Anglo–American Defence Cooperation in 1957' in T. Gorst, L. Johnman and W. Lucas (eds.), *Postwar Britain 1945–1964: Themes and Perspectives*, Pinter Publishers, London, 1989, pp. 203–20.

5   Macmillan, *op.cit.*, p. 461.

6   T. Botti, *The Long Wait: The Forging of the Anglo–American Nuclear Alliance, 1945–1958*, Greenwood Press, New York, 1987, pp. 213–28.

7   Report of the Conference of Experts to Study the Methods of Detecting Violations of a Possible Agreement on the Suspension of Nuclear Tests, *Cmnd. 551*, HMSO, London, October 1958.

8   'The Conference of Experts, having considered a control system for detecting violations of a possible agreement on the suspension of nuclear tests, has come to the conclusion that the methods for detecting nuclear explosions available at the present time, namely, the method of collecting samples of radioactive debris, the methods of recording seismic, acoustic and hydro-acoustic waves, and the radio-signal method, along with the use of on-site inspection of unidentified events which could be suspected of being nuclear explosions, make it possible to detect and identify nuclear explosions, including low yield explosions (1 to 5 kilotons). The Conference has therefore come to the conclusion that it is technically feasible to establish ... a workable and effective control system to detect violation of an agreement on the world-wide suspension of nuclear weapons tests.'

9   *Geneva Conference on the Discontinuities of Nuclear Weapons Test: History and Analysis of Negotiations*, Department of State Publication 7258, Washington, DC, 1961, p. 31.

10   *Seismic Verification*, Department of External Affairs, Canada, 1986, p. 28.

11   R. Mason, 'Nuclear Weapons: Non-Proliferation, Technologies and Test Ban Treaties', *Disarmament*, XII, p. 36. See also *Hansard*, 27 April 1959, cols. 898–1028 for details of the then British approach to the Test Ban Conference.

12   See statement by Selwyn Lloyd, the then Secretary of State for

Foreign Affairs, *Hansard*, 27 April 1959, col. 899.

13   *ibid.*

14   *ibid.*, cols. 899–900.

15   *ibid.* For further details of the OSI debate, especially for the US position see, *Geneva Conference on the Discontinuance of Nuclear Weapon Tests*, Department of State Publication 7258, Washington, DC, 1961.

16   H. Macmillan, *At the End of the Day, 1961–1963*, Macmillan, London, 1973, p. 173.

17   W. Waldegrave, 'The Partial Test-Ban Treaty: A British View', *Disarmament*, XII, p. 3.

18   Fetter, *op.cit.*, p. 6.

19   Waldegrave, *op.cit.*, p. 4.

20   For the text of the PTBT see J. Goldblat, *Arms Control Agreements: A Handbook*, Taylor & Francis for SIPRI, London, 1983, pp. 142–3.

21   'Nuclear Notebook', *The Bulletin of the Atomic Scientist*, April 1989, p. 48.

22   J. Simpson, *The Independent Nuclear State: the US, Britain, and the Military Atom*, 2nd ed., Macmillan, London, 1986, p. 167.

23   'Nuclear Notebook', *op.cit.* The moratorium lasted from 1965 through to 1974. Little attempt was made to pressure the other nuclear weapon states to follow suit.

24   It should be noted, however, that at time of writing neither of these treaties (which limit underground explosions to 150 kilotons) have been ratified by the US Congress, although both parties (and the UK) have conformed to the threshold limit.

25   H. York, *Making Weapons Talking Peace*, Basic Books, New York, 1987, p. 301.

26   S. Fetter, *Towards a Comprehensive Test Ban*, Ballinger Publishing Co., Cambridge, MA, 1988, p. 114.

27   J. Goldblat, 'What it Would Take to Ban Testing', *Bulletin of the Atomic Scientists*, October 1988, pp. 25–7.

28   J. Edmonds, 'Proliferation and Test Bans' in J. Howe (ed.), *Armed Peace: The Search for World Security*, Macmillan, London, 1984, p. 78.

29   York, *op.cit.*, p. 302.

30   *ibid.*

31   'Luce Calls for N-Test Moratorium', *Guardian*, 30 August 1985.

32   York, *op.cit.*, p. 306.

33   *ibid.*, p. 312.

34   The necessity to test weapons to prove that their performance has not been degraded has recently been questioned. See 'Evidence Supporting Nuclear Tests is Challenged', *The New York Times*, 20 June 1988, p. 17.

35   *Hansard*, Vol. 960 , 17 January 1979, cols. 1692–3.

36   D. Mellor, 'Nuclear Weapons', *Hansard*, Written Answers, House of Commons, 27 June 1988. See also statement by William Waldegrave, Minister of State at the Foreign and Commonwealth Office, at the Conference on Disarmament in Geneva on 15 June 1989. For text see *Quarterly Review*, No. 14, Arms Control and Disarmament Research Unit, Foreign and Commonwealth Office, London, July 1989.

37   'Luce Calls for N-Test Moratorium', *Guardian*, 30 August 1985.
38   C. Archambeau, 'Verification of a Low-Yield Nuclear Test Ban' in J. Goldblat and D. Cox (eds.), *Nuclear Weapons Tests: Prohibition or Limitation?*, Oxford University Press for SIPRI, Oxford, 1988, pp. 273–96.
39   T. Renton MP, 'Britain's Approach to Arms Control', *Contemporary Review*, February 1987, p. 69.

UK arms control and disarmament policy on chemical and biological weapons[1]

Introduction

The UK is ostensibly committed, '... to the objective of General and Complete Disarmament (GCD) under strict and effective international control.'[2] To this end, the UK has been a signatory to the major multilateral treaties which have been negotiated in recent years. These include: the Partial Test Ban Treaty (PTBT); the Treaty on the Non-Proliferation of Nuclear Weapons (NPT); the Biological Weapons Convention (BWC); the Environmental Modification Convention (ENMOD); and area treaties, like those banning the placement of weapons of mass destruction in Outer Space and on the Seabed. One of the glaring omissions in this list of multilateral treaties is one which effectively bans chemical weapons (CW) from the military arsenals of the world.

There have recently been some rather gloomy prognostications that the world is currently on the verge of a CW arms race, both horizontally and vertically.[3] It is argued that in some quarters CW are rapidly becoming seen as the 'poor man's atomic bomb', thus prompting horizontal proliferation.[4] Both the US and the Soviet Union are also said to be in the process of improving their own CW capabilities, thus creating a pressure for vertical proliferation.[5] Added to this, there is conclusive evidence of their recent use in warfare in the Iran–Iraq war,[6] and some less conclusive evidence of their reported use in conflicts elsewhere.[7] This disquieting situation suggests that the problem of chemical and biological warefare (CBW) is now a more pressing issue than it was ten years ago.

At the declaratory level, the central objectives of current UK CBW policy are the clarification and strengthening of the 1925 Geneva Protocol and the successful conclusion of a treaty banning CW to supplement the treaty which banned BW in 1972.[8] These objectives have formed the backbone of the UK's CBW policy, irrespective of changes in government and changes in the status of CBW in the doctrines of the world's military forces.[9] The UK's policy on CBW[10] and, more specifically, its approach to CW and BW arms control and disarmament is interesting for several reasons, not the least of which is that the UK is one of the few countries to have had an offensive CW stockpile and to have then disarmed it.[11] How this policy evolved, and how the UK has since dealt with its disarmed status, therefore provide the major themes for discussion. This, in turn, leads to an assessment of whether UK policy on CW can be seen as a catalyst or retarder[12] in the effort to negotiate a multilateral chemical weapons treaty. Is the UK a 'model' disarmed CBW state in the sense that it has no offensive CBW capability? Or was the UK's decision to abandon its CW capability predicated on the grounds that a more potent security guarantor was available to it in its possession of nuclear weapons? If a CWT was negotiated would those states denied a CW capability search for alternative sources of security in the form of nuclear weapons?

The development of CBW policy in the 1950s[13]

It is officially stated that the UK stopped production of CW in 1956.[14] This policy was not initiated because of universal considerations but because of factors which were specific to the UK at the time. While moral objections to CW may well have influenced the UK decision to disarm, other less noble arguments seem to account for the decision. Sterling Seagrave, for example, suggests that the UK's decision to disarm can be traced to '... economic reasons as [the UK] retrenched from empire and struggled to find a new national identity'.[15] A similar explanation is also advanced by Robert Harris and Jeremy Paxman who argue that the UK's decision, '... although largely based on economic considerations, came to be seen as a moral gesture. This decision, in later years vaunted as an example of the moral courage of the nation, was, at best, a half truth.'[16] This explanation appears more salient when other factors are also considered. The UK's unilateral action, for it was dependent on no reciprocal action by any other state or by adherence to an arms control treaty, coincides with the early stages of the UK nuclear weapons programme. This was a costly programme at a time when financial reserves were already stretched by the UK's wide-ranging defence commitments. Between 1952 and 1954, in particular, subsequent economic crises in the UK necessitated a very hard look at ways in which these burdensome defence commitments could be reduced. Papers released in the PRO indicate that the pragmatics of balancing the budgetary books were a major guiding principle in defence planning circles at this time.[17] It would seem, therefore, that the UK made a decision to scrap its offensive CW arsenal (the maintenance and improvements of which at this time would also have been costly), in favour of channelling more resources into the on-going nuclear weapons and other defence-related development programmes. This assessment becomes more compelling when other, predominantly military considerations regarding the UK's CBW policy, are seen within the context of the UK's wider defence and security policy debate in the 1940s and 1950s.

Towards the end of the war, UK military thinking emphasised the disadvantages of CBW.[18] Concern was expressed about the negative effects associated with the preparation for such forms of warfare, particularly on the morale of the military forces.[19] There was a further concern about the labour intensity required in the manufacture of CW and BW.[20] There were also doubts about the military effectiveness of CBW in various theatres of war.[21] Given the debatable military utility of CBW and problems in the preparation for engaging in such forms of warfare, it was argued that the emphasis should be placed on defensive rather than offensive capabilities.

Some of the basic assumptions in this analysis carried over into peacetime thinking, but it was not the final word. Under the chairmanship of Sir Henry Tizard, a committee met between January–July 1946 to discuss the UK's immediate post-war strategic planning priorities. Known as the Tizard Report, the findings of this committee saw BW as having certain distinct advantages, particularly against specific targets in the Soviet Union:

The tremendous destructive power of the atomic bomb and the devastating effects against live targets expected from biological weapons, which can be produced with relatively small effort in terms of manpower on the part of the attacker, lead us to infer that the most profitable objects of attack by the new weapons will normally be concentrations of populations, centres of distribution and communication.[22]

But in 1946 the UK did not possess an atomic capability, whereas it was in a position to develop BW on a large-scale if necessary.

By the mid-1950s, however, the UK was well on the way to

developing an atomic stockpile and the arguments in favour of nuclear deterrent strategies and the rationales which underpin them were then beginning to be accepted in the West as a means of war prevention. But it was war prevention at a number of different levels, not just at the nuclear.[23] The upshot of this argument was that nuclear weapons provided the best possible method for deterring all forms of war, from the conventional right through to the nuclear (including, also, a CBW attack). If a state was in possession of a nuclear weapons capability, an offensive CW capability might thus be considered superfluous. It might also be seen as destabilising, as a CBW capability might serve to lower the nuclear threshold. As weapons of mass destruction CBW might not be regarded as analogous to nuclear weapons.[24] Conversely, they might also be considered to be more potent than conventional weapons. Viewed from this perspective, chemical weapons represent an intermediate step between conventional and nuclear weapons. By removing CBW altogether a 'fire-break' between conventional and nuclear weapons would therefore be established.

The relationship between CBW and nuclear capabilities was clearly a factor in early post-war UK decision-making. In 1954, for example, one strategic assessment concluded that: 'While the Soviet Union may well be capable of initiating biological and chemical warfare, it seems very unlikely that they will do so as long as they have nuclear weapons at their disposal.'[25] One of the first public pronouncements in the UK of this relationship was made by Denis Healey in a statement to Parliament in 1970. The then UK Defence Secretary stated that:

NATO as a whole has chemical weapons available to it because the US maintains an offensive chemical capability. However, I believe that both the former and the present government in Britain were right not to stockpile offensive chemical weapons in the UK. If the House really considers the situation, I believe that it will recognize that it is almost inconceivable that enemy forces would use chemical weapons against NATO forces except in circumstances of a mass invasion in which event even more terrible weapons would surely come into play.[26]

When taken together, the arguments outlined above provide a compelling explanation of the UK's decision to eventually dispense with its offensive CBW capability: faced with the uncertainties of the retreat from empire; the growing costs of a huge defence commitment; the availability to the UK of nuclear weapons; and the negative effects associated with such forms of warfare, the UK decided that there was little or no place for CBW in its future strategic planning priorities. In relation to the CW decision in particular, the UK dismantled its remaining offensive CW stockpile, together with much of its supporting infrastructure. Once the process of dismantling was complete the UK was left with only a residual CW capability, deemed necessary for defensive purposes. But just how residual and for what purposes it has been designed to serve has been a topic of some speculation and dispute.

The UK's residual CBW infrastructure

The only establishment in the UK currently dealing with CBW is the Chemical Defence Experimental Establishment (CDEE) at Porton Down in Wiltshire (founded in 1916 in the midst of the First World War).[27] The Ministry of Defence (MoD) acknowledges that research into CBW does take place at Porton Down. The official statement is that this research is conducted for defensive purposes only. This was elaborated in *A Report of the Select Committee on Science and Technology* of May 6, 1968. The Report outlined the work of the military experimental officers based at Porton Down as being:

... to represent and interpret in detail the functional requirements of their service's equipment in the CW defence field and to inform and advise their service of technological advances in these fields which can influence policy and functional requirements for equipment.[28]

This justification has been challenged by Harris and Paxman, however, who claim the distinction made by the MoD between 'defensive' and 'offensive' research is not so clear cut:

This distinction, critical to the preservation of a 'respectable' image for chemical warfare research, was ... meaningless, since Porton Down was actively developing new weapons for the British army based onNazi nerve gases ... The Weapons Unit at Porton Down was dominated by attempts to develop new methods of delivering GB nerve gas to an enemy. They tested dozens of possible weapons – mortar bombs, artillery shells, aircraft bombs ...[29]

Until very recently little was publicly known about the extent of past and present UK CW capabilities. This had fuelled much speculation regarding the UK's CW activities, as the above quotation from Harris and Paxman's book indicates. However, in a surprisingly forthright UK working paper, presented in the context of the forum discussing CW arms control and disarmament in Geneva, extensive details of the UK's wartime and post-war CW capabilities have been made publicly available.

The paper states that during the Second World War approximately 60,000 tons of CW agents were manufactured – of which about two thirds was mustard gas.[30] It further states that in the years after the war ended this agent was disposed of by dumping at sea.[31] The factories used in the production of these agents were also made inoperative.[32]

In 1950 a pilot plant was established at Nancekuke in Cornwall. Utilising the research work which had been conducted at the Sutton Oak Research Establishment, the Nancekuke plant was used to study 'the feasibility of producing the nerve agent GB'.[33] The principal objectives of this pilot programme were to, '... establish data for the design of a larger scale production facility (fifty tons/week) ... and to study the storage stability of the bulk agent'.[34]

Between January 1954 and January 1956, the Nancekuke plant produced a total of twenty tons of GB. This agent was then stored for a further ten years after which time it was ascertained that the agent had an approximate storage stability period of twenty years. Once this research was completed the agent was then destroyed, except for the small quantities transferred to Porton Down for further research. From 1956 the Nancekuke plant was used only for research purposes and was eventually dismantled in 1976.[35]

As far as the actual production of weapons was concerned the paper stated: 'Although an experimental weapon charging facility to handle 25 pounder shells was installed it was only trialled with stimulants. No weapons were charged with GB or any other nerve agent'.[36]

The larger plant which would have enabled the UK to go into the full-scale production of the nerve agent was never built. However, the pilot programme had ascertained that the UK was able to go into full production if the case arose. Once this had been established to the satisfaction of the MoD the UK never resorted to that option, probably because of the economic and strategic arguments outlined earlier. This being the case, the UK's decision to get out of the CW field becomes rather more a decision not to go into production than a decision to disarm *per se*, although the end result is the same.[37] At the contingency level, the UK had established that the resumption of offensive CW production could be achieved at short notice. And given the UK's large industrial chemicals industry, which would be capable of producing a make-shift CW capability, this was clearly deemed sufficient. But if the UK were seriously to consider embarking on a large-scale programme of CW rearmament today there can be little doubt that sizeable resources would have to be spent on the construction of a new CW production plant to accommodate this programme (such as the one the US has recently constructed at Pine Bluff, Arkansas, for its binary CW programme). However, there would appear to be no plans for any such contingency in the UK at the present time.

Thus, the UK can be considered a 'model' disarmed CW state. But this situation raises another interesting set of questions concerning how the non-possession of an offensive CW capability has affected the UK's policy and, more especially, its bargaining ability in the CBW arms control and disarmament talks themselves?[38]

UK CBW arms control and disarmament policy from 1968 onwards

It was not until the NPT was opened for signature in 1968 that the search for a CBW ban was really begun in earnest. With nuclear weapons seemingly brought under the umbrella of multilateral control, the way was open for a similar concerted effort to reach an agreement on CBW. UK policy initiatives were instrumental in providing much of the foundation which underpinned the CBW arms control and disarmament talks in these early stages.

The main thrust of the UK's position was presented to the Eighteen Nation Disarmament Conference (ENDC) in 1968. It argued that the current international law on CBW was inadequate and needed further clarification and strengthening.[39] Two methods of doing this were suggested: one was to update the Geneva Protocol; the other was to keep the Protocol as it stood, and further supplement it by negotiating additional agreements. The UK made it quite clear that it preferred the latter course of action.[40]

There are several reasons why the UK pressed for this course of action. The first relates to the Anglo–American 'special relationship'. At the time, the US was not party to the Geneva Protocol (as it had not been ratified by Congress) and was also heavily embroiled in the Vietnam war where it was using certain types of herbicide and riot control agents. The UK may have pressed for the second option so as not to draw too much attention to US policy.[41]

A second reason was a recognition by the UK of the difficulties entailed in updating the Geneva Protocols. Given the ambiguity of the Geneva Protocols and that CBW issues touch on the highly sensitive area of each individual state's national security, the UK deemed it unlikely that an effort at updating the Protocols would have been an avenue for successful negotiations. The UK argued at the ENDC discussions that the problems of advancing restraints on CBW could be made 'less intractable by considering chemical and microbiological methods of warfare separately.'[42] The UK went on to outline the requirements for a BW treaty which was designed to be the first step towards strengthening the international law on CBW. This treaty, the UK argued, was intended to, '... supplement but not supersede the 1925 Geneva Protocol.'[43]

The UK recommendation to separate chemical from biological weapons clearly had its routes in the annals of military history. CW had a well-documented history of use in war. BW has always tended to have rather dubious military utility because they can have very long-term and very unpredictable effects. For these reasons there has long been a traditional reluctance on the part of military forces to engage in any form of biological warfare.[44] This being the case, the UK argued that because CW had become an everyday part of military training and life, the chances were that governments would show considerable reluctance (due to the difficulties associated with verification, especially in relation to the global chemical industry) when it came down to negotiating their removal. On the other hand, BW were not at that time regarded as significant in military terms and posed fewer problems for verification. This meant that there would probably be less reluctance to negotiate them away. Thus the UK position was that a piecemeal approach, dealing with BW first and leaving CW for later negotiation, would be the most propitious way for the negotiations to proceed.

Many of the UK's NATO allies were not overly convinced of the wisdom of this approach, preferring instead to press for a ban on chemical and biological weapons to be negotiated jointly. However, the most vehement objections came from the Soviet Union and several of the non-aligned countries. The USSR, especially, was deeply suspicious of the UK's motives for suggesting the split. Thus, for a time it looked as though the piecemeal approach would be rejected.

The UK position also included several other interesting

suggestions. The working paper of 1968 suggested the establishment of an international inspectorate to be responsible for monitoring compliance to the treaty.[45] It would be established under the auspices of the United Nations' and 'investigate allegations made by a party to the Convention which appeared to establish a *prima facie* case that another party had acted in breach of the obligations established in the Convention'.[46] In the Draft BWC, tabled by the UK in 1969, provision was made for the United Nations Secretary-General to investigate allegations of breach of the Convention and for a report to be placed before the Security Council.[47] The UK's Draft Convention prohibited future research on offensive biological weapons and would have required signatory states to renounce the use of such weapons.

The tabling of the UK's draft convention on biological warfare (BWC) in August 1969[48] had a profound affect in the US where pressure was mounting on the Nixon administration to clarify its CBW policy. The impact was such that in 1969 the US administration announced that it was going to unilaterally disarm its BW stockpile. President Nixon stated that the US CBW policy would in future: renounce the first use of lethal weapons and incapacitating agents; renounce the use of lethal biological agents and biological warfare; engage only in defensive biological research and develop recommendations for the disposal of existing stocks of bacteriological weapons.[49] Just as significantly, the US stated that it would accept the UK's proposal for a piecemeal approach to BW and CW as well as the suggestion of dealing with the former category first.[50]

Soviet opposition to the now combined UK–US negotiating stance lasted until Spring 1971 when the Soviet Union eventually accepted the proposal for separate treatment of the two types of weapon.[51] Once CBW disarmament became a firm fixture on the international agenda, events moved quickly. Late in 1971 the US and USSR presented their own draft of a BWC. But this particular Draft Convention did not meet with the full approval of the UK. As Elisa Harris has observed:

British concerns about the US–Soviet draft treaty centred on three issues, the absence of a ban on offensive biological weapons research, the absence of an explicit renunciation of the use of biological and toxin weapons, and the absence of authority for the UN Secretary General to investigate allegations of such use.[52]

In particular, the UK was concerned that the joint US–Soviet formula represented a 'watered-down' version of the provisions contained within in its own Draft regarding future research and verification procedures.[53] But these objections were to no avail. On 10 April, 1972, the *Convention on the Prohibition of the Development, Production and Stockpiling of Bacteriological (biological) and Toxin Weapons (BWC)*, based largely on the US–Soviet draft treaty, was opened for signature and eventually came into force on 26 March, 1975.[54] Up to this juncture at least, the UK's argument for the piecemeal approach would appear to have met with considerable success. However, it was not until the CW talks got underway that it soon became evident that the real problems were only just beginning.

The real focus of attention in the CW talks has been the policies pursued by the US and the Soviet Union, both of which have extensive chemical warfare capabilities. This aspect notwithstanding, the UK has undoubtedly been very active in these talks, pursuing a somewhat low-key stance between 1972 and 1976, and a much higher profile from 1976 onwards.[55] A number of proposals have been tabled by successive UK governments in this forum which suggests that the UK does put considerable store in the attainment of a multilateral CW treaty.

The aims of UK policy in the CW talks were first outlined in comprehensive form in the UK Draft CW Convention presented to the Conference of the Committee on Disarmament on 4 August, 1976.[56] The Draft Convention noted the pressing need for an '... effective prohibition of chemical weapons', but that the only way this could be achieved was for an agreement aimed at, '... general and complete disarmament (of chemical weapons) under strict and effective international control'.[57] Thus the idea of a permanent disarmament organisation was once more promulgated by the UK. This time it was to be in the form of an International Consultative Committee (ICC), which would oversee the agreement. However, as Nicholas Sims has observed:

The principal innovation of the UK Draft Convention concerned its timetable. It envisaged states assuming certain obligations merely upon *signing* the eventual Convention. They would notify one another of their CW agents, if any, and their production facilities, and they would halt production. These notifications would not be verified (except, presumably, by traditional means where states' intelligence capability permitted). The idea was that the declarations and the freeze on CW production would give states the confidence needed to ratify their signatures and thereby bring the

Convention into force, at which stage the remaining obligations – including acceptance of inspection – would come into effect.[58]

One of the most intractable issues in the talks thus far has centred on the issue of the inspection measures that would accompany the CWC. Progress has been made, however. Some form of on-site inspection (OSI) is now regarded as an essential component of any future CWC. This position is strongly advocated by the West but is increasingly being accepted in the Soviet bloc as well. Where divergence still remains is in relation to the precise details of the OSI, in particular between the US and the Soviet positions. The US has insisted that any future CW agreement would be conditional upon the Soviet Union accepting fairly rigorous measures for OSI.[59] In large part, these demands have been conditioned by what the US regards as the inadequacies of the inspection measures in the BWC. These concerns were heightened as a result of an unusual outbreak of anthrax in the Soviet Union at Sverdlovsk (an area where it was thought that BW might be stockpiled) in 1979.[60]

The Soviet Union has traditionally taken the view that the kinds of inspection demanded by the US are too intrusive. Indeed, the term 'legalised espionage' is often used in this context to describe the Soviet view of this type of inspection. But over the years this position has begun to change: to the extent that the Soviet Union now embraces a view of verification on several arms control related issues not too dissimilar from viewpoints held in the West. The most obvious example of this change is to be found in the inspection measures incorporated in the Intermediate Nuclear Forces (INF) Treaty.[61]

It is specifically in those areas related to the verification and compliance of the CWC that the UK has been most obviously active. Following the agreement on the BWC, the UK government undertook a number of working papers to study the feasibility of certain types of verification procedure to accompany a future CW agreement. These ranged in terms of the specificity of the verification procedures required. While many of the early working papers examined the possibilities for National Technical Means (NTM) and other less intrusive forms of verification,[62] the later ones (especially post-Sverdlovsk) have tended to focus more on some form of OSI and also on how satisfactory compliance to a future agreement can be effectively maintained.[63] This position was elaborated more fully in a working paper submitted to the Committee on Disarmament (CD) in February, 1982:

The United Kingdom believes that, as is the case in many arms control agreements, it is necessary for all States party to a Convention to have reasonable confidence in the compliance of all other States parties, and that the provisions of a CW would therefore need to include adequate measures for its verification. The United Kingdom considers that verification measures would be necessary for each stage of implementation – that is for declaration and destruction of stockpiles and production facilities – and thereafter to monitor that continued compliance of States to the provisions of the Convention dealing with non-production of chemical weapons, including the monitoring of permitted uses of chemical warfare agents and dual-purpose agents. It is also essential that the Convention has an effective complaints procedure for the handling of any doubts which might arise about the implementation of the Convention.[64]

The question of what form the OSI will take has thus become a major theme of recent UK working papers and initiatives. In 1984 the UK position was firmly stated:

To be effective and to maintain international confidence the proposed Convention will include procedures for mandatory routine international on-site inspection. However, to ensure that the Convention is properly observed in every respect, an additional element of challenge inspection is essential. The latter cannot be substituted for routine *international on-site inspection*. But it can be an effective way of dealing with instances of suspected non-compliance which would not necessarily be revealed by regular inspection of declared facilities.[65]

This position was elaborated further in 1986 with the intention of overcoming the impasse which had developed between the US and Soviet delegations over the strict verification procedures proposed by the US. The basic thrust of the UK's position is explained by John Walker:

In order to try to move the negotiations forward ... the UK (has) suggested that, should any party request clarification or resolution of any matter causing doubts about compliance, each state party receiving such a request should be obliged to demonstrate to others, the requesting party in particular, that it was in full compliance with the convention ... this could mean that in some very exceptional circumstances ... a limited right of refusal of inspection might be valid.[66]

Another element in the UK's policy regarding CBW arms control and disarmament was the behind the scenes diplomatic effort to co-ordinate the various viewpoints of NATO Alliance, particularly between the US and Western Europe. Given the objectives of UK policy in the CBW field, this role is inevitably an important one, especially in recent years when the CBW re-armament option has begun to receive a much higher profile on the NATO agenda.

To create further confidence that an inspection system could be implemented to the satisfaction of all parties to the CWC, the UK has also been involved in certain bilateral initiatives with the Soviet Union, outside the framework of the multilateral CD negotiations. In May 1988 the UK opened the Porton Down research establishment and the Chemical Training Centre in Dorset to a team of Soviet officials for a confidence-building inspection tour. In July 1988, the Soviet Union reciprocated by allowing a team from the UK to conduct an inspection tour of the Soviet chemical warfare centre at Shikhany.[67]

In addition to these initiatives in the inspection sphere, the UK has clearly been keen to keep the momentum of the negotiations moving forward in the area of compliance too. Building on the work of a previous paper presented by the Netherlands,[68] the UK, in 1985, tabled a paper outlining the institutional and procedural arrangements it deemed necessary for the effective operation of the proposed CWC.[69] The paper called for the establishment of an 'International Organisation for the Prohibition of Chemical Weapons', to be responsible for, '... implementing all aspects of the Convention.'[70] This Organisation would have three essential components: a consultative committee; an executive council; and a secretariat, which would have the responsibility for carrying out, '(i) routine inspection of declared chemical facilities ... and (ii) immediate challenge inspections of declared and undeclared facilities and locations.'[71]

As one of the principal tasks of the secretariat would be to carry out verification procedures in the civilian chemical industries, the UK has also attempted to create confidence that this too can be implemented effectively to the satisfaction of all parties. In 1979 several experts were invited to inspect a civilian chemical facility in the UK.[72] Similarly, in August 1988, responding to an earlier paper presented by the Federal Republic of Germany calling for an exchange of data, the UK gave yet a further signal of its intentions in the Geneva talks by tabling a working paper outlining the precise details of the civil chemical facilities in the UK producing chemicals relevant to the CWC.[73] Almost simultaneously, the UK submitted a paper to the UN Secretary-General's Group of Experts meeting in

Geneva calling for automatic investigations by the UN of allegations of use of CW.[74] These proposals are therefore very much in keeping with the UK CBW policy that has been evolving over the years and which sees the establishment of an international CBW disarmament 'regime' as the best method of preventing CBW.

Conclusion

The question of the role of any one state in the CBW talks is inevitably always going to be difficult to evaluate. These talks take place in a multilateral environment and concern a group of weapons which have a direct effect on the security considerations of states. Precisely for these reasons a CWC has been enormously difficult to negotiate. However, throughout these talks the UK does appear to have been very active, both in the negotiating forums themselves and behind the scenes working diplomatically between the various delegations. In addition to this, the UK has also persistently pursued one negotiating course, multilateral CBW disarmament. Even when the rearmament option was considered, it was soon rejected in favour of continuing with its stated preferred negotiating objectives. This position has been consistently adopted, irrespective of changes of government.

However, the UK's enthusiasm for multilateral CBW disarmament and its decision to get out of the offensive CBW business has much to do with particular circumstances related to the UK's economic and strategic situation in the aftermath of the Second World War. This unilateral decision was taken at a time when the UK's defence budget was already stretched by other defence commitments. The UK's decision was thus predicated primarily on the grounds that the costs of going into full-scale CW production at this particular period would offset resources being channelled into other more vital areas of defence, especially the nuclear weapons programme. A contributory factor to the decision was the UK's past, especially wartime, military experiences regarding CW. These experiences cast doubt on the military rationales for retaining an offensive CW capability. Such an assessment inevitably has to be conjectural because no information has been released to the PRO on this topic. But the information that is available suggests that these considerations must have weighed heavily in UK decision-making circles at this time.

In the Geneva talks aimed at achieving such a ban on CBW the UK has subsequently pursued a very active strategy, especially since 1968. Why such an active strategy has been pursued can in large part be attributed to the UK's non-possession of an offensive CBW capability. It may well be, therefore, that not having certain categories of weapons allows a country to countenance types of arms control and disarmament proposal that it would not accept if it were in possession of such weapons. Certainly in the CBW talks it has been those negotiating parties with militarily significant stockpiles of such weapons which have been the most constrained in their approach to these talks. The UK has seemingly been under no such strictures, with the available information suggesting that in terms of a negotiating strategy, the UK has been almost unerring in its endeavour to play out the role of catalyst in the CBW talks.

Notes

1   The author would like to express his grateful thanks to the following people: to Helen Leigh, who provided invaluable research assistance; Dr. Edward Spiers for his detailed comments on specific aspects of the paper; to Professor Ian Bellany who commented on a very early draft; and finally, to the members of the Southampton Arms Control Study Group for their encouragement and support in the final writing of this chapter.

2   See *Quarterly Reviews*, UK Arms Control and Disarmament Unit, Foreign and Commonwealth Office, London.

3   It was this concern which precipitated a conference on chemical weapons which convened in Paris in January 1989. A total of 149 countries participated in the conference. One of the major issues of the conference, however, was the linkage between chemical and nuclear weapons. The Arab countries in particular argued in favour of retention of chemical weapons as a counter to the alleged stockpiling of nuclear weapons by Israel. See *Financial Times*, 9 January 1989; *International Herald Tribune*, 13 January 1989.

4   For an account which highlights these developments see, N. C. Livingstone and J. D. Douglas, *CBW: The Poor Man's Atomic Bomb*, Institute for Foreign Policy Analysis, Cambridge, MA, 1984.

5   For recent statements and analyses of the US and Soviet Union positions on CW programmes and modernisation see: *Chemical Warfare. Progress and Problems in Defensive Capability*, Report to the Chairman Committee on Foreign Affairs, House of Representatives, GAO/PEMD-86-11, US General Accounting Office, Washington DC, July 1986; B. Roberts (ed.), *Chemical Warfare Policy: Beyond the Binary Production Decision, Significant Issues Series*, IX, Center for Strategic and International Studies, Georgetown University, Washington DC, 1987; H. Stringer, *Deterring Chemical Warfare: U.S. Policy Options for the 1990s*, Institute for Foreign

Policy Analysis, Cambridge, MA and Washington DC: 1986; E. M. Spiers, *Chemical Warfare*, Macmillan, London, 1986; NATO Chemical Weapons Policy and Posture, *ADIU Occasional Paper No. 4*, Brighton, 1986; J. Hemsley, *The Soviet Biochemical Threat to NATO*; and 'A new generation of CB munitions', *Jane's Defence Weekly*, 30 April, 1988, pp. 852–3.

6 See United Nations Security Council, *Report of the Specialists Appointed by the Secretary-General to Investigate Allegations by the Islamic Republic of Iran Concerning the Use of Chemical Weapons*, S/16433, 26 March 1984.

7 In recent years there have been several US reports and statements regarding the use of CW in South-East Asia and Afghanistan. These reports also usually implicate the Soviet Union in the allegations.

8 For example, Richard Luce, Minister of State, Foreign and Commonwealth Office, 'Chemical Weapons: Negotiating a Total Ban', *NATO Review*, No. 3, 1985, pp. 1–5.

9 As far as is known, only on one occasion in recent years has the UK government seriously considered the chemical rearmament option, which was then rejected. At a Press Conference on 2 April 1980, the then Defence Secretary, Francis Pym, stated that the UK was considering whether to revive the UK's offensive chemical weapons capability as a deterrent to the growing threat of Soviet chemical warfare capabilities. See *The Times*, 3 April 1980. According to Brian Becket, the rearmament option was not about whether or not the UK was '… to produce and develop its own CW weapons, but rather whether to purchase, store and deploy a new generation of American weapons if and when the US commits itself to a CW programme'. See B. Becket, 'Chemical warfare: a battle of nerves', New Scientist, 21 August 1980, pp. 596–9. However, on 17 June 1980 both Mr Pym and the Prime Minister reassured the House of Commons that the UK had no plans for chemical weapons rearmament, *Parliamentary Debates Oral Answers*, 17 June 1980 . For an analysis of this particular review of the UK's CW policy see N. A. Sims, 'Britain, Chemical Weapons and Disarmament', *ADIU Report*, II, July/August 1980). A report in the *New Statesman* in 1985, however, alleged that the question of the UK's CW re-armament was once more back on the government agenda. This was later flatly denied by the Prime Minister. See *Guardian*, 11 January 1985.

10 For a brief but detailed outline of CBW see *Chemical/Biological Warfare (CBW), ADIU Factsheets No.5*, ADIU, University of Sussex, Brighton, March 1984.

11 Julian Perry Robinson identifies the other countries as being Germany, Italy, Canada, Turkey, Greece, and Spain. See *NATO Chemical Weapons Policy and Posture, ADIU Occasional Paper No. 4*, ADIU, Brighton, 1986, p. 25.

12 The terms catalyst and retarder are used in chemical science to describe specific chemical reactions. A catalyst is a substance which acts to speed up a reaction. A retarder, on the other hand, has the opposite effect, having specific properties which act to slow down the chemical reaction.

13 For reasons, presumably of military security and current political sensitivity, very little information on the UK's postwar CW decision-making

has appeared in the UK Public Records Office (PRO). Inferences therefore have to be drawn from the information which is available. However, there have been occasional references to the UK's CW policy in the Chiefs of Staff (COS) and the Prime Minister's Private Office papers. These are often couched within the wider context of the UK security debate in the 1950s and therefore provide useful pointers to UK military and political thinking at the decision-making level.

14 'Past Production of Chemical Warfare Agents in the UK', *UK Working Paper for Conference on Disarmament*, August 1988, p. 2.

15 S. Seagrave, *Yellow Rain: Chemical Warfare – the deadliest arms race*, Sphere Books Ltd, London, 1982, p. 202.

16 R. Harris and J. Paxman, *A Higher Form of Killing: The Secret Story of Gas and Germ Warfare*, Chatto and Windus, London, 1982, p. 183.

17 Although these papers make no specific reference to CBW capabilities, ways were clearly being sought to reduce the UK's burgeoning defence commitments. See PRO Budget Committee Papers 1953: T171/429 (1952–3) Budget Memoranda; T 171/430 Budget Memoranda; T171/431 (1953) Budget Memoranda; T171/431 (1952–3) Minutes of Meeting; T171/432 (1952–3) and T171/433 (1953) Miscellaneous briefing papers on memoranda. Budget Committee Papers 1954: T171/442 (1953–4) Memoranda; T171/443 (1954) Memoranda. See also: T225/72, T225/73, T225/74, T225/75 considerations on defence estimates; and T225/76 Defence budget in the event of cessation of US aid; T225/201, T225/202, T225/203 Defence programme and the balance of payments; T225/240 Preparation of defence budget 1953; T225/298 Preparation of defence budget 1954.

18 *Prime Minister's Private Office, PREM 3/89, 'Chemical Warfare (II)', Feb. 1944 – June 1945*. This PRO document provides a rare insight into UK military thinking on CBW.

19 See especially, PREM 3/89, *Report – Military considerations affecting the initiation of chemical and other special forms of warfare*.

20 *PREM 3/89*. In his study of the UK and CW, Andy Thomas, has noted the hazardous nature of the work undertaken by civilians in the chemical weapons factories during the First World War, especially during the production of mustard gas. See *Effects of Chemical Warfare: A selective review and bibliography of British state papers*, Taylor & Francis for SIPRI, London and Philadelphia, pp. 23–9. Thus it might be argued that there were also possible negative effects to the morale of the civilian workforce engaged in CBW production activities, a consideration which might also have been influential in post-war UK thinking.

21 *ibid*.

22 Quoted in *The Times*, 15 June 1981. The main report from which this quote was taken is, *Future Developments in Weapons and Methods of War*, Submitted to the Joint Chiefs of Staff July 1946. See also Harris and Paxman, *op.cit*., pp. 149–50.

23 For an analysis of the impact of nuclear weapons on the UK's defence policy during the early 1950s see N. Wheeler, *The Roles played by the British Chiefs of Staff Committee in the Evolution of Britain's Nuclear*

Weapon Planning and Policy-making, 1945–55 (Unpublished PhD thesis, University of Southampton, 1988), especially chapter six, and Ian Clark and Nicholas J. Wheeler, *The British Origins of Nuclear Strategy, 1945–55*, Oxford University Press, Oxford, 1989.

24 Although the UN classification makes no such distinctions.

25 *CAB 131/14*, p. 4, July 1954.

26 *Parliamentary Debates* (Commons) Statement by the Rt. Hon. Denis Healey, 801 (6 May 1970): 389.

27 Basic training for CBW is undertaken at the Chemical Training Centre at Winterbourne Gunner in Dorset.

28 Quoted in J. Cookson and J. Nottingham, *A Survey of Chemical and Biological Warfare*, Sheed and Ward, London and Sydney, 1969, p. 103.

29 Harris and Paxman, *op.cit.*, p. 177.

30 These agents were produced at seven Ministry of Supply factories established at Randle, Valley, Springfields, Wade, Rocksavage, Millhouse and Roydmills. The Research Establishment at Sutton Oak was also involved in the operational activities. 'UK Working Paper For Conference on Disarmament', *op.cit.*, p. 1.

31 *ibid.*, pp. 1–2.

32 *ibid.*, p. 2.

33 *ibid.*

34 *ibid.*

35 *ibid.*, pp. 2–4.

36 *ibid.*

37 Even then Harris and Paxman argue the UK had already taken alternative action as early as 1947 to maintain a handle on any new or unforeseen CW developments by signing a Trilateral Agreement with the US and Canada (later the Quadrilateral Agreement when Australia also joined) which linked the UK to any US offensive chemical warfare developments. *op.cit.*, pp. 174–5.

38 The term disarmament has been included here because the aim of these talks (at least from the UK's point of view), is total disarmament. Whereas treaties like the NPT and the PTBT can be understood within the context of multilateral arms control (and not necessarily disarmament), the CBW talks, on the other hand, have been directed towards the objective of multilateral disarmament. For a more detailed discussion of this point, see N. A. Sims, *Morality and Biological Warfare: The Moral Status of Biological Warfare and the Norm of Non-Possession of Biological Weapons*, Paper presented to the Conference on 'Morality and Warfare', Centre for the Study of Arms Control and International Security, University of Lancaster, 17 December 1986.

39 See the speech by Mr Fred Mulley, the UK delegate to the Eighteen Nation Disarmament Conference (ENDC) On 16 July 1968. Plenary Session 381, *Further Documents on Disarmament: The Disarmament Negotiations July–December, 1968, Cmnd. 4141.*, pp. 56–64.

40 *ibid.*

41 US ratification of the Geneva Protocol eventually occurred in 1975.

42 'UK Working Paper Dated 6 August on Microbiological Warfare',

Document No. 8, Cmnd. 4141.

43 *ibid.*

44 For further elaboration of these points see Sims, *op.cit.*

45 'UK Working Paper Dated 6 August on Microbiological Warfare', *op.cit.*, paragraph 8. This idea had its roots in UK proposals on the question of CBW disarmament in the 1920s and 1930s, thus suggesting a long historical lineage to UK thinking on CBW verification measures.

46 *ibid.*

47 'Draft Convention for the Prohibition of Biological Methods of Warfare with Associated Draft Security Council Resolution' tabled by the UK in the Conference of the Eighteen-Nation Committee on Disarmament in Geneva on 10 July 1969, *Miscellaneous No. 27 (1969), Cmnd. 4113*, Article III.

48 *Documents on Disarmament, 1969*, pp. 431–4. See also statement by Mr Porter, the UK delegate to the CCD, *Documents on Disarmament, 1969*, pp. 436–40.

49 For complete texts of the US policy statements of November 1969 and February 1970, see *The Prevention of CBW. The Problem of Chemical and Biological Warfare*, Vol. V, Almquist and Wiksell for SIPRI, Stockholm, pp. 275–7.

50 'News Conference Remarks by President Nixon on Chemical and Biological Weapons, 25 November, 1969', *Documents on Disarmament, 1969*, pp. 590–2.

51 *CB Disarmament Negotiations, op.cit.*, p. 316.

52 Elisa D. Harris, 'Chemical and Biological Arms Control: The Role of the Allies', in J. Roper and F. Hampson (eds.), *Arms Control and the Allies* (forthcoming).

53 See N. A. Sims, *Biological and Toxin Weapons: Issues in the 1986 Review*, Faraday Discussion Paper No. 7, The Council for Arms Control, London, 1986.

54 For full text see J. Goldblat, *Arms Control Agreements. A Handbook*, Taylor and Francis for SIPRI, London, 1983, pp. 163–6.

55 N. A. Sims, 'Britain, Chemical Weapons and Disarmament', *op.cit.*

56 *CCD/512*. In 1979 this became the Committee on Disarmament (CD).

57 *ibid.*

58 'Britain, Chemical Weapons and Disarmament', *op.cit.*, p. 1.

59 See especially the US *Draft Convention on the Prohibition of chemical weapons, CD/500*, 1984. This convention calls for: (1) that all stocks of chemical weapons had been destroyed; (2) that all declared production facilities had been destroyed; (3) that all declared stocks constituted all the stocks; (4) that the declared facilities were all the facilities.

60 To add further speculation to the issue, the Soviet government has refused access to US inspectors so that they could investigate the cause of the outbreak.

61 Signs of changes in the Soviet Union's view of OSI in the CW field have also started to appear. In 1984, for example, the Soviet Union stated that it was prepared to accept, '... systematic international on-site verification of the destruction of stocks at a special facility, with the permanent presence at the facility of the representatives of international control.' See *The United Nations Disarmament Yearbook*, Vol. IX, 1984, p. 316. But this did not go far enough to satisfy US demands. More recently, the Soviet Union has accepted significant CW OSI verification proposals tabled by the West, including mandatory challenge inspections without the right of refusal. See *The Independent*, 12 August 1987.

62   For those papers dealing with the feasibility of observing compliance by National Technical Means (NTM) and other less intrusive forms of verification see: 'Remote Detection of the Testing of Chemical Weapons by Satellite-based Scanning Systems', *Cmnd.5344*, Doc.No.4, 1973; and 'Working Paper by the UK on the Feasibility of Extraterritorial surveillance of chemical weapon tests by air monitoring at the border', *CCD/502*.

63   For those dealing with some form of OSI see 'Visit to Britain by Chemical Weapons Experts (14–16 March 1979),' *CD/15*; 'Working Paper on Verification and the Monitoring of Compliance in a Chemical Weapons Convention', *CD/244*; 'Verification of Non-Production of Chemical Weapons', *CD/353*; 'Chemical Weapons Convention: verification and compliance – the challenge element', *CD/431*; 'Verification of non-production of chemical weapons,' *CD/514*; 'Chemical Weapons Convention: Verification and Compliance – The Challenge Element', *CD/715*; and 'Making the Chemical Weapons Ban Effective', *CD/769*.

64   *CD/244*, para. 2.

65   *CD/431, op.cit.*

66   'A Chemical Weapons Ban? The Role of the US, the Soviet Union and the UK', *Topic: Journal of the Liberal Arts*, XXXX, 1986, p. 45.

67   *Guardian*, 1 July 1988.

68   See 'Size and Structure of a Chemical Disarmament Inspectorate', *CD/445*.

69   *CD/589, op.cit.*

70   *ibid.*

71   *ibid.* For a very detailed analysis of the ideas associated with the establishment of such an Organisation, see N. A. Sims, *International Organization for Chemical Disarmament*, Oxford University Press for SIPRI, Oxford, 1987.

72   'Visit to Britain by Chemical Weapons Experts (14–16 March 1979)', *op.cit.*

73   'Provision of Data Relevant to the Chemical Weapons Convention', *Working Paper for Conference on Disarmament*, August 1988.

74   The UK's argument was that such an investigations procedure would: (a) circumvent the need for a political decision to investigate each time an allegation of CBW use is made; (b) enable more accurate and conclusive evidence to be collected; (c) provide a more concrete basis for an international response against states violating the 1925 Geneva Protocol or other relevant international obligations; and thus (d) deter CBW use. 'Procedures For The Investigation Of The Use Of Chemical Or Biological Weapons', submitted 15 August 1988.

Britain and conventional arms transfer restraint[1]

Introduction

Britain has what appears to be an ambivalent attitude towards both conventional arms transfers and conventional arms transfer control. This ambivalence stems from two competing aspects of British security policy. On the one hand, it is a middle-sized weapons supplier to whom sales abroad are of great importance. On the other hand, Britain perceives itself to be a reasonably important actor in the international system, particularly in the area of arms control negotiations. As previous chapters have noted, this view is largely a consequence of its status as a nuclear weapons power.

However, Britain's ambivalence is more apparent than real. Since the end of the Second World War there has been a general bipartisan consensus on arms transfer policies, making it, until fairly recently, a non-issue in political debate and in the newspapers. On the occasions when arms transfer issues do make the news it is usually because British weapons have reached countries under a weapons embargo (for example South Africa, and Libya) or non-state groups such as the Contra Guerrillas.[2] Additionally, sales successes tend to be uncritically praised in the press, as in the case of the 1988 arms sale to Saudi Arabia.[3] In contrast to the situation in the US, if the matter does arise in political debate it is usually in terms of criticisms of sales opportunities missed.

Rationales for transfer

The primary motivation for arms sales tends to be economic. For Britain, arms sales are a valuable source of foreign exchange and contribute to the balance of trade. Brzoska and Ohlson note that successive governments have also highlighted sales as a means by which to extend production runs in order to achieve economies of scale (which reduces the cost of weapons to the armed services) and ensure that the services can obtain sufficient quantities while also recouping some of the monies spent on research and development.[4] Arms sales abroad are also seen as a means of maintaining domestic employment and technical skills in the defence industries.

In addition to the economic justifications, there are also political rationales. Arms transfers are seen as a means of maintaining links with strategically and economically important states such as those in the Persian Gulf. And as Pierre notes:

There remains a general sense that having an arms industry is an attribute of an important middle-level power, that the ability to manufacture advanced technology is another source of strength and that the arms industry may somehow enhance Britain's flexibility in foreign and military affairs.[5]

Consequently British arms export policy has consistently favoured sales where they have been prudential. Britain's arms transfer policy is managed to yield the maximum economic and political benefit without compromising British security or foreign policy goals.

Yet as Britain enters the 1990s, its ability to maintain sovereign control of this policy will be thrown into doubt. In order to assess the factors that will impinge on British policy in the future, it is necessary to understand the current state of arms transfers. Three different facets of the arms transfer issue need to be examined. First, regardless of how clever the marketing strategies employed by the British government may be, macroeconomic factors are a major determinant of the levels of sales. Thus in order to look to the 1990s it is necessary to assess the current and future state of the international arms transfer market and Britain's ability to compete in it. Second, as recent events have shown, the attitudes of consortium partners will affect Britain's ability to sell arms to certain countries. As co-production increasingly becomes a necessity, the arms transfer policies of partners are another potential brake on arms sales. Third, an important determinant of the quantity and quality of British sales is the US attitude towards technology transfer. British arms sales are becoming increasingly constrained by US demands to protect sensitive western technology from being transferred either directly or indirectly to the Eastern bloc.[6] The US imposition of legal constraints concerning sensitive technology transfers directly through extraterritorial legislation and indirectly through CoCom (the

West's co-ordinating committee on export controls) is a clear illustration of the limitations of Britain's freedom to act in this area.

This means that Britain's arms transfer policy has developed and evolved in the context of arms transfer management and sometimes restriction, but not restraint.[7] But increasing concerns about the volume of arms sales and the proliferation of conventional weapons technologies, in particular ballistic missile technology, has raised the question of whether it is possible to move from a policy of arms transfer *management* to arms transfer *reduction* in the 1990s. One possibility is the increasing interest in linking conventional arms transfer issues with concerns to prevent nuclear proliferation as illustrated in Britain's involvement in the Seven Power Missile Agreement.

Past attempts at conventional arms transfer control

There have been few British attempts at conventional arms transfer control – unilateral, bilateral or multilateral – in the post-war period. This reflects the perception that nuclear arms control is more important; a lack of agreement about the need for conventional arms transfer control; and a consequent lack of political will to achieve such agreement.

Britain has consistently expressed a preference for multilateral approaches to the control of arms transfers, rather than unilateral efforts because of the belief that the British share of the market is too small for a unilateral control effort to have any impact. Working with other states, several arms embargoes have been imposed in the past: on sales to South Africa (although British weapons are still reaching the country);[8] on Nigeria during the Biafran war; on Idi Amin's Uganda; on Pinochet's Chile between 1974 and 1980 (now a favoured customer following the improvement in relations brought about following the logistical assistance Chile gave the British during the Falklands war); on Iran following the Revolution in 1979; and on Libya in 1986. It seems that most of these embargoes have been reactive – forced on the government by the tide of public opinion, a UN mandate or pressure from other governments.

There have been other attempts at multilateral control of arms transfers. One example is the 1950 Tripartite Declaration on the Middle East. This has been heralded by some as a precedent for arms transfer control. However, this was primarily a market-sharing arrangement between Britain, the US and France and was thus arms transfer management rather than reduction.[9] Britain has been involved in attempts to establish multilateral arms transfer negotiations through the UN, though it is difficult to judge its commitment to this approach.[10] Since 1965, Britain has consistently argued in favoured of the establishment of an international arms trade registry. However, this enthusiasm at the international level sits uneasily with Britain's unwillingness at the domestic level to reveal details of arms transfer agreements.[11]

The one major post-war attempt to negotiate a conventional arms transfer agreement outside the UN framework was the effort by the Carter administration in 1977. President Carter had campaigned on the promise of reducing the global trade in arms through both unilateral US measures and negotiated global restraints. Before approaching the Soviet Union and requesting negotiations on arms transfer control, the Carter administration sought the support of its arms transferring Western allies. The administration received a variety of responses from its allies ranging from the refusal of the French to even discuss the issue, to the British who expressed a degree of interest.[12]

A cynical interpretation of the British response would be that the government felt it safe to agree, secure in the knowledge that the responses of the other European allies made the idea a non-starter. It also could be argued that the British response had more to do with being the good ally than any genuine enthusiasm for the idea. As John Rowe of the US Defence Security Assistance Agency noted, the British reaction was that they 'would go along with it, if it made the US happy they were willing to play'.[13] However, two factors serve to partially undermine this interpretation. First, the Callaghan government had on several occasions expressed a genuine interest in arms transfer restraint and did seem committed to the notion of controlling the international arms trade. Second, there was no assurance that the talks would not go ahead on a trilateral basis, as a unified response from the European allies was not necessarily a prerequisite for action.

As a result of the lack of allied enthusiasm, the talks took place as a series of bilateral discussions between the US and the Soviet Union, with the US regularly reporting back to its European allies. The talks ended in deadlock in 1979. What is important to note, however, is that despite the importance of arms sales for its economy and in

particular its defence industry, Britain appeared willing in principle
to enter into negotiations on arms transfer control. Although the
reason may involve less of a concern to negotiate controls than a
desire to please the US, British concurrence sets a potential precedent
for the future. Before examining the possibility of Britain's participation in future efforts at arms transfer control, it is necessary to
discuss the internal decision-making process and the international
market structure relating to arms transfers.

Arms transfer procedures and policies

The process by which British conventional arms transfers are made
has been extensively documented elsewhere.[14] However, a brief
outline of the procedures is useful to indicate the thrust of government policy. The British defence industry has both public and private
sectors. While the public sector has been reduced by the Conservative government through the privatisation of the Royal Ordnance
factories and Rolls Royce, the line of demarcation is not as clear as it
might seem. For example, it is known that the Ministry of Defence
(MoD) has been using private companies to 'front' in the supply of
specialist weapons and to conduct sensitive sales abroad.[15] Additionally, the government owns companies such as International Military Services (IMS) which act as intermediaries and thus deflect
criticisms away from the state.[16]

The British government is committed to selling arms abroad and it
receives a high priority within the Ministry of Defence. In 1968 the
Defence Sales Organisation (DSO) was created to stimulate arms
exports and has 'sought to bring the marketing and promotion
techniques of private industry to government.'[17] In 1986 the DSO
was renamed the Defence Export Services Organisation (DESO).
The DESO's head now comes on secondment from the British
defence industry and the current head is Alan Thomas, President and
Chief Executive of Raytheon Europe.[18] The techniques the DESO
employs include the staging of arms trade fairs and the use of Royal
Navy ships as floating promotions. According to Pierre, 'The clear
disposition is to make sales whenever and wherever possible. The
style is aggressive and achievement-orientated.'[19]

The export of military goods is controlled by the government
through the Export Of Goods (Control) Order. Licences are granted
by the Department of Trade after consultation with the Ministry of

Defence, The Foreign and Commonwealth Office and other interested departments. But as Brzoska and Ohlson note, 'in practice it is the MoD which dominates arms sales policy'.[20] Before, during and after an arms transfer, government policy is never to comment on individual sales or total sales to particular countries as this is be judged to be a matter of 'commercial confidence'.[21]

Within this organisational framework a series of procedures and guidelines have developed in relation to arms transfers. There are two aspects of these arms transfer procedures which it is important to examine. First, there are general guidelines by which the majority of arms transfers are judged. However, this should not be taken to mean that there is a comprehensive set of rules which govern British arms transfers; this is far from the case. Indeed, most arms transfer requests are judged on an individual basis. Second, there are the methods of dealing with the large or politically controversial sales which are not covered by these guidelines.

General policy guidelines are apparently 'determined and constantly updated, as a consequence of liaison between MoD and the FCO within the general framework of government policy'.[22] As Edmonds explains:

> ... there exists within Whitehall a well understood and clear set of guidelines that are compatible with government policy and against which arms export proposals can be judged with competence and at a relatively low bureaucratic level. This is a function which is carried out separately by the departments concerned, often working on precedent, without reference to higher authority.[23]

Most of the 7,000 applications made each year for arms export licences are handled by the Board of Trade's Export Licensing Board. In the main, decisions are made on a case by case basis which, according to Pierre, 'reflects the essential pragmatism of the British style of government'.[24] The lack of an overall policy was justified by the MoD as a consequence of the 'highly competitive character of the international trade in defence equipment' and the fact that 'changes in the situation of countries abroad may occur very quickly'.[25]

There are, however, certain constraints on potential sales, which are rarely admitted and are certainly not codified in any form. The circumstances under which sales would be affected were listed by the then Foreign Office Minister Douglas Hurd as: if the arms transfers would pose a threat to Britain or NATO; if the arms transfers would contravene UN mandated embargoes; and if the arms transfers ran up against special political considerations (such as opposition of other states in the region to sales). In addition to these, certain subsidiary issues are considered: what are the implications of sales for regional stability; what is the role to which equipment could be put; would the arms transfers affect the safeguard of British dependencies; and finally, would the arms transfer have implications for multilateral efforts at arms transfer management.[26] Furthermore, in the case of arms sales to 'Warsaw Pact or other communist countries, consultation and CoCom (Co-ordinating Committee on Export Controls) regulations devised by the Western bloc are employed'.[27]

In most cases, however, the pragmatic approach means that these constraints are imposed on a selective basis, normally in response to a particular political context. According to Pearson:

Britain ... imposes end-use certification only in certain sales contracts where danger of re-export is considered great. It professes to rely on intelligence information to track down harmful re-exports and the threat of future sales bans to discourage them.[28]

However, approximately 3 per cent of arms transfer applications require close scrutiny or special attention as a result of these constraints.[29] In these cases where the arms transfer is deemed to be sensitive in nature, the decision is taken by ministers, either informally or in inter-ministerial committees. If a decision still cannot be reached then the Cabinet will be consulted. In addition, decision-making on arms transfers may be affected by the collaborative nature of the venture. As Pearson notes: 'if equipment is being jointly produced in collaboration with foreign firms or governments, inter-governmental consultation about sales may be necessary.'[30]

This arms transfer framework is not without contradictions or problems. For example, the government's stated reason for not having rigid guidelines is that it can react quickly to changes in the international environment. Yet this goal is contradicted by a decision-making process in which low-level bureaucrats apply standard operating procedures and work on the basis of precedent. Similarly, the emphasis on low-level decision-making means that it is only at a late stage in the arms transfer process that questions relating to technology transfer and the need for consultation with other governments are considered. Both the issues are discussed below.

The role of the international arms market in determining sales levels

The international arms transfer market has undergone significant changes in the post-war period. Of particular relevance as indicators of what is likely to happen in the 1990s are the changes which have occurred in the last two decades. These changes are best analysed in terms of the structure and operation of the market.

The major change in the structure of the market has been an increase in the number of supplier states. New supplier states have emerged spurred by the desire for independence and/or political and economic necessity. Important new suppliers include Argentina, Brazil, Egypt, Israel and South Africa. Purchasing from these developing suppliers is an attractive proposition to Third World states seeking to diversify their sources of supply in order to minimise superpower leverage. An additional advantage is that the weaponry tends to be low-tech, which suits the recipient as it is cheaper, easier to maintain and more appropriate to local conditions. At the other end of the market, there has been a trend towards increasingly complex and sophisticated weaponry. The superpowers have what is still an unassailable grip on this aspect of the arms transfer market.

The major consequence of these two structural features is that the middle-ground of the arms transfer market, occupied by secondary suppliers such as Britain, France, and West Germany is under threat from both above and below. Secondary suppliers face ever greater competition in the high and low-tech markets and there is increasingly cut-throat competition between them for a share of the ever-diminishing middle-ground.

In the 1970s, Britain's share of the arms transfer market declined and France overtook it to become the third largest supplier. This was a consequence of Britain's inability to benefit from the expansion of the international arms market during those years. SIPRI highlights several reasons for this: Britain was not a major supplier to the Middle East (the major growth area); Britain's diminished international stature worked against increasing arms sales; the Labour government pursued a policy of restraint between 1974 and 1979; and, importantly, British weapon systems were at the high-tech end of the arms market, where there was less expansion. Since then, however, Britain has been fighting to increase its sales abroad. As SIPRI points out: 'The British share of exports of major weapons increased in the mid-1980s because of a massive sales drive by the conservative government which came to power in 1979'.[31] Despite some fluctuations in sales levels, the Conservative government has been generally successful in maintaining and increasing the British share of the market. Particularly crucial to this have been the two massive sales of weapons to Saudi Arabia in 1986 and 1988. These sales returned Britain to the position of third largest supplier.

The British government has used three major strategies to maintain and attempt to increase its share of the market. First, it has employed creative marketing techniques. Second, the British government has made available favourable credit arrangements.[32] Third, it has ensured that the weapons on offer are up-to-date and thus attractive to would-be recipients. In combination with the secrecy which routinely surrounds British arms transfers, these techniques have thus far enabled Britain to maintain a significant market share.

On the basis of this three-pronged approach, the DSEO has been willing and able to go to considerable lengths in order to secure sales. For example, a key part of the recent deal to sell to Saudi Arabia Tornado fighters and other defence equipment was an agreement that the England football team would fly to Riyadh to play a friendly match and that the English Football Association would play an active part in promoting the game in Saudi Arabia.[33] Similarly, a £1 billion arms package to Malaysia in danger of collapse seems to have been saved by increased provision of landing rights for the Malaysian Airline System at Heathrow.[34] These examples of creative marketing are indicative of the importance attached to sales.[35]

In spite of these efforts, British arms sales to the Third World have been declining since the early 1980s. This is largely a consequence of the global economic recession, the debt problems of would-be recipients and the completion of many Third World procurement cycles.[36] Coupled with the increased number of suppliers, this means that Britain faces increasing difficulties in maintaining its share of the market into the 1990s.

One means which has been employed by secondary suppliers such as Britain in an attempt to keep their market positions relates to changes in the operation of the market. Many secondary suppliers are exhibiting greater willingness to export production facilities and engage in technology transfers. This move is necessitated by the fact that recipient countries paying for weapons are now demanding more for their money. If the secondary suppliers refuse, there are other states willing to step in and fill orders. Although this sharing of technology has the effect of maintaining market positions in the short term, in the long term it undermines the secondary suppliers as it enables rival suppliers to emerge.

Another change in the operation of the market is the increased role of offsets in arms transfer deals. For example, Britain's 1988 Tornado sale to Saudi Arabia included an offset agreement in which Britain has pledged to encourage £1 billion of private investment in Saudi Arabia.[37] The increased use of offsets is another indication of the change from a sellers to a buyers market.

Overall then, the prognosis is not good from the perspective of the British government. It would seem that the 1990s will be a time of increasing competition for an ever-diminishing market. Although thus far Britain has been able to maintain its market share through the techniques set out above, this may not hold true in the future. Given the increasing costs of producing high-tech weapon systems, Britain will have to assess its ability to continue competing in the high-tech market in the 1990s. A decision to maintain its competitive profile in the high-tech market is not without costs. It would necessitate an increase in the research and development budget and an expansion of Britain's industrial base. Failure to do either is likely to increase Britain's dependence on advanced US technology. This dependence would increase the pressure imposed on arms transfer policies by US concerns about technology transfer, further diminish its independence of action and have an impact on the structure and functioning of its domestic economy. Given that much of the arms industry is privatised, this is a decision which the government cannot take on its own.

One possible solution is increasing co-production agreements with other secondary suppliers. This allows a means of sharing research and development costs and making use of different countries' areas of expertise in an effort to maintain a competitive profile in the international arms transfer market. However, this approach is not necessarily a trouble-free course of action, as was evident in the difficulties with West Germany over the sale of Tornado aircraft to Jordan. The implications for the future are clear: if Britain goes further down the road to co-production, arms transfer arrangements will become increasingly complex as a result of the need to co-ordinate different policies on arms transfers.[38]

British transfers and issues of sensitive technology

One of the most significant factors affecting British arms transfer policy is that Britain is a supplier towards the high-tech end of the market. These advanced weapons systems rely on technology that is indigenously produced and acquired from abroad, particularly the US. Until recently, over 50 per cent of Britain's total research and development (R&D) budget was devoted to defence.[39] The high level of R&D places British defence industries among the most advanced in Western Europe and in some areas, such as electronics and tank protection, it is more advanced than even the US.[40]

This has occurred at a time when there was heightened concerns, particularly in the US, about the erosion of the Western Alliance's technological lead over the East through technology transfers. The aspect of technology transfer which concerns the US most is the leaking of advanced technologies to the Soviet Union, Eastern bloc states or countries with communist sympathies. It has been estimated that technology transfers to the Soviet Union were costing NATO, and particularly the US, between $20bn and $50bn annually in extra military spending in order to it maintain a five to ten year technology lead.[41]

Moreover, the reduction in lead-times as a result of technology transfers is:

compounded by the increased real costs required to recapture US technological superiority. Weapons replacement and modernization before anticipated life-cycles have been completed create not only substantial monetary costs, but also additional expenses in the form of transatlantic tensions and *greater European concerns over increased dependency on the US technological base.*[42]

Although protection of US technology was a stated aim of the Carter administration, it was not until the Reagan administration that the issue assumed its current status. The definition of sensitive technology adopted by the Reagan administration was somewhat broader than the one that had operated before and included so-called dual use technologies (i.e. those with both about civil and military applications) such as microelectronics and computers.[43] The US considers it necessary to guard both types of technology because civilian technology is running ahead of military developments. For the US and its allies,

... this change from military to civilian technological predominance presents new problems. The technologies most sought by the Soviet Union have been developed first for use within the private sector. Hence, pressure for trade with the Soviet bloc may result in the transfer of significant technologies even before they are applied to weapons systems in the US and Western Europe.[44]

In addition to urging the Western allies to guard their civil and military high technology, one of the main planks in the US policy was upgrading the role played by the Co-ordinating Committee on Multilateral Export Controls (CoCom). This organisation, made up of all members of NATO (except Iceland) plus Japan, monitors and co-ordinates the protection of technology to prevent its acquisition by the Soviet Union, its East European allies and on occasion other states such as China, Cuba, North Korea, Vietnam and Kampuchea. Following the 1979 Soviet invasion of Afghanistan the member states agreed that there should be no transfers of any dual technologies on the CoCom list. This was known as the 'no exceptions' rule.

The US has also employed direct action in order to preserve the West's advantage. The Reagan administration used the 1979 Export Administration Act and the stringent amendments to it of 1985 as its major weapon in the fight against loss of technology. In addition to the amended 1979 Act, an Office of Export Enforcement was established to monitor goods and technologies of US origin and guard against unwanted technology transfer. This office demands that any British company seeks US permission before re-transferring goods or technology of US origin from Britain.[45] Conformity with this procedure is required even when the receiving state is another CoCom member. This imposition of US extra-territoriality is viewed by many as an infringement of state sovereignty and aroused considerable resentment in Europe.[46]

The US appears to have been largely successful in imposing unilateral controls on goods and technology of US origin and has been able to monitor re-transfers. One of the reasons it has been able to do so is that companies fear that contravention of the legislation would result in a cut-off of US technology and loss of access to the US market. For example, Washington declared that any company moving equipment *even within Britain* without US permission would be placed on the US export denials list.[47] This has proved to be a powerful inhibitor to companies contemplating sales disapproved of by the US.

Additionally, Washington has sought to isolate *countries* who leak technology to the Eastern bloc by a similar blacklisting process.[48] Loss of access to the US market would be particularly serious in the military field as America is Britain's major Western recipient. This is likely to be a powerful restraint – more implicit than explicit – upon British arms transfers, as countries that refuse to co-operate will be stranded in a 'technological wilderness.'[49] One consequence is that UK firms have become more assiduous in applying US restrictions than US firms.[50] The other is that the British government has become increasingly involved in protecting sensitive technologies in an effort to reassert its sovereign control over the issue and remove the justification for US claims of extra-territoriality.[51] In line with US concerns about technology transfer, Britain has introduced a new policy on the export of software which means that any company intending to export to the Soviet Union, China, Eastern European countries, other communist countries and socialist countries such as Nicaragua, will have to obtain a licence from the British government.[52]

However, by 1989 Britain was chaffing under the CoCom 'no exception rule' on the transfer of dual technologies. In April 1989 it directly challenged the rule by granting an export licence for a proposed sale of £450 million of high-tech construction and processing equipment to the Soviet Union despite US objections to the sale.[53] Additionally, both Britain and France introduced new measures to streamline intra-CoCom trade. In May 1989 the US finally agreed to the ending of the 'no exceptions' rule – apparently paving the way for millions of pounds worth of sales to be made.[54]

It is difficult to assess the impact of US attempts to control technology transfer – both direct and indirect – on the level of British conventional arms transfers because of the secrecy which surrounds British arms transfer decision-making. Moreover, the case-by-case basis of British decision-making makes it impossible to know what concerns lead to the rejection of a particular arms transfer request. It seems, however, that the US concern to protect sensitive technology, coupled with British interests in monitoring technology transfer have resulted in new standard operating procedures being introduced lower down the bureaucratic chain in the British arms transfer decision making machinery. As Richard Perle revealed: 'If you now go to London, you will find a technology transfer unit in the Ministry of Defence that did not exist as recently as [1985]. There are fifteen or eighteen people busy at work there.'[55]

Technology transfer, rather than being a final consideration for sensitive sales, now seems to be a primary consideration in all potential transfers. This change in bureaucratic procedure by the British government, in addition to pressure on individual firms and the tightening up of CoCom's lists, all indicate that Britain now takes into account technology transfer concerns when deciding whether to grant an export licence for a particular transfer. But given the recent changes in the Soviet Union and Eastern Europe, and the UK's tendency towards liberal interpretations of the rules, it is unlikely that this will provide a significant break on UK arms transfers.

Conventional arms transfer control and non-proliferation

The last factor which may affect UK arms transfer policy is the growing linkage between concerns over conventional technology transfers and nuclear proliferation issues. Until recently it appeared as though there was a contradiction between the nuclear non-proliferation policies of the Western nations and their conventional arms transfer policies. This contradiction was induced by the 'Doves Dilemma'. This referred to the dilemma, or perhaps more appropriately blackmail, faced by western decision-makers when a country threatened to 'go nuclear' unless supplied with advanced conventional weapons technology.[56] The result was that although the West did not transfer fissile material, it did transfer the technology, parts and indeed whole missiles which could contribute to a nuclear weapons delivery system. This meant, in effect, that countries receiving advanced weaponry as an incentive to remain out of the 'nuclear club' were being given the components for sophisticated weapons delivery system. The issue has once again come onto the international agenda with the sale by the PRC of Silkworm missiles to Iran and with Iraq's Condor 2 ballistic missile programme.

In April 1987, seven Western governments – Great Britain, Canada, France, The Federal Republic of Germany, Italy, Japan and the US – simultaneously announced their decision to tighten up their arms transfer policies with the intention of controlling the proliferation of missiles capable of delivering nuclear weapons.[57] The agreement, which took four years to negotiate and had been in secret operation since 1985,[58] had its roots in the 'Callaghan accords' agreed on at the Guadeloupe Summit of 1979. Over the next six years this initiative evolved into the Seven Power Missile Agreement or the Missile Technology Control Regime as it is now called. The agreement contains guidelines to control the transfer of equipment and technology which could make a contribution to any missile system capable of delivering a nuclear weapon. Indeed, the agreement stipulates controls over even relatively outdated missile technologies, as these are thought to be just as strategically important. A statement by the British Foreign and Commonwealth Office indicated that Britain, along with the other signatories, would take the following factors into account when contemplating an export application: nuclear proliferation concerns; the capabilities and objectives of the missile and space programmes of the recipient state; the significance of the transfer in terms of the potential development of nuclear weapons delivery systems other than manned aircraft; the assessment of the end-use of the transfers, including the relevant assurances of the recipient states; and finally, the applicability of relevant multilateral agreements.[59]

The missile agreement of 1987 is unlikely to have a great impact upon British conventional arms transfers. SIPRI figures indicate that between 1981 and 1985 missiles were only two per cent of total arms sales. In addition, Britain's missile sales have been in decline since the end of the 1970s.[60] Moreover, the agreement does not totally prohibit sales, it merely tightens up the regulations – particularly end-use – which govern such sales. The fact that there were few costs to Britain in signing the agreement could in part explain Britain's willingness to accept arms control in an area it has sought to protect in the past.

Nevertheless, the agreement is significant as it lays the basis for further efforts at controlling the transfer of advanced weapons technology. It has been suggested that the next moves in this area should be to impose restrictions on the sale of advanced combat aircraft capable of delivering a nuclear weapon. As Spector points out, foreign-supplied advanced combat aircraft 'effectively transform the inchoate nuclear-weapons capabilities of these undeclared nuclear states into concrete military threats, greatly intensifying the risks of regional nuclear confrontation'.[61] However, given its recent aggressive marketing of Tornado, Britain is unlikely to support such an effort. In addition, because the arms market now favours recipients, a suppliers' regime of this sort will be difficult to maintain.

Moreover, such efforts may run up against the spirit if not the letter of the NPT. Implicit within the treaty was the assumption that there would be a free market in conventional weapons. As Smith has noted:

Underlying the explicit bargain was a tacit agreement: non-nuclear weapons states would not seek to acquire nuclear weapons so long as the nuclear states (both the economically dominant and militarily dominant states) sustained a robust and expanding international economy and a system of relatively free trade in conventional weaponry.[62]

Even if the current missile agreement is not viewed in this light, any further controls – such as those envisaged to cover the sale of manned bombers – might be seen by the Third World as an effort by the West to maintain its military dominance over the South. The desire for and the concern over dual technologies may therefore work its way into discussions at the NPT Review Conference. Ironically, the effort to shore up the non-proliferation regime by making a direct connection between advanced conventional technology and the problems of nuclear proliferation may serve to exacerbate the pre-existing tensions within the NPT regime.

Conclusions

The above review seems to indicate that the prospects for Britain moving from arms transfer management to arms transfer reduction are not very good. However, trends in the international arms market, difficulties of co-production and concerns over technology transfer are all imposing different kinds of pressures and constraints on British arms transfers and it may be that these factors – beyond the control of the British government – together impose a form of arms transfer restraint.

However, despite the positive move towards restraint by linking conventional arms transfer policies with concerns to prevent horizontal nuclear proliferation, we are unlikely to see any major efforts on the UK's part to further advance arms transfer controls. Britain's ambivalent approach allows it the flexibility to appear concerned about the global increase in conventional arms spending while maintaining a policy of aggressively marketing Britain's wares in the global arms bazaar. The only consideration which might impel Britain to participate in future negotiations would be the concern to minimise the restraints placed upon the types of weapons that Britain supplies. Consequently, it is difficult to foresee any dramatic changes in British conventional arms transfer policies.

Notes

1   The author would like to thank members of the Southampton Arms Control Study Group, Cornelia Navari and Jean Grugel for their comments on an earlier version of this chapter.

2   See 'UK link in SA arms chain', *Observer*, 8 November 1987.

3   Compare, for example, Mark Urban and Mary Fagan, 'Britain wins £10bn Saudi arms order', *The Independent*, 9 July 1988, p. 1; David Fairhall, 'Britain signs £6 billion Saudi arms contract', *Guardian*, 9 July 1988, p. 1; and Michael Evans, 'Weapons for Saudi Arabia Britain's biggest arms sale', *The Times*, 9 July 1988, p. 1. Critical analysis of the implication of the sale came from correspondents abroad reporting the reactions of foreign governments, see for example, Charles Richards (Jerusalem), 'UK weapons sale to Saudis under fire from Jerusalem', *The Independent*, 11 July 1988, p. 10 and Michael Binyon (Washington), 'White House anger over loss of 30 billion arms deal', *The Times*, 9 July 1988, p. 7.

4   However, many of the economic rationales for arms transfers are not without challenge. A parliamentary committee looking into the conventional wisdom that exports significantly reduce unit costs found evidence to doubt its validity. Additionally, even if the economic advantages do accrue as proponents of transfers assert, there are nevertheless costs involved. Specifically, the need for sales abroad has had an effect on the types of weaponry available to the British armed services. According to Brzoska and Ohlson, 'The government has encouraged the development of weapons especially designed for export and British procurement agencies are asked to bear in mind that weapons for the British armed forces should also be attractive to foreign customers'. See Michael Brzoska and Thomas Ohlson, *Arms Transfers to the Third World 1971–1985*, OUP for SIPRI, Oxford, 1987. Moreover, British defence readiness has also suffered on occasion so that British industry can fulfil orders. A prime example of this was the 1985 sale of Tornados to Saudi Arabia when twenty completed Tornados destined for the Royal Air Force were diverted to the Saudis.

5   Andrew J. Pierre, *The Global Politics of Arms Sales*, Princeton University Press, Princeton, NJ, 1982, p. 102.

6   The recent renegotiation with the Japanese on the co-development of the FSX fighter aircraft indicates that the US is equally exercised about maintaining a technological lead over its allies as its adversaries.

7   Frederic Pearson 'Problems and prospects of arms transfer limitations among second-tier suppliers: the cases of France, the UK and the Federal Republic of Germany' in Thomas Ohlson (ed.), *Arms Transfer Limitations and Third World Security*, OUP for SIPRI, Oxford, 1988, p. 129.

8   Frederic S. Pearson, 'The question of control in British defence sales policy', *International Affairs*, LIX, Spring 1983, p. 226.

9   Pearson, 'Problems and prospects of arms transfers limitation', p. 143, n 47.

10   *ibid.*, pp. 143–4.

11   One of the major problems in undertaking a study of British conventional arms transfers is the lack of accurate information. As Pierre notes 'the

whole subject is shrouded in official secrecy'. In the annual figures released by the government, no explanation is provided regarding the proportion of weapons versus services in the sum or to whom the sales are to be made. Nor is it obvious whether the figures include offsets. Moreover, as Taylor has noted, British statistics only include those items which can be identified as 'military' through the Customs and Excise tariff. As a consequence of this, items such as aircraft engines and parts are not included in the totals as they are not distinguishable from similar civilian goods. Slightly more information is available about deliveries completed; however, the government also gives this information in terms of millions of pounds and, unless weapons can be accurately priced, this gives little indication of the numbers of weapons involved. An additional problem is that the actual destination of a particular transfer is often not released; the annual statement on defence specify only totals to continents. Thus, in order to get a reasonably accurate idea of British arms transfers it is necessary to turn to publications such as those of the US' Arms Control and Disarmament Agency (ACDA), the Stockholm International Peace Research Institute (SIPRI) and the International Institute of Strategic Studies. Although these sources are not without their own well-documented faults, they nevertheless provide more detailed information than is available from official published government sources. See Pierre *op. cit.*, p. 101. and Trevor Taylor, 'Research Note : British Arms Exports and Research and Development Costs', *Survival*, XXII, November/December 1980, pp. 259–62.

12   Jo L. Husbands and Anne Hessing Cahn, 'The CATT Talks: An Experiment in Mutual Arms Trade Restraint', in Ohlson (ed.), *op. cit.*, pp. 116–17.

13   Interview with John Rowe of the US Defence Security Assistance Agency, Washington DC, 2 December 1985.

14   See, for example, Pearson, 'The question of control', Martin Edmonds 'The British Government and Arms Sales' *ADIU Report IV*, November/December 1982; and House of Commons Foreign Affairs Committee, *Overseas Arms Sales : Foreign Policy Aspects*, Minutes of Evidence, 4 March 1981.

15   See David Pallister, 'MoD used private firms for sensitive deals', *Guardian*, 4 December 1987.

16   For a detailed examination of the activities of IMS see Pearson, *op. cit.*

17   See Pierre, *op. cit.*, p. 103.

18   'New DESO Head', *Campaign Against the Arms Trade* (Newsletter No 96), 6 April 1989, p. 4.

19   Pierre, *op. cit.*, p.104.

20   See Brzoska and Ohlson, *op. cit.*, pp. 70–1.

21   *Campaign Against The Arms Trade*, Newsletter No. 92, 11 August 1988, p. 4. The British government's belief in 'commercial confidence' was an important factor in Saudi Arabia's decision in 1988 to purchase Tornado fighters.

22   *ibid.*

23   Edmonds, *op. cit.*

24   Pierre, *op. cit.*, p.106.

25   Memorandum from the MOD to the Defence and External Affairs Sub-committee of the House of Commons. Quoted in Pierre, *ibid.*

26   Pearson, 'The question of control', p. 226.

27   *ibid.*, p. 214.

28   Pearson, 'Problems and prospects', p. 134.

29   Edmonds, *op.cit.*

30   Pearson, *op.cit.*, p. 214.

31   See Brzoska and Ohlson, *op.cit.*, p. 68.

32   Bank loans for weapons can be underwritten by the Exports Credit Guarantee Committee after the Treasury has given approval, *ibid.*, p. 71.

33   'BAe and Football', *Campaign Against the Arms Trade*, Newsletter No.94, 8 December 1988.

34   'Malaysia', *Campaign Against the Arms Trade*, Newsletter No. 96, 6 April 1989.

35   Concern has been expressed that the British government is prepared to use underhand tactics to ensure sales. For example, the aforementioned sale of Tornado aircraft to Saudi Arabia is subject to an investigation by the National Audit Office because of the size of the deal, the involvement of the two governments in what is primarily a private sector operation and the fact that Saudi Arabia is to pay for part of the deal in oil. Significantly the Labour Party has called for the scope of the investigation to be increased to include the question of fees paid in order to secure the deal. Labour's Allan Rogers stated: 'I am quite confident that commissions have been paid in the Saudi deal ... It seems to me that the present government are hell-bent on developing defence exports to such an extent that they may well sign a deal and get involved in tactics for which, in the past, they have criticised other countries.' See John Pienaar, 'Inquiry into £15bn UK-Saudi arms deal', *The Independent*, 27 April 1989, p. 8.

36   See Brzoska and Ohlson, *op.cit.*, p.36.

37   'Saudi Arabia', *Campaign Against the Arms Trade*, Newsletter No. 97, 15 June 1989.

38   For a discussion of recent tensions between the UK and the Federal Republic see David White, 'Why Bonn has raised its voice', *Financial Times*, 22 September 1989.

39   The 1988 Cabinet Office annual review of R&D revealed that the defence share of the budget will dip to 47.8 per cent in 1989. Despite this fall, the British proportion of R&D monies going to defence is by far the highest in Europe – with France running a distant second at 33 per cent – and is second only to that of the US in the Western world. See Peter Large, 'State spending on R&D still falling', *Guardian*, 28 July 1988.

40   See Brzoska and Ohlson, *op.cit.*, p. 72.

41   Melvyn Westlake, 'The Great Hi-Tech Scam', *South Magazine*, April 1988, p. 11.

42   *East–West Trade and Technology Transfer: New Challenges For The United States*, A Conference Report of the second annual forum Co-sponsored by The Institute for Foreign Policy Analysis Inc. and the International Security Studies Programme, The Fletcher School of Law and

Joanna Spear189Diplomacy, Tufts University, 23–24 September 1985, p. 3 (emphasis added).

43   Alan Cane, 'Soviet Union buys "expert" software', *Financial Times*, 20 March 1989, p. 10.

44   *East–West Trade and Technology Transfer: New Challenges For The United States*, p. 2.

45   For an account of how the issue came to the fore in Britain see Kevin Cahill, *Trade Wars: The High Technology Scandal Of The 1980s*, W.H. Allen and Co. Ltd, London, 1986.

46   Melvyn Westlake, *op.cit.* The impact of US attempts to enforce end-use conditions on dual-capable technologies has been particularly felt by the British computer industry. See Alan Cane, *op.cit.*

47   Such a list certainly exists. According to *South Magazine*, 'At one time 154 companies outside the US and even more in it, were said to be listed. A longer separate register, compiled by the CIA, was said to contain the names of over 300 companies in 30 countries involved in diverting technology to the USSR.' Westlake, *op.cit,*. p. 11.

48   Cahill, *op.cit,*. p. 16.

49   Westlake, op.cit., p. 9.

50   Cahill, *op.cit.*, p. 192.

51   John Hooper, 'Government's new curbs on sales of software', *Guardian*, 17 July 1985.

52   The Export of Goods (Control) Order 1987 (SI. 1987/2070).

53   Alex Brummer, 'British sale to Moscow upsets US', *Guardian*, 28 April 1989, p. 12.

54   Mary Fagan, 'Bush decision boosts UK's high-tech export prospects', *The Independent*, 1 May 1989.

55   Speech by Richard Perle, *East–West Trade and Technology Transfer: New Challenges for the United States*, p. 27.

56   Roger K. Smith, 'Explaining the Non-proliferation Regime: Anomalies for Contemporary International Relations Theory', *International Organization*, XXXXI, 1987, p. 258.

57   David Fairhall, 'UK in Missile Export Ban', *Guardian*, 17 April 1987 and David Buchan, 'New Curbs on Export of Nuclear Arms Technology', *Financial Times*, 18 April 1987.

58   'Seven Countries Maintain Secrecy On Missile Ban', *International Herald Tribune*, 19 April 1987.

59   *Missile Technology Export Control*, Statement by the Foreign and Commonwealth Office, 16 April 1987. These concerns recently lead the UK to refuse a grant to the Space Research Corporation to open a plant in Belfast. The reason was concern over the role SRC may have played in supplying advanced weapon systems technology to South Africa which was used in its first nuclear test over the south Atlantic 10 years ago. See David Pallister, 'Missile fears block grant to firm', *Guardian*, 16 September 1989.

60   Pearson, *op.cit.*, p. 220.

61   Leonard Spector, 'Foreign-Supplied Combat Aircraft: Will They Drop the Third World Bomb?', *Journal of International Affairs*, XXXX, Summer 1986, Special Issue on the Arms Trade.

62   Smith, *op.cit.*, p. 258.

Part III:

Conclusions

UK security and arms control policy in the 1990s: dilemmas and prospects

Introduction: four approaches to arms control

In assessing the possibilities for UK arms control policy in the 1990s it is worth recalling the contending approaches which have characterised the debates regarding British security and defence policies. Phil Williams in the opening chapter of this volume identifies two broad approaches which characterise British attitudes towards arms control: the conservative and the radical. Croft and Dunn, in their chapter on defence budgets, identify a further two: the managerial and the reformist. Though each has deeper roots than the current debates, these four approaches have been evident in the debate on UK security and arms control policy over the last ten years. Each of these approaches offers a different understanding of the nature and purpose of arms control; each offers a different assessment of the changes that have taken place in the international and strategic environment and the possibilities they create; and each offers a different set of recommendations for policy in the arms control issue areas discussed in the preceding chapters.

The conservative approach adopts an essentially status quo orientation. It is comfortable with the set of assumptions developed during, and premised on the Cold War. The goal of policy within this context is to reassert the validity of these assumptions and the necessity for maintaining military capabilities in line with such assumptions. Essentially, this entails a deep-seated commitment to the necessity of nuclear deterrence and in particular the enhancement of the credibility of extended deterrence and Flexible Response via the continual modernisation of capabilities. This cautious, indeed pessimistic approach is not particularly pro-arms control. It views arms control narrowly as a means of codifying and reasserting the strategic relationships which developed in the post-war period.

The managerial approach starts from two basic premises. The first is that there are real differences which separate East from West and that these cannot be solved through arms control processes. The second is that nuclear weapons are a fact of life. The two combine together to undermine any possibility of real disarmament. Moreover, such an outcome is seen by the managerial approach as being undesirable. It is nuclear weapons, they claim, that have kept the peace in post-war Europe. Nevertheless, the managerial approach sees a limited but useful role for arms control in maintaining the credibility of deterrence. Its purpose is not to change the satisfactory post-war international security order but to ensure its smooth operation. It places greatest emphasis on confidence building measures which leave the basic military and deterrent structures of security intact, while enhancing its stability. The managerial approach recognises a series of tensions in simultaneously pursuing both deterrence and arms control objectives. There is always the possibility that certain deterrence strategies may undermine the possibilities for arms control, or that the momentum and outcome of arms control processes may undermine rather than reinforce strategic stability. For this reason, the managerial approach tends to be more interested in arms control *negotiations* rather than arms control *agreements*; arms control *processes* rather than arms control *outcomes*.

The reformists argue that not only can arms control processes be linked to major changes in the international system but they can also play an important role in producing, directing and channelling such changes. This approach is critical of the emphasis on merely limiting weapons and argues that arms control must incorporate real elements of disarmament. The reformists argue that a self-reinforcing cycle of change can be induced, in which arms control processes help to mitigate threat perceptions which in turn produces a more positive climate for further arms control measures, which leads to real changes in force capabilities and structures, which serves to further alter threat perceptions and so on. The argument seeks to highlight the contradiction within existing approaches and encourages the reassessment and reformulation of defence and security policies in the light of changed military and political circumstances. The most important component in this process would be the rethinking of the nature of security and the content of security policies.

The radical approach argues that the arms control process is essentially status quo oriented and therefore politically suspect if not morally bankrupt. It argues that what is need is the development of new concepts as a logical pre-condition and necessary outgrowth of the desire to promote dramatic change in the international system. The impetus for further changes in political and strategic environments can best be promoted through dramatic unilateral gestures. The radical approach argues that unilateralism has several distinct advantages: the policies can be tailored to the specific security needs of individual states; they can be implemented at an optimum point; and they do not require complicated negotiations entailing intrusive verification.

Challenges to the post-war consensus

The core of Britain's post-war official security policy has revolved around the conservative and managerial approaches. This can be clearly seen in the justification offered for Britain's nuclear deterrent. It is difficult to identify *the* reason for Britain's possession of nuclear weapons. Instead, there are a series of complex and cross-cutting justifications. As the previous chapters highlight, some of the basic assumptions and rationales underpinning post-war UK policy are: (1) that Britain is a major power in the international system; (2) that the possession of nuclear weapons is a necessary accoutrement for a power of Britain's stature; (3) that the possession of nuclear weapons will act as a deterrent against the Soviet Union; (4) that the possession of nuclear weapons provides a means of influencing US strategic, defence and arms control policy; (5) that the possession of nuclear weapons gives Britain a influence in NATO policy and constitutes a second centre of decision-making within the Alliance; (6) that the possession of nuclear weapons in a nuclear armed world is the ultimate guarantor of UK security; and (7) that a denuclearised world is not possible or indeed desirable. The final point is perhaps the most important consideration in characterising Britain's post-war arms control policy as oscillating between conservative and managerial approaches. If there are multiple justifications for Britain's deterrent, they all point to a single rationale for its arms control policy: to keep Britain's nuclear weapons out of the arms control process, to prevent any constraints being placed on Britain's possession of, and its ability to modernise its nuclear weapons, and, as an ancillary proposition, to prevent the denuclearisation of Europe. These policy objectives are based on perceptions of threats and an understanding of the nature of security which derive from the Cold War security system.

What has become equally evident over the last decade is the breakdown of the post-war bipartisan consensus which underpinned these policies – what Phil Williams has referred to as the 'bonfire of the certainties'. The reason for this breakdown in the bipartisan post-war consensus on arms control and security policy is a series of challenges from a variety of directions.

First, it was challenged domestically by the rise of CND.[1] With its opposition to the 1979 'Dual Track' decision, especially the deployment of Cruise Missiles in the UK, and the decision to purchase Trident, the arguments of CND were reinforced by the general concern with the rhetoric and policies of the Reagan administration and general public support for more active and genuine pursuit of arms control policies by the West. It was also challenged from within by the Labour Party's adoption of unilateralism as party policy.

Second, the post-war consensus was challenged by changes in the international strategic and political environment including: the changes in Soviet leadership and policy; the Reykjavik summit; the INF Agreement; the Federal Republics's views on the modernisation of SNF; and the changes in Eastern Europe. The challenges from Soviet policy started under Andropov, as the Soviets managed to make the West appear to be the major impediment to arms control, focusing particularly on the INF deployment but also Reagan's Strategic Defence Initiative. The challenges became more substantive once Gorbachev came to power. The Soviet acceptance of NATO's disingenuous 'double zero' INF proposals, in conjunction with the domestic policies of *perestroika* and *glasnost*, caused serious disquiet to the comfortable nostrums of the Soviet threat.

The Gorbachev–Reagan discussions at the Reykjavik summit on the elimination of all ballistic missiles over a ten year period came as a tremendous shock to the core of the UK's policies. The contemplation by its US ally of such a proposal posed a serious threat to Trident as the successor to Polaris and therefore to Britain's ability to stay in the nuclear business. Such was the concern over these discussions and Reagan's more visionary arms control policies, that the Prime Minister arranged a hasty meeting with Reagan at Camp David in order to reaffirm a series of basic principles for US arms control policy. Needless to say, Reagan administration officials differed in their interpretation as to the substantive meaning of the four points agreed by Thatcher and Reagan.

The bipartisan consensus was also challenged, in the long-term, by the successful conclusion of the INF Treaty. While having publicly declared its support for US and NATO policy with regard to INF, the UK government was seriously dismayed by the prospect of a whole tier of nuclear weapons being removed from Europe. Having argued for the initial deployment as necessary for the continuing credibility of extended deterrence and Flexible Response, the INF Treaty was viewed as leaving a gapping hole in NATO's deterrent posture. In short, INF was seen as the thin edge of the denuclearisation wedge. Countering this nascent process would require the modernisation of SNF and the substitution of stand-off air launched missiles. However, this would be made more difficult as a consequence of the precedents set by the INF treaty and by the public pressure for further arms control agreements.

The seriousness of these challenges became evident in Britain's position in the NATO discussions regarding the follow-on to the Lance missile. In an effort to forestall the further denuclearisation via the 'third zero' the Thatcher government argued that further nuclear arms control in Europe must be contingent on progress in dealing with the conventional imbalance and chemical weapons. The UK's vehement adherence to this line in opposition to the view of the West Germans produced fairly acrimonious exchanges between the NATO allies. The decision announced at the May 1989 NATO summit might be seen at one level as a success for the Thatcher government. However, it was a rather limited success. The formula adopted by NATO was not as strict as the British wanted. Moreover, the speed with which the CFE talks have moved has undermined whatever hope there was that they might be a means towards forestalling SNF negotiations. Indeed, the opposite is likely to be the case. The result is that SNF could be on the arms control agenda sooner than Britain had hoped for, or wanted, and with it increasing pressure for a fundamental reassessment of NATO's nuclear strategy.

The changes in Eastern Europe pose a further long-term difficulty for UK policy. The dramatic domestic political changes in Eastern Europe and the announcement of cuts in defence spending and military forces by several East European countries serve to reinforce the general perception, initiated by Gorbachev's reforms, that the

Cold War is ending or has ended and that the threat from the East, both politically and militarily is subsiding. This undermines some of the basic declared justifications for Britain's security and arms control policies.

In the face of these challenges and changes, there has been some degree of change in UK attitudes. Significantly, there was a shift away from the rather harsh 'Evil Empire' rhetoric of the early Thatcher years once Mrs Thatcher decided that Gorbachev was a man the West could 'do business with'. However, despite the apparent enthusiasm for Gorbachev's reform, the underlying policy objectives have remained unaltered: to ensure that Britain's nuclear status is not threatened or constrained by whatever arms control agreements materialise between the US and Soviet Union. The emphasis of UK policy is still on stabilising East–West security via the procurement and deployment of new weapon systems, rather than grasping that the bases of European security are fundamentally shifting away from such an orientation.

The effect of the changes which have taken place over the last five years is paradoxical. In the short-term, it makes the objectives of the managerial approach easier to achieve. In the long term, the changes taking place are so profound that they have created a momentum which will propel any negotiation process seeking to simply manage change into reassessing the very structure of post-war relations themselves. Using the openings created by the changes in the East to consolidate prudential positions in the West is a process that is unlikely to stay within these confines. Despite the best hopes of the managerial approach, traditional approaches to security and arms control negotiations are unlikely to contain the processes of structural change which has been set in motion. Nor is it desirable to simply hope for or rely upon the natural braking mechanism which exists within the current processes of change: the difficulties with making *perestroika* a functioning reality in both the Soviet Union and Eastern Europe and the tensions within the Western alliance. A reliance on such factors will simply serve to exacerbate a situation in which a fundamental transformation of the system is taking place without any strategy for directing or channelling it to produce constructive outcomes.

Moreover, the implications of these changes are not somewhere off in the distance but are likely to have a direct impact on UK policy by the early to mid-1990s. The effectiveness of the UK's response will depend significantly on its ability to develop coherent and inter-related security and arms control policies. For many years the radical approach has advocated the demise of alliance blocs in Europe, while the conservative and managerial approaches have presumed their continued existence. Neither group is well placed to deal with the enormity of the changes which have taken place. Each is time bound within a set of assumptions that appear increasingly contingent in nature. This creates an imperative for innovative thinking regarding the framework for European security, which is to be developed in place of the decaying post-war system.

The effort to develop innovative ideas to manage and guide the transformation of the structure of security must constitute the core concern of Britain's security policy in the 1990s. Fundamental to this change must be the recognition that the UK's security is, indeed, bound up with that of Europe's rather than with that of the US. The impact of the 'special relationship', and in particular the dimension of technological reliance on the US in the nuclear field, has distorted Britain's security interests and security policies. The nature of the changes taking place is likely to compel a recognition and reorientation towards defining, pursuing and promoting UK security within a European context. The implication of these challenges is that if Britain is to take advantage of, and play a leading role in, the movement towards a European security framework based on mutual security, then its security and arms control policies will have to move increasingly towards the reformist approach. They will have to provide answers to challenging questions regarding the requirements of security and stability in Europe in a post-Cold War world. The impact of a reformist approach on security and arms control policy is evident if we examine some of the issues discussed in the preceding chapters.

Arms control policy

The central premise of UK and NATO policy has been the reliability of the Soviet Union as 'the enemy'. This threat perception provided the rationale for the UK's past security and arms control policies. It required continual force modernisation while allowing a public rhetoric in favour of arms control, with the private recognition that the prospects of substantial reductions were limited and that any real progress was unlikely.

The premise of a reformist approach to security and arms control policy is that the Soviet threat is no longer compelling. Gorbachev's foreign policy has severely eroded the image of the Soviet Union as an expansionist power bent on world hegemony. This has been reinforced by changes in Eastern Europe and the manner in which the Soviet Union has handled and encouraged them, as well as its policies regarding regional conflicts. In fact, Gorbachev's reforms pose an acute dilemma for the Western Alliance. On the one hand, it cannot but help to welcome the changes which Gorbachev and his like-minded colleagues in the Soviet Union and Eastern Europe are instituting. On the other hand, the success of these policies undermines the basis of the Atlantic Alliance. The changing political and economic circumstances of Europe, in particular the changing Soviet threat, means that the requirements of deterrence will change. This will be true at both the strategic and theatre levels.

Strategic arms control

Due to the way in which strategic arms control negotiations have developed over the last three to four years, it will be increasingly difficult for the UK to maintain its past policy of standing outside of arms control negotiations. To sustain such a position in the 1990s will create and reinforce public perceptions of obstructionist policies on the part of the UK. As Jonathan Alford argued in 1983, there are few grounds, either in equity or politics, for Britain's nuclear capabilities being excluded from proportional reductions.[2] It is no longer possible to rely on the SALT, INF and START I scenarios of fudging the status of the UK's deterrent and thereby hoping to avoid its inclusion in future arms control agreements. Changes in domestic and international public opinion, East–West relations, US–Soviet strategic relations, the arms control environment and European security have all moved inexorably to a point where UK forces will have to be taken into account. The longer the UK refrains from developing a positive approach, the greater the political pressures it will face domestically and internationally to participate. Not to do so would only serve to isolate the UK: further undermining its 'special relationship' with the US, limiting the role it can play as an intermediary between the US and the Soviet Union, and reinforcing Continental perceptions of the UK as a reluctant European ally.

But as Wheeler and Croft note in their respective chapters, the difficult question is precisely what role the UK can play in strategic arms control. Given that the UK characterises its SLBM based nuclear deterrent as 'minimum' there would seem to be little room for manoeuvre. However, with the purchase of the Trident D-5 missile, there is a substantial increase in actual and potential nuclear capabilities on the part of the UK. This expansion of capabilities at a time when the US and the Soviet Union are negotiating substantial reductions in START places increasing pressure on the inclusion of the UK's nuclear forces in post-START negotiations sometime in the early 1990s. But it also provides the UK with flexibility and leeway in developing eventual negotiating positions.

The obvious possibility, given the expenditures already made on Trident, would be to develop arms control policies in a manner which is consistent with definitions of what constitutes a minimum deterrent. This could entail any combination of negotiated limitations on warhead numbers, on megatonnage, on useable missile tubes and on the number of boats.

At the moment, the Thatcher government has said that it will only deploy eight warheads on each Trident D-5 missile.[3] This means that the number of warheads on station will increase from 48 to 128 with the Trident programme. The total number of warheads will increase from a maximum of 192 with Chevaline to 512 with the D-5.[4] Within the confines of post-START strategic arms control negotiations, the increased number of warheads provides flexibility for Britain's negotiating position. Various proposals have been put forward for limiting the number of warheads. One school of thought suggests that warhead numbers should be limited to six per missile. This would provide a total deterrent force of 384 warheads with 96 highly accurate warheads on station at any given moment. The basis for this proposal is that it would constitute the minimum necessary to have a reasonable chance of overcoming Moscow's ABM system. It would also provide scope for additional cuts proportionate to further US–Soviet reductions. Others, including the Labour Party, have argued for cutting the number of warheads back to current levels. This would place a limit of three warheads per missile. The argument behind such an approach is that, if the UK deterrent of 48 warheads on station has been credible up to now and given that there has been no upgrading in the Moscow ABM system, then 48 warheads of increased accuracy and megatonnage are all that is needed to maintain the existing minimum deterrent. The obvious difficulty that such proposals encounter is that of verification.

The second possibility is to negotiate a limitation on the number of missile carried by each Trident submarine. This would entail sealing missile tubes up and would have the advantage of being easily verified. If current UK capabilities are taken as the bench mark of what constitutes a 'minimum deterrent', then depending on the number of warheads per missile it would theoretically be possible to have as few as six launch tubes available per boat. However, given the budget resources allocated to the purchase of Trident and the resources necessary to maintain it, such an approach would constitute an extravagant waste of scarce resources in order to maintain a minimum deterrent.

The third possibility would be negotiating limitations on megatonnage as this represents the most dramatic aspect of the increase in UK deterrent capabilities as a result of the decision to purchase Trident. Each Polaris missile has three 200 kt warheads, with each Polaris submarine capable of delivering a total of 9.6 mgt. The gross megatonnage available with Polaris is 38.4 mgt. Each Trident D-5 missile will carry eight 475 kt warheads. This means that each Trident submarine will be capable of delivering 60.8 mgt, or nearly twice the Polaris total. The total megatonnage available under Trident will be 243.2 mgt. However, there are difficulties with a concentration on megatonnage. Despite the efforts of certain enthusiasts in the 1970s, there has been no satisfactory way of making megatonnage the direct focus of arms control negotiations. The greatest difficulties would be with verification. In addition, pressure to deploy anything other than the 475 kt warhead currently under development would be unacceptable to the government, as the UK has only one warhead design available. Moreover, reductions in megatonnage would occur naturally with limitations on either warhead number or available missile tubes, thus making this an unlikely avenue for focused attention.

The last possibility is a limitation on the number of Trident submarines commissioned. The question of the number of overall boats is a particular point of contention. Originally, five Polaris boats were to be purchased under the terms of the Nassau Agreement. The Wilson government cancelled the fifth boat on the basis that, with refit schedules, four boats provided the minimum necessary to maintain a credible deterrent on station at all times. The 'four boat criteria' in turn became the basis for the purchase of

Trident. However, there are grounds for arguing that advances in submarine technology and the longer-term service capability of the Trident submarine make it *technologically* possible to move towards a three boat SLBM force. The prime argument against such a shift has more to do with the difficulty of maintaining the morale and concentration of the Trident crews enduring longer tours of duty than with questions of strategic necessity.

Taking the maximum combination of the above possibilities, the UK could move to a 'minimum deterrent' of a three-boat, sixteen-missile, three-warhead SLBM force, with no loss of credibility or survivability. More problematic is the question of what such a negotiated reduction would achieve in terms of meaningful reductions from the Soviets. This would require close co-ordination of arms control policies and negotiating positions with the US. But due to the UK's technical reliance on the US, this is something which it may be compelled to do in any case.

The difficulty for the UK in such 'deep cut' scenarios is the possibility of the US and the Soviet Union agreeing to an ABM/SDI regime that allowed for the limited deployment of enhanced ballistic missile defence systems. An upgrading of the ABM system around Moscow could create difficulties for the credibility of a minimal UK deterrent – *but only if the Moscow criterion is maintained*. But, even if there are no significant changes in BMD deployments, the changes in the political and strategic environments may make it desirable to move away from the tight Moscow criterion to a much broader definition of 'targeting Soviet state power'. Given the nature of the changes in the political environment, the decline of the Soviet threat makes the Moscow criterion increasingly irrelevant. Once a broader interpretation is given to the requirement that the UK be able to threaten 'key aspects of Soviet state power', then required specifications of the UK deterrent become amenable to change, which in turn opens up arms control possibilities.[5]

The Trident modernisation programme also offers possibilities for reaching an accord on a CTBT or a significantly enhanced PTBT. With the completion of the Trident warhead design in the early to mid-1990s, a CTBT of limited duration and including stockpile reliability tests would affect the UK only at the margins. The greatest impact would be at the sub-strategic level as the UK sought to develop and test a replacement for the WE-177. However, with the Trident modernisation and a START regime in place, a window of opportunity similar to those in the early 1960s and 1970s would exist in the mid-1990s for reaching a CTB agreement.

The point of the above discussion is not to detail every possible scenario but to highlight the flexibility in negotiating positions available to the UK for participating in post-START strategic arms control negotiations in the early to mid 1990s. Moreover, such arms control postures are not without advantages to those steeped in the conservative or managerial approaches. The major benefit would be a multilateral legitimisation of Britain's nuclear status and the configuration of its nuclear capabilities which might well put it beyond the bounds of domestic political debates. The advantages for the reformer is that they would signify a fundamental shift in the UK's attitude towards arms control, reinforce the changes in the strategic environment codified by a START agreement, sustain the momentum of arms control processes and would not prevent negotiating a complete withdrawal of the UK's strategic capabilities in future negotiations. Rather than being seen as an impediment, the UK's deterrent would be incorporated into a new security regime.

European arms control

A central determinant of European security is the structure and deployment of the military balance as a consequence of conventional and nuclear arms control negotiations and the linkage to decisions of force modernisation in the context of scarce resource allocation. Within this nexus the one factor that is clearly changing is the structure of military confrontation in Europe. The implication of this is profound: the era of extended deterrence is coming to a close.[6] If such change is not to dictate strategies, then we need to think through the structure of security which will replace the Cold War system in Europe. This will necessitate the UK accepting and promoting more flexible processes of negotiated security rather than concentrating efforts on yet another attempt to shore up the postwar structures through force modernisation or limited political initiatives.

At the European level, the UK's security and arms control policies, along with those of its allies, will have to be geared towards managing the winding down of heightened military confrontation and facilitating the shift towards alternative bases of European security. It will have to assimilate and fully utilise the role that arms control can play as an integral part in managing the required changes in deterrent postures. Most importantly, it will have to recognise that the changes taking place in the political and strategic environments entail a fundamental rethinking of NATO's strategic doctrines and in particular a reassessment of the nuclear premises and biases of Flexible Response.

Flexible Response has always represented a fudge, an 'agreement to disagree over strategy'.[7] It is the doctrinal embodiment of an inability to agree on and deploy the necessary level of conventional forces and the military versus the political role of nuclear weapons. It is possible to argue that throughout the 1960s and 1970s, the ambiguities of Flexible Response adequately served its purpose of militarily committing the US to Europe and reassuring the European allies. But since the early 1980s it has faced increasing pressures: over the sharing of risks, conventional force levels, the neutron bomb, INF deployment and the INF negotiations. It is not surprising that it should undergo significant pressure. As the wider strategic context undergoes fundamental change, the ambiguities which were once the strength of Flexible Response have become a hinderance in moving towards a restructuring of European security. It is open to question how well it can stand up to such pressures, or even if it is desirable that it should do so.

Behind the debates on the future viability of Flexible Response lies deeper concerns about the future direction of European security. It is possible to chart the dynamics of European security from its roots in the *Ostpolitik* of the 1960s through to the detente process of the 1970s. These fostered changes in European security which provided further impetus for changes in Eastern Europe and the Soviet Union. Once this process was set in motion the Cold War structure of security was in terminal decline. Indeed, it could be argued that the very stability engendered by the Cold War contained the seeds of its own destruction. Once strategic stability could be taken for granted, it was possible to ease political, economic, social and military tensions between East and West. But doing so set in motion a series of forces which in the long term would be corrosive of the very conditions which made the process of change possible. This has created a dynamic of change which has been difficult to stop and may be even more difficult to control without rethinking that nature of security.

The UK's policies in reaction to these pressures have represented a lack of vision and innovation. There have been two distinct but interrelated strands to the UK's policies. First, it has promoted force modernisation over arms control and hesitatingly embraced arms control processes with the hope that agreements would not be forthcoming. Any other course would undermine or upset the basic strategic assumptions and threat assessments which underpin its security policies. But support for the UK position within the Alliance is limited and declining. Second, it has emphasised CBM's as the most desirable form of arms control. The UK believes that these address significant security concerns – such as capabilities to mount surprise attacks – without fundamentally altering the framework of security. The first fails to come to grips with the profound changes taking place in Europe. The second fails to recognise that even CBMs are corrosive of the strategic assumptions on which they are premised and which they seek to maintain and reinforce. Both represent a failure to develop a comprehensive and integrated concept of security and arms control.

More recently, the UK has sought to reinforce an artificial distinction between conventional and nuclear arms control by insisting that there be substantial progress on conventional arms control before the SNF question is addressed. But the UK insistence on separate conventional arms control prior to negotiations on SNF may well backfire. The attempt to address new problems with old solutions has invested the follow-on to the Lance question with greater political significance than it militarily merits. Moreover, given the apparent success of the INF approach, it is difficult to envisage proposals for the modernisation of SNF forces without an accompanying arms control track. The long-term consequence of the UK's policy will be to undermine the very status quo it sought to maintain.

A more imaginative approach is required which would encompass a serious reassessment of the nature and requirements of UK and European security, the pursuit of arms control at both the nuclear and conventional level, and a shift towards greater reliance on long-range deterrent platforms. Britain would be better served if it embraced the opportunities created by the CFE process for transcending the post-war security structures in Europe. There would be distinct advantages in an arms control policy which resulted in the reduction or elimination of SNF and significant asymmetrical reductions in NATO and WTO conventional forces. In addition to the opportunity to trade 88 Lance launchers for the WTO's 1,4000 launchers, it provides the opportunity to move away from the destabilising reliance on the early use of nuclear weapons and would promote a shift towards more flexible and survivable platforms.

Through a more positive approach to arms control, the UK and its allies can hope to have a significant impact on drastically reducing and restructuring the military threats it faces. Arms control processes can assist in translating psychological and political transformations into the restructuring of the military balance to enhance stability and common security. It will allow NATO and the WTO to pursue a conventional stability in which neither is capable of large-scale offensive operations. This, in turn, provides a context in which NATO can renounce the first use of nuclear weapons and move on to a wholesale reassessment of its strategic doctrines recognising the interdependent nature of European security. Thus, the choice between modernisation and negotiation which the UK has sought to emphasise is a false dichotomy. Instead, the focus needs to be on negotiation as a means of managing force modernisation and reductions in the context of change security requirements.

As a consequence of the INF Treaty, the CFE negotiations, the possibility of the elimination of SNF, and the likely reductions in strategic weapons via START, the focus has shifted away from the need to constantly reinforce extended deterrence via military hardware towards the need to redefine the framework of European security. As further political change takes place in the East, there will be increasing pressures for NATO to reassess and redefine the nature of the threat it faces and is meant to deal with, and more importantly, the strategic doctrines on which it relies. The long-term shift to some pattern of non-provocative or defensive defence now seems an inevitability.

This process has set in motion a movement away from security in Europe being premised solely on nuclear deterrence towards the redefinition of security premised on new political spaces and opportunities. Moreover, it has led to a recognition that security can no longer be defined simply as stability. On that criteria, European security would best be gainsaid via an unchanging political and strategic environment. This may have been the unstated desire of Western foreign policy and defence decision-makers, but clearly was incompatible with publicly-stated support for domestic change in the Soviet Union, for changes in its foreign policy behaviour and, in particular, for changes in the nature of its relationship with its East European allies.

This requires a significant shift in attitudes and thinking. Ultimately, it questions the continuance of NATO, at least in its present incarnation of an Alliance reliant on the early use of nuclear weapons. The assumptions that Western Europe is essential to US security interests or that the US is central to the maintenance of security in Europe in the 1990s are assumptions which are coming to be more widely questioned on both sides of the Atlantic. As the nature of the Soviet threat diminishes and changes, it is corrosive of the consensus on which the Alliance was founded and on which its military doctrine developed.

Thus there is the need for a new consensus on the nature and purpose of the Alliance, based on a recognition that the real threats to European security lie in disorderly change at the political level rather than orderly change at the military level. The Alliance needs to be less concerned with how to deal with a direct Soviet/WTO attack on Western Europe and more concerned with how it will react to and cope with the rising political, ethnic and economic turmoil in the Soviet Union and Eastern Europe. It needs to address the security needs of Europe as a whole and not just those of Western Europe. Without such a reorientation, the Alliance itself will be seen as increasingly irrelevant to the security needs and interests of its members. The failure to rethink European security could be a radical disjunction between the structure of alliances and the aspirations of those living within them. While it is true that these processes of change cannot be managed by arms control processes, a more reformist or even radical approach to arms control will make the UK more receptive to the changes taking place and enhance its ability to guide them in positive directions.

The above changes indicate the need for a fundamental reassessment of the modalities of UK security policies. This would entail a debate about Britain's role in the international system, its policy objectives and the level of forces required. The most sensible means of engaging in such a process would be a full-scale defence review. Indeed, the political and strategic changes taking place may not only provide the incentive for a defence review, but necessitate one. Multilateral negotiations may have a negative impact on proposed force modernisations, making it more difficult to gain funding for equipment which might eventually be negotiated away. These difficulties are compounded by the breakdown in the post-war bipartisan defence consensus. Not only is there unease over reliance on nuclear deterrence and further nuclear modernisation, but as a result of the CFE negotiations there is decreasing pressure to replace reductions in nuclear weapons with increased spending on conventional weapons. A reassessment of UK security and arms control policies via a defence review would provide some possibility of resolving the tension between resources and commitments – a tension which is not unique to the UK.

While the above discussion has focused on the arms control issues relating to strategic weapons and European security, a change in the basic orientation of Britain's security policy would also have implications for its arms control policies in other areas. The more Britain moved away from the 'nuclear fix', the more flexible its positions would become on questions relating to non-proliferation, the desirability and prerequisites of a CTBT,the further advancement of a CBW regime and restraints on arms transfers.

Conclusions

It might be argued that the dilemmas discussed above are unlikely to materialise or lead to significant changes in the UK's security and arms control policy. A START agreement has not been completed and is unlikely to be before 1991; while the CFE negotiations show great promise, a final agreement is a long way off; negotiations on SNF have not even started; significant differences between East and West still remain over chemical weapons; and *perestroika* has run into serious problems. All of these might provide comfort for those who wish to argue that no fundamental change in UK policy is required or desired. But before adopting such a sanguine approach it would be best to recall the state of East–West relations, arms control negotiations and international security in the mid-1980s and contrast it with what seemed possible then and what has happened in the intervening years.

It is for these reasons that the discussions in this volume will not bring much comfort to those who have continually sought to reassert the validity of Cold War assumptions. They should provide an impetus to those who see the present phase of East–West relations as offering the possibility of moving significantly beyond the outcomes of detente in the 1970s. There is now the genuine prospect of restructuring the security framework in Europe which will shift it away from the Cold War system of relations. It is for this reason that Britain's security and arms control policy in the 1990s must assume a character of facilitating, managing and institutionalising changes in both European and international security.

Moreover, the changing political and strategic environments pose dilemmas and problems not only for governments of a Conservative political persuasion. The issues and dilemmas discussed in this volume will have to be dealt with by any British government in the 1990s – whether it is Conservative, Labour or coalition. The problem is that the West in general and the UK in particular have not been very adept at developing a coherent policy in relation to the possibilities offered by the changes taking place in the international and strategic environment. Those policies they have developed are still premised on narrowly defined security interests. The danger is that current UK security and arms control policy not only assumes a status quo but actually seeks to reinforce it. But the risks that Europe faces in the 1990s can only be managed through co-operative security policies and through dialogues in which competing security interests are explored. In the 1990s, the UK faces the challenge and necessity of developing a coherent and innovative approach to security which will allow it not simply to react to changes in European security, but to foster, direct and channel them. It is an open question whether it is a challenge that Britain's foreign and defence policy decision-makers are up to.

Notes

1   Needless to say, there were earlier periods of challenges to UK security policy from within. In the late 1950s and early 1960s, its policy was attack during the first active period of CND. The bipartisan consensus was also attacked by Labour in opposition under Wilson. However, once in power, the Wilson and Callaghan Labour governments made the decision not only to maintain Britain's deterrent but to modernise it with Chevaline. However, it did so with some subtle and significant changes in the rationales for the UK deterrent.
2   Jonathan Alford, 'The place of British and French nuclear weapons in arms control', *International Affairs*, LX, 1983/84. It is worth noting that Alford made this argument at a time of tremendous pessimism regarding the possibilities for arms control. The changing political and strategic climate makes his argument even more apposite today.
3   This is the maximum number of warheads that would have been available on the Trident C-4, the initial choice to replace Polaris/Chevaline.

4 The Thatcher government has continually sought to emphasise that even with 50 per cent cuts under a START treaty, the UK SLBM deterrent *after* modernisation will still represent less than 10 per cent of Soviet strategic capability.

5 Paradoxically, some have argued that a broader interpretation would require enhanced strategic capabilities in order to provide coverage of an increased number of targets.

6 See Aspen Study Group, *After the INF Treaty: conventional forces and arms control in European security*, University Press of America, London, 1988.

7 Leon Sigal, *Nuclear Forces in Europe*, The Brookings Institute, Washington DC, 1984, p.14.

Index